Marygrove
EX LIBRIS

WALL STREET
20th Century

WALL STREET

20th CENTURY

SPONSORED BY

THE INVESTMENT ASSOCIATION OF NEW YORK

THE WHITE HOUSE
WASHINGTON

The economy of the American people has served this nation faithfully and well. It stands as living evidence of the toil of this generation and those who have gone before. It has yielded the material counterpart to the dignity that is every American's birthright. It has afforded not only material comfort, but the resources to provide a challenging life of the mind and of the spirit. It has provided the strength to make our homes secure against those who would attack us and destroy our way of life. It has given us the means to work unceasingly for a just and lasting peace among the nations of the world.

All this we can keep and strengthen by our faith and by our exertions. May we so conduct ourselves today that, when we look back upon this time, we can say: We met the test.

One salient fact should be clear. We can never pep-talk our way to prosperity. No one here is proposing that we try. We are simply suggesting that businesses do what is clearly in their own interest. We are suggesting, further, that it be done in the time-honored American way of self-reliance and self-starting initiative. Our economy has grown strong because our people have made jobs for each other and have not relied on the government to try to do it for them.

Our economy is the result of millions of decisions we all make every day about producing, earning, saving, investing and spending. Both our individual prosperity, and our nation's prosperity, rest directly on the decisions all of us are making now.

But remember: these are fast-moving times. The faint-hearted and the doubters who hang back today are apt tomorrow to be trampled in the dust of progress. It has been the tough-minded optimists whom history has proved right in America.

Dwight D. Eisenhower

QUOTATIONS FROM STATEMENTS MADE BY PRESIDENT EISENHOWER

WALL STREET | 20th Century

A republication of the Yale Daily News' WALL STREET *1955*

March 15, 1960

The Investment Association wishes to thank the Yale Daily News for extending to us the opportunity of revising and distributing this volume. As with the original issue, many people spent long hours on this non-profit undertaking. I should like to express my particular appreciation to William Ruane and to Donald Fordyce who met problem after problem with tireless energy. These men, together with the executive board of the Investment Association, devoted considerable time--in addition to their normal investment activities--to make this edition available. The financial support given by many investment firms, whose names are listed on a following page, have made economically feasible this publication and its extensive free distribution of over 40,000 copies. In addition to professional competency, William Ottley's contributions far exceeded his official responsibility to the design and lay out of this handsome edition. It is difficult to exaggerage the efforts and wise counsel that were rendered in all phases of the publication by John Neumark, the creator of the original issue, "Wall Street 1955". Finally, we are particularly indebted to Amyas Ames, Robert C. Johnson, Harold H. Sherburne, Kenneth Williams, MacMillan Co. and Doremus & Co., whose assistance and encouragement were of great help to our organization.

The motivating concept behind this new issue was Ruane's conviction that a significant need existed for a comprehensive treatment of all aspects of the securities industry. The volume was envisioned as having great value, not only to students and professors of economics and finance, but also to trainees in financial institutions and libraries serving the general public. After extensive research, the publication of the Yale Daily News' 1955 Board, "Wall Street 1955", appeared most ideally suited for our undertaking. Ten thousand copies of that volume had been distributed to college seniors and after it went out of print, a large demand materialized. Believing that a real service could be rendered to the financial community by republishing this edition and making it widely available, the Investment Association obtained a copyright from the Yale Daily News. Subsequently, a number of layout and textual changes were devised in order to make "Wall Street/20th Century" more timeless and comprehensive. The royalty funds accruing to the Yale Daily News as a result of this undertaking have been set aside to provide pensions for those on its permanent staff.

It is my hope that this book will serve the purpose of creating greater understanding of the securities business and its key role in our nation's economy.

Sincerely,

Worthington Mayo-Smith

Worthington Mayo-Smith

WM-S:mp

TABLE OF CONTENTS

TABLE OF CONTENTS *continued*

SPONSORS

Abbott, Proctor & Paine
Adler, Coleman & Co.
Allen & Company
A. C. Allyn and Company, Incorporated
Arnhold & S. Bleichroeder, Inc.
Asiel & Co.
Auchincloss, Parker & Redpath
Bache & Co.
Baker, Weeks & Co.
Bear, Stearns & Co.
A. G. Becker & Co. Incorporated
Blair & Co. Incorporated
Blyth & Co., Inc.
Brown Brothers Harriman & Co.
W. E. Burnet & Co.
Burnham and Company
Burns Bros. & Denton, Inc.
Carlisle & Jacquelin
Clark, Dodge & Co.
DeCoppet & Doremus
DeHaven & Townsend, Crouter & Bodine
C. J. Devine & Co.
Dick & Merle-Smith
R. S. Dickson & Company, Incorporated
Dillon, Read & Co. Inc.
Discount Corporation of New York
Distributors Group, Incorporated
Dominick & Dominick
Drexel & Co.
Dreyfus & Co.
Francis I. duPont & Co.
Eastman Dillon, Union Securities & Co.
F. Eberstadt & Co.
Equitable Securities Corporation
Estabrook & Co.
Faulkner, Dawkins & Sullivan
The First Boston Corporation
Freeman & Company
Glore, Forgan & Co.
Goldman, Sachs & Co.
Goodbody & Co.
Granbery, Marache & Co.
Gregory & Sons
Halle & Stieglitz
Hallgarten & Co.
Halsey, Stuart & Co., Inc.
Harriman Ripley & Co., Incorporated
Harris, Upham & Co.
Hayden, Stone & Co.
Hemphill, Noyes & Co.
H. Hentz & Co.
Hirsch & Co.
Hornblower & Weeks
E. F. Hutton & Company
W. E. Hutton & Co.
Investment Bankers Association
Jesup & Lamont
Josephthal & Co.
A. M. Kidder & Co., Inc.
Kidder, Peabody & Co.
Kuhn, Loeb & Co.
W. C. Langley & Co.
Lazard Freres & Co.
Lee Higginson Corporation
Lehman Brothers
Carl M. Loeb Rhoades & Co.
Lord, Abbett & Co.
Carl Marks & Co. Inc.
McDonnell & Co. Incorporated
McLeod, Young, Weir, Incorporated
Merrill Lynch, Pierce, Fenner & Smith Incorporated
Merrill, Turben & Co., Inc.
Model, Roland & Stone
Morgan Stanley & Co.
W. H. Morton & Co. Incorporated
National Securities & Research Corporation
Neuberger & Berman
New York Hanseatic Corporation
New York Stock Exchange
Paine, Webber, Jackson & Curtis
Carl H. Pforzheimer & Co.
W. C. Pitfield & Co., Inc.
R. W. Pressprich & Co.
Reynolds & Co.
Riter & Co.
L. F. Rothschild & Co.
Salomon Bros. & Hutzler
Shearson, Hammill & Co.
Shields & Company
Singer, Bean & Mackie, Inc.
Smith, Barney & Co.
F. S. Smithers & Co.
Steiner, Rouse & Co.
C. E. Unterberg Towbin Co.
Vance, Sanders & Co., Inc.
Wagner, Stott & Co.
G. H. Walker & Co.
Walston & Co., Inc.
Weeden & Co.
Wertheim & Co.
White, Weld & Co.
H. N. Whitney, Goadby & Co.
Arthur Wiesenberger & Co.
Robert Winthrop & Co.
Dean Witter & Co.
Wood, Gundy & Co., Inc.

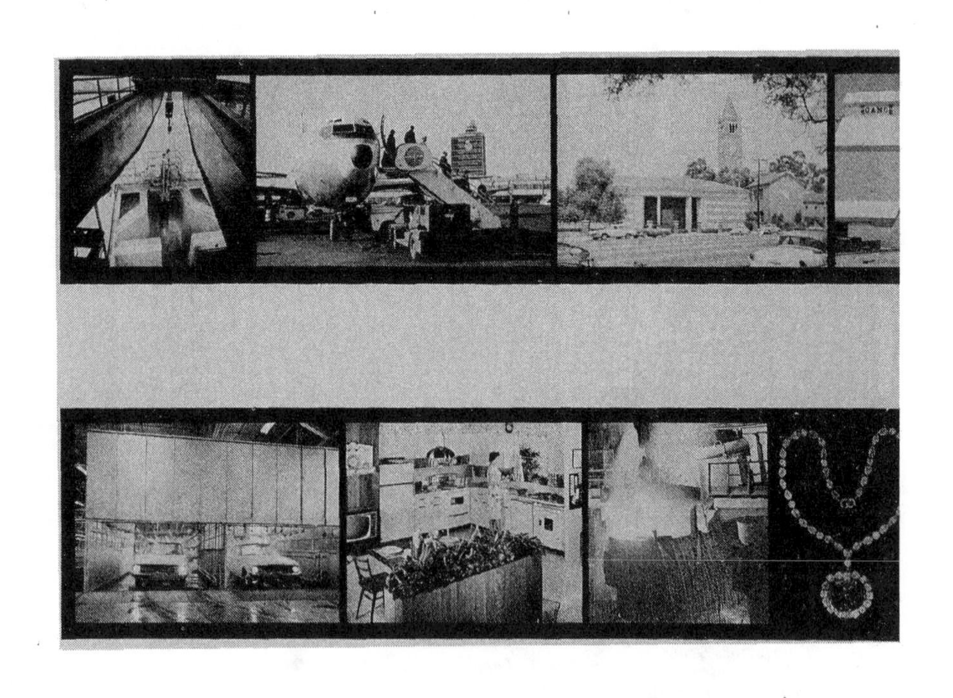

part 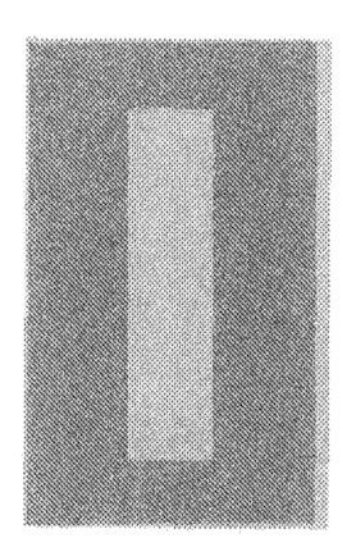

ECONOMICS AND FINANCE

Education for War, Peace and the Future

REFLECTIONS

Bernard M. Baruch

SOME MEN and women start out early in life knowing what they want to be, and their lives become tales of how they made their ambitions come true. That, plainly, has not been true of my career. In my personal ambitions I have been constantly beset by conflicting desires. The turns my life took have been determined as much as anything by the rush of events.

Although I didn't realize it at the time, when I first came onto the Wall Street scene, it was at the end of one era in our country's history and at the beginning of a new one. The dominant financial figures of the day—Morgan, Harriman, Ryan, Hill, Duke, Rockefeller—were at the summit of their power and prestige.

"Why can't I?"

Watching them and hearing of their exploits, I thought to myself, "If they can do it, why can't I?" I tried my best to emulate them, particularly Edward Harriman, who seemed to me to be the epitome of all that was dashing. The son of a minister, he had started from scratch, as I had. He bet on horses, races, prizefights, and elections—things I also liked to do.

But I was never able to become a second Harriman. Perhaps I just wasn't the man. However, I think that the conditions which made possible the "robber barons," or "Lords of Creation," as they have been termed by some writers, were slipping away. The years in which the United States emerged as a world power also climaxed the era of unrestrained individualism in American finance.

After the turn of the century, for one thing, the financial arena became too huge to be dominated by any one man or even group of men. If in 1907 a Morgan still could stem a panic, when the 1929 flood broke loose no one man could hold it back.

This change could be seen in the stock market itself. In 1898 something like 60 per cent

BERNARD M. BARUCH has served country and community for many years—today he is honored as "advisor to presidents" for service to every chief executive since Wilson. He was also U. S. representative on the United Nations Atomic Energy Commission. Mr. Baruch is a prolific author; his most recent was a best-seller in 1959: "My Own Story."

The government learned in World War I a new role, as the country awoke to a new national purpose. Here's a model of the Stock Exchange in support of the 1917 Bond drive.

of the securities listed on the Big Board were of railroads. This, of course, reflected the fact that the main business of America in the period after the Civil War was the physical spanning and conquest of the continent. By 1914 railroads represented less than 40 per of the Stock Exchange's listings, by 1925 about 17 per cent, and by 1957 only 13 per cent.

Up to World War One, almost the only financing of foreign governments done in this country had been for Britain during the Boer War, and for Japan in connection with the Russo-Japanese War. Today, of course, the United States is the most important single center of foreign financing.

The nation awoke

But the times were also awakening a sense of social responsibility in the whole country. The titans who had made vast fortunes had begun to give their money away—something they often found more difficult to do wisely than to make it. More important were the many social changes and currents of feeling which found expression in the progressive ideas of Theodore Roosevelt and Woodrow Wilson.

But the real turning point in my thinking—and I believe in the thinking of American businessmen generally—was World War One. The war forced a shelving of the old *laissez-faire* tradition and thrust the government into a wholly new role. What was done in those war years was never to be completely forgotten. Afterward, whenever an emergency arose, whether it was a domestic crisis like the Great Depression or a Second World War, the country turned back to the pattern of action by the government which had first been developed during World War One.

I, of course, was one of the human instruments through which this revolution in national thinking in the role of government was registered. It was not that I was particularly far-sighted. When World War One broke out I certainly was no global thinker. Military strategy meant little or nothing to me; nor did I have any comprehension of what needed to be done to mobilize a nation's economy for a total war.

A wholly new approach was needed, one which envisioned every factory and all raw materials, every business leader and worker as part of one gigantic industrial army.

A responsibility for preparedness

When the Advisory Commission of the Council of National Defense was set up, I was made a member and was given the responsibility for seeing that the raw materials would be available for our preparedness program. Since raw materials enter into the manufacture of everything, I found myself concerned with every part of the economy. I quickly learned that the tasks given me could not be accomplished by business-as-usual methods.

What I learned I somehow had to pass on to other businessmen. It was no easy job. At some of our earlier meetings, whenever a labor leader spoke up he would be interrupted by the businessmen on the commission. I often found myself saying, "Please let Mr. Gompers finish. I would like to hear what he has to say."

In this new industrial army, men who were generals of finance or business often had to play the role of lieutenants and sergeants. Many of our business leaders had grown accustomed to thinking of themselves as virtually laws unto themselves, brooking no interference by the government or anyone else with how they ran their factories or plants. It was not easy to explain to such men why they had to shed their fiercely individualistic ways and take orders from the government or cooperate with their competitors.

I did not always succeed in making these business leaders adopt the larger view of the national interest. There was Henry Ford, for example. I went to see him at his hotel in Washington to explain why, since the steel used for automobiles was needed for war, the production of civilian cars would have to be curtailed.

Ford insisted that he could make cars and munitions at the same time. "Just tell me what you want and I'll make it," he declared.

Although I tried to explain why there just wasn't enough steel for both the war and civilian cars, he remained unconvinced.

"Let things alone" was no solution

When the First World War was over, the American people in general and businessmen in particular tried to go back to things as they had been before the war broke out. I did not. My main reason, I suppose, was that I had found public service so much more satisfying than making money. But I could also see that the war had left in its wake many problems which could not be solved by a "let-things-alone" philosophy.

When I think back over these and the many other difficulties we have had to wrestle with —from the problems of the depression and a Second World War to the cold war with Russia —I am struck by the fact that most of them revolve around one crucial interrelationship—that of war and peace.

In our governmental skills we never really have caught up with the forces and problems unloosed by two world wars. Whatever has been done, more remained to be done. It has been as if we were chasing a train which we never seem able to catch.

We must look upon the crucial trial we now face as, in essence, a test of our ability to govern ourselves. We do not suffer from any lack of material resources. The sheer power, both for constructive and destructive purposes, which man commands is unprecedented. What we lack is the ability to control and direct this power and these vast productive resources which are ours.

This test of our ability to govern ourselves is really threefold.

♦ First, it is a test of values, of what things we will give up in order to make other things secure.

♦ Second, it is a test of our reasoning powers, of whether we have the wit to think our problems through to an effective solution.

♦ Third, it is a test of self-discipline, of our ability to stand by our values and see our policies through, whatever the personal cost.

The issue of how much should be spent on our national defense provides a fairly good illustration of all three aspects of this trial.

Some persons have contended that "our economy can stand only so much." But during both world wars we demonstrated that our economy could support an infinitely heavier effort than anyone has yet proposed be done in the struggle for peace. The physical resources at the disposal of ourselves and our allies exceed what the Soviets and their satellites can command. I, for one, will never concede that we cannot do as much in defense of our freedoms as any enemy may be doing to destroy those freedoms.

Talk of the need for discipline and of the need to think may seem old-fashioned preaching. This tendency to shrug off these old truths is another part of what troubles our society. Many of us listen to these truths and nod our heads at their verity, but do nothing to put them into practice. Since we do not think through what would be required to apply these old truths, they remain mere words.

Education evades discipline

Sadly, the dominant trends in education seem to be operating to aggravate this neglect. Instead of teaching young people to think, too many of our schools assume that their task is done if students are kept interested. Curriculums have been enriched to cover every conceivable subject, while discipline has come to be frowned upon. Along with the growth of specialized schools seeking to turn out technical experts has come an illusion that the mere amassing of information is a sign of being well-educated.

The point that I am trying to make is that information without judgment and thought is of little value.

To be able to exercise sound judgment, one must keep the total picture in focus. Our better educators are coming to realize that what is needed is not a familiarity with specialized detail but this ability to see our varied problems as parts of one interrelated whole. Almost nothing in our world stands alone. Everything tends to cut athwart of everything else. If action on any particular front is to be truly effective, usually a host of other actions are required on supporting fronts.

This struggle for the total as opposed to the piecemeal approach was the central issue in the long and, sad to say, unsuccessful fight to prevent inflation during World War Two. Congress and most of the officials in the executive branch argued that monetary controls alone would suffice or that only a few prices had to be controlled, while wages and farm prices could be left largely uncontrolled. Against this bits-and-pieces approach, I warned that a whole series of actions across the entire economy was needed, as parts of a single, synchronized mobilization of all our resources.

A total approach to peacemaking

When World War Two ended I again took up the battle for a total approach—this time in relation to the peacemaking. Even as we had devised a global strategy to win the war,

How much for defense? Today's cost for preparedness dwarfs all prior experience. From left: "Texas Towers," constructed at sea to buy warning time against air attack; the F-100, first of the "Century" jets, shown here being tested at Muroc Dry Lake; the Titan under test in Sacramento, first second-generation U. S. missile; the intermediate range THOR takes off from Cape Canaveral—total development is reckoned in multi-billions.

President Wilson meets with the Advisory Commission of the Council for National Defense. Flanking Wilson are Treasury Secretary McAdoo and Navy Secretary Josephus Daniels; Baruch is seated at right, Food Administrator Herbert Hoover stands at left.

I urged that the equivalent of such a strategy be worked out to embrace every aspect of the struggle for peace, so that we could employ the strength that was ours to the greatest advantage. Many officials made speeches about the need for "total diplomacy." But the painstaking task of piecing together all the many interrelationships of a unified, global strategy has not yet been carried through.

One reason for this failure is our yearning for quick and easy solutions. It has taken some time for the American public to learn that there are no short-cuts to world peace. The task of preventing a third world war will engage us through our whole lives and the lives of our children.

With every action that is proposed we would do well to ask ourselves not only how much it can be expected to accomplish, but what it is that it *cannot* do.

It is also important to make certain that our efforts are directed at the decisive core of the problem and not on distracting side issues. The more complex the difficulties we face, the more important it becomes to bear this in mind, for it is human nature to try to evade what we cannot cope with.

Mankind has always sought to substitute energy for reason, as if running faster will give one a better sense of direction. Periodically we should stop and ask ourselves if our efforts are focused upon the crux of the problem—the things that must be settled if there is to be a manageable solution—or if we are expending our energies on side issues which cannot yield a decision, no matter what their outcome.

A guiding philosophy

This, of course, is enormously important in the struggle for peace. In the making of peace, I believe, there are two issues which overshadow all others. Unless these two issues can be resolved, no basis of enduring peace is possible.

A few years ago I delivered a lecture before some college students in which I tried to sum up the philosophy that has guided me.

I pointed to the cyclical succession of wars and peace, booms and busts, enslavement and freedom that have characterized human history. After each of these breakdowns there was always a rebuilding which lifted man to new heights of accomplishment—at least by material standards.

Today, however, we wonder whether our civilization could stand another cyclical breakdown. In place of the old averaging out of collapse and recovery we yearn for some system of sustained progress. This, I believe, is the dominant yearning of our time.

To break free of this cycle of breakdown and buildup, we must free ourselves of man's age-old tendency to swing from one extreme to another. We must seek out the course of disciplined reason that avoids both dumb submission and blind revolt.

I believe in reason, not because of the wisdom that men have demonstrated in the past, but because it remains man's best tool for governing himself. It is not mere chance that, whenever society is swept by some madness, reason falls as the first victim. Neither perfection nor utopia are within man's grasp. But if the frenzy of soaring hope can never be realized, we can also avoid the panic of plunging despair—if we learn to think our problems through, decide what it is that we value most, and organize ourselves—both as individuals and as a nation—to see that first things come first.

From "Baruch: My Own Story", published by Henry Holt & Co., New York, Chapter 22.

Economic Growth in a Competitive Economy

THE UPWARD-MOBILE U. S. A.

Robert B. Anderson

FUTURE PROGRESS in this nation must be based on the solid foundation of a reasonably stable currency. Sound money, and the maintenance of the purchasing power of the dollar that it implies, is properly a goal in itself. The millions of Americans who hold savings in the form of life insurance contracts, Government savings bonds, savings accounts in financial institutions, social security, and in other forms are entitled to the assurance that these invested dollars will not shrink in value because of inflation. But sound money is more than an end in itself; it is absolutely essential if our other important economic objectives—as well as non-economic objectives such as our national security—are to be realized as fully as is possible.

We are dedicated to the attainment of three important economic goals—

- Continuity of job opportunities for those able, willing, and seeking to work;
- A sustainable rate of economic growth;
- Reasonable stability of price levels.

Each of these objectives is important. Each is fundamentally related to the others.

The desirability of promoting continuity of job opportunities and stability in the purchasing power of the dollar has been emphasized for years. Only recently has continuing economic growth been recognized as a major economic objective. Some observers appear to believe that economic growth at a dramatic and unprecedented rate is of such overriding importance that it must be achieved at *any* cost. According to this view, Government should utilize all of its capabilities and powers to guarantee a record-breaking rate of growth, year in and year out, regardless of other developments in our competitive economy.

ROBERT B. ANDERSON, Secretary of the Treasury under President Eisenhower, is headquartered in this neo-classic building in Washington. Anderson earlier served as Navy Secretary and Deputy Secretary of Defense. He has also held many appointive offices in his native state of Texas.

U. S. progress suffers when goods that people do not want compete for savings and investment. Secretary Anderson contrasts the military (here, a Hawk missile for use against low-flying aircraft, and already obsolescent in the missile age) with public facilities (the new Stanford University Medical Center, designed by famed architect Edward Stone, paid for by individual savings). Far more tax dollars go to fill government corn silos with unwanted corn than are available to spur aviation progress—Pan Am's world jet goes around the globe 173 days faster than 1924 trip made by the historic biplane "New Orleans."

The economy thrives on freedom

This view is wholly inconsistent with our basic ideals. The strength of our economy stems from reliance on the integrity, wisdom, and initiative of the *individual*—not the directives of an all-wise government. Just as our political system is one of free choice, in that each individual is free to select the party and candidate of his choosing, so is our economic system one of free choice. The consumer, by casting his dollar votes in the market place, selects the goods to be produced, their quantities and characteristics.

The economy thrives on growth

Growth cannot be *forced* in a free choice economy. The essence of economic freedom is the right to dispose of our incomes as we see fit—to consume or to save, to invest or not to invest. These decisions, arrived at freely and independently by millions of people and institutions, are a central and highly important factor in the growth process.

If we are to maintain our freedoms, the Government cannot be the predominant factor in our Nation's economic advancement. Its role must be to foster and facilitate growth—not to force it. Economic growth at an artificial rate, forced through unsound practices, can only cause the loss of some of our most cherished economic freedoms—or inflation—or both.

While Government cannot force growth in a free economy, it can do much to promote sound, sustainable economic progress. We can realize maximum success in this endeavor only if we understand the nature of growth and the forces that influence it in our type of economy.

Economic growth is usually thought of in terms of the annual increase in real gross national product—that is, growth in the dollar value of total output, adjusted for changes in price levels. For some purposes this is a good measure of economic growth; for others it is not.

This particular measure of growth is deficient, in the first place, because it tells us nothing about the nature of the growth that takes place. This is simply another way of saying that promotion of growth for its own sake could result in an unwanted type of growth. An increase in output, to be meaningful, must consist of the useful goods and services that people want and are able to buy.

Secondly, a broad, aggregate measure of growth provides only a partial clue as to whether the growth that takes place is sustainable. If an upsurge in output proceeds at an unsustainable pace, and if strong pressures on prices are allowed to build up, we run the risk of falling back to a lower level of output.

We must look behind the broad measures of growth. We must ask searching questions about its characteristics.

The "how" and "why" of desirable economic growth

When growth has taken place, how much did consumption expand relative to Government use of goods and services? How much of the Government portion consisted of military hardware as opposed to schools, highways, and other public facilities? How much of the increase in output was composed of goods that people did not want—goods which ended up in Government warehouses, being given away, destroyed, or sold for less than true value? What portion of total output was devoted to enlargement and modernization of business plant and equipment and to research? How much of our effort had to be devoted merely to maintenance of plant and equipment, as opposed to net new additions?

There are other important questions. How were the fruits of the growth in output distributed among various groups in the economy? Was the growth characterized by distortions and imbalances that would hamper future growth? To what extent was temporary growth stimulated by actions that impinged on the free choice of individuals and institutions?

These questions indicate that economic growth, in terms of a specific figure, is not an end in itself. It must be growth of the right kind. It must be sustainable. It must have a reasonable distribution.

In an economy so highly dynamic and complex as ours, with its primary emphasis on the freedom of individual decisions, the factors influencing the rate of growth are necessarily manifold and complex.

The pace of technological advance is one of the more important factors. No one can study the economic history of this or of any other advanced industrial nation without being impressed by the vital contributions of the inventor, the innovator, and the engineer. Man's ingenuity in tackling and solving his problems lies at the heart of the growth process.

Technological advance alone, however, cannot assure a high rate of growth. The best ideas and the best techniques are of little benefit if the means are not available to translate them into operating processes. This requires capital; and true capital can only grow out of saving and productive investment.

The cruciality of a high rate of saving to the growth process leads to an important but, apparently, little understood principle of economics. From the standpoint of an individual, every act of saving means that much less consumption. The more he consumes, the less he saves; the more he saves, the less he consumes. Consequently, if we insist on a dramatic and unprecedented rate of economic growth in the future, we must frankly admit to ourselves that this requires a higher rate of saving at the present time.

This principle has important implications today. There appear to be some observers who believe that, on top of providing adequately for national defense and devoting a considerably larger volume of current output to public projects, we can achieve a dramatic rate of growth in the private sector. Perhaps we can; but it seems clear to me that this can occur only if we are willing to increase our saving.

A third important requisite for a high and sustained rate of growth is efficient and continuous use of our economic resources. Inefficiencies in use of resources can carry a heavy toll in terms of lost output. Moreover, idle manpower and equipment—a characteristic of the adjustment periods that result from efforts to grow too fast—represent production that is irretrievably lost. Recession is the number one enemy of sustained growth.

To sum up, economic growth in a free choice, competitive economy tends to vary directly with the pace of technological advance, the rate of saving and capital formation, and the efficient and continuous use of our economic resources. An effective Government program to foster growth should operate largely through these basic determinants.

The moving forces which promote growth in a free economy are basically the same as those that account for economic progress on the part of the individual. The individual's desire for a higher and more secure standard of living for himself and for his family is the basic stimulus; this is the prime mover. To this end he studies, plans, works, saves and invests. He searches out new ways of doing things, developing new techniques and processes. Where such instincts as these are strong, the forces promoting growth in society as a whole are strong. Where they are weak, the impetus for growth is also weak.

We are dedicated to the proposition that the desire of the individual to improve the standard of living for himself and for his family is strongest in an atmosphere of freedom. Consequently, the first task of Government in fostering growth is to safeguard and strengthen freedom. The proper role of Government is to provide an atmosphere conducive to growth, not to force unsound and unsustainable growth through direct intervention in markets or through an improvident enlargement of the public sector of the economy. Governmental efforts to promote growth that rely on, or subsequently lead to, excessive intervention in and direction of market forces can in the long run only impede the kind of growth that is desirable and sustainable.

Sharp competition brings healthy growth

Government can also promote rapid, healthy growth by fostering competition in the economy. Competition sharpens interest in reducing costs and in developing more efficient methods of production. It places a premium on skills in business management. It stimulates business investment in new plant and equipment, both as a means of economizing in the production process by use of more efficient machinery, and by enlarging capacity in order to capture a larger share of the market. Healthy, vigorous, and widespread competition, in short, is the primary stimulant to efficiency in use of our economic resources, both human and material, through technological advance and by stamping out waste and inefficiency.

There are other ways in which the Government can promote healthy and sustainable economic growth. I am hopeful that a study of the tax system, recently undertaken by the Congress and in which the Treasury is cooperating, will lead to significant and beneficial results. Moreover, the Government can and should do much to eliminate waste, not only in its own operations, but in Government-supported or -regulated activities.

All of these are important methods of aiding growth in a free choice economy. I am convinced, however, that one of the most significant Governmental contributions to economic progress involves use of fiscal, monetary, and debt management powers to promote stability in the value of the dollar and relatively complete and continuous use of our economic resources.

Confidence in the integrity of the dollar is basic to a high rate of sustainable growth. As I noted earlier, a high rate of capital formation in turn depends upon saving. Incentives to save in traditional forms—in savings accounts, bonds, and through purchasing insurance—may have been somewhat impaired by a disturbing conviction on the part of some people that inflation is inevitable. This is a mistaken conviction. But if we should ever allow a lack of confidence to develop in the future value of the dollar, the desire to save in traditional forms will be weakened. Growth will be impeded.

Full confidence in the future value of the dollar can be maintained only if we remain constantly alert to all of the forces and practices that promote inflation. Some of these forces and practices may have grown out of changes in the economy in recent years; further study may be necessary before they can

"COMPETITION SHARPENS INTEREST—PLACES A PREMIUM ON SKILLS IN BUSINESS MANAGEMENT . . ."

To meet the competition from giant Coke, Pepsi-Cola built an even bigger sign than the traditional weather bureau operated by Coca-Cola at Columbus Circle, New York. Management moved further, revamped the entire Pepsi "image" from quantity to quality, and in the ten years between the ads shown here, Pepsi's net increased nine-fold! Coca-Cola responded energetically; result: the entire market enlarged by skillful management and free competition.

be identified and before appropriate policies to control them can be devised.

Some observers point to the high degree of price stability of the late '50's as proof that we are not now confronted with monetary inflation. This general price stability should be carefully evaluated. A rise in the cost of many goods and services has been offset by declining prices for farm products and food. This is, at best, a precarious balance. Moreover, the important point is that effective control of inflation requires actions to restrain inflationary pressures as they develop. To wait until the pressures have permeated the economy, and have finally emerged in the form of price increases, is "to close the barn door after the horse is already part way out."

Actions to limit inflationary pressures during periods of strong business activity will, in addition to protecting the purchasing power of the dollar, foster sustained growth in still another important way. Restraint and self-discipline today will help assure that the current healthy advance in business activity does not rise to an unsustainable rate and then fall back. This is the best possible assurance that our economic resources will remain in continuous and efficient use. The severity of a recession reflects primarily the build-up of unsustainable expansion in the preceding period of prosperity. By exercising restraint and moderation during periods of prosperous business, we can keep booms from getting out of hand. This will minimize the impact of later adjustments.

Our nation is constantly confronted with a critical choice:

♦ We can choose sound Government financial policies that will foster growth—not of the temporary, unsustainable type, but long-lasting and rewarding.

♦ Or we can choose the temporary expedient of excessive Government spending and money creation during a period of strong business activity. Such practices can readily lead to inflation, which will ultimately dry up the flow of genuine savings and lead to recession—the number one enemy of growth. As has been proved in country after country, the road of currency depreciation leads inevitably to serious and long-lasting difficulties.

The choice before us is a momentous one. At stake for all of our people are the job opportunities, rising incomes, and the security of savings set aside for later years. At stake also is the safety of our country and of the free world, for in the last analysis this too depends upon the economic strength of America.

A Debt to the Public

THE SPECIAL RESPONSIBILITY OF MEN IN FINANCE

Prescott S. Bush

PRESCOTT S. BUSH is a partner of Brown Brothers, Harriman & Co., and director of many corporations. He has been the United States Senator from Connecticut since 1952 and is a member of the Senate Committee on Banking and Currency. He graduated from Yale in 1917.

BECAUSE most of my active business life, until 1952, was spent in the financial community of the United States, I am very much impressed with the responsibility which men in finance owe to the general public.

When one speaks of "men in finance," the phrase includes not only the commercial banks, but the whole financial community of the country. That means banks, trust companies, savings banks, and savings and loan associations. It means pension funds and insurance companies of all kinds. And, of course, it means the investment organization in all its phases: brokerage, underwriting, distribution of securities, and investment trust management.

"His word is as good as his bond." That is an old saying which one frequently hears about a respected citizen. I mention it here because one should be able to say it of any man in finance. Of course, it should be true of all citizens—of all men in all business enterprises. But I mention it in connection with the financial world because there is no place where such huge sums of money are transferred by word of mouth as in "Wall Street," which is the accepted nickname for the financial world of the United States. In the investment field, financial commitments are made on the telephone every day involving millions and millions of dollars. These are usually confirmed in writing or at least a notice of them is sent out in writing. Nevertheless, an individual can buy thousands of shares of stock every day without signing a paper. His word must be as good as his bond in the investment field.

Your word: worth millions

Brokers, dealers, buyers for institutions, bankers—all shift hundreds of millions of dollars each day by the spoken word. So it is essential that the field of finance must continue to attract men of character and integrity, in order that the high standards established over the years in the field of finance may be maintained in the years ahead. The maintenance of these high standards is a public responsibility.

Most institutions in the financial world have their doors open to the public. Anyone can walk in and attempt to do business. Credit, of course, and reputation must be established to the satisfaction of the financial organizations. But the doors are open to the public. More than that, in most financial fields, intensive advertising and sales campaigns are conducted, hoping to persuade people to "come in and see us."

The public responsibility of the men in finance is not simply to be "money honest." Indeed, the law will deal with those who are not, and one seldom finds them in finance. The responsibility goes further, and places on the financier in any one of these fields an obligation to protect the interest of the client, or customer. He must advise him fairly. He must prevent him from making commitments beyond his capacity, beyond his resources, beyond his ability to perform and pay.

He shouldn't lend him too much money. He shouldn't sell him too much insurance. He shouldn't sell him too many stocks, and none of doubtful value.

So, because of this public responsibility, the the field of finance should attract the very best from our universities and our graduate schools of business. It is an attractive field. Generally speaking, it brings one into contact with successful people in all walks of life.

I have no hesitancy in saying that it is an agreeable and congenial industry in which to work out one's destiny. In order for it to remain that way, and to maintain its stature and importance in our American scheme of economic life, the men in finance must be conscious of their public responsibility—and that responsibility includes participation in public affairs. A great contribution to the common good can be made by men trained in finance on all levels of government—local, state, and national. Wise management of the people's money is essential to sound progress. It means "getting into politics," which many businessmen have been reluctant to do. But it is my conviction that the businessmen, including the men in finance, who complain about politics and politicians cannot do so with fairness if they are unwilling to dare the hazards of political life.

A FEATHER FOR CHASE

Financial institutions today mount major advertising and public relations campaigns to disprove dusty reputations for stuffiness. Few have been as successful in persuading people to "come in and see us" as the Chase (now Chase Manhattan) Bank, a pioneer in personality.

A memorable instance was when Chase turned their then-current campaign into the talked-about ad pictured here. In the summer of 1953 a rufous-necked hornbill from Siam ecaped from a pet shop, and flapped around Wall Street's skyscrapers all day, as clerks and secretaries craned to watch its antics. The bird, as big as a turkey, finally flew into the arms of a *New York Times* photographer waiting beside Chase's 28th-floor window ledge. The result: the ornithological curiosity turned into the stunt of the year.

Below, Chase board chairman John J. McCloy talks to stockholders after a recent annual meeting where 400 Chase stockholders gathered to get to know *their* bank better.

Headquarters of the Federal Reserve System, Washington, D. C.

The Ever-Adapting System

THE NEW CAPITALISM

William McC. Martin, Jr.

AS IN THE STORY of the elephant and the blind man, Capitalism would be differently identified or evaluated depending upon where the would-be evaluator touched it or it touched him. Almost everyone possessed of all of his faculties, however, would know the animal when he encountered it. Few would venture to define or explain it. That it is of ancient lineage is certain. That it has undergone evolution or adaptation, without extinction, is equally true. Whether it be considered benign or malignant obviously depends largely upon the individual's personal experience with it, as well as upon his economic and ethical ideas.

Doubtless in the early days of Athens or Rome, Capitalism's rapid dissolution was predicted—even as today—either by those who wanted it to survive but feared it was being dealt mortal blows by its pretended friends, or by those who, hoping for its destruction, openly or covertly sought to sabotage it, and if that failed, to bring it down by force of arms. Down through the ages, those who are against it, except perhaps for the nihilists, profess to believe that some other "ism" would better serve mankind.

If, as it seems to be widely assumed, there is in the United States today a dangerous body of Americans who wish to supplant Capitalism with some economic-social system of untried worth or even one of demonstrated failure, it is strange; for no people in all history have produced such material abundance and enjoyed such well-being as the American people—although America's span of time has been short as history is measured. That men can be corrupted, by money, to espouse any cause is far from surprising. But it is far from plausible that a prosperous people, with freedom of thought, of speech, of opportunity, of choice, people whose ears or eyes tell them of the terror and deprivations behind the Iron Curtain, should of their own free choice wish to abolish the system under which this well-being has come about, and to experiment with something else in its stead.

Adaptability—key to success

All analogies are, no doubt, false, but to liken the capitalistic system to a living, progressing, and changing organism does not seem to me to be inappropriate. Its outstanding characteristic is, I think, its adaptability. It has and can develop evil. It has and can greatly outweigh the evil by the good. It is the creature and the servant of man. He can kill it, or he can continue to eradicate its evils and foster and enlarge its benefits. It reflects his moral and ethical values, just as it gives the greatest spur to his ambition, enterprise, inventiveness, and desire for progress.

Since Capitalism has always had this adaptability, I find it rather misleading to speak of the "New Capitalism." Have we not, rather, adapted the old Capitalism to our modern-day needs, without destroying its fundamental characteristics—private ownership of the physical means of production, production by private enterprise for private profit, and fair, open competition in the market place? We have contrived certain devices—such as bank credit—and certain regulatory harnesses or disciplines which, if overdone, could cripple and stop its progress, but if applied only so far as needed to avoid excesses or unfairness, may make for steady headway and the avoidance of pitfalls. We are fond, as a people, of speaking of the "New Capitalism," as did Theodore Roosevelt, or the "New Freedom" of Woodrow Wilson, or the "New Deal" of Franklin Roosevelt—but the adjective implies adjustment or adaptation to current conditions rather than some *de novo* concept or system. Like the "new look" of the automobile, for example, the outward appearance has been changed, perhaps radically, but the basic principles of propulsion remain the same.

Let us take a quick glance over our shoulders to note just a few of the phenomenal strides of progress under our free institutions.

Three-quarters of a century ago, we did not have automobiles, electric lights, radio, television, gasoline tractors, airplanes, wonder drugs, frozen fruits, vegetables, meats, even waffles. The fantastic world of plastics and synthetic yarns was unknown. The telephone was a novel rarity. The atom and the hydrogen bombs were not even a gleam in the eye of the scientist.

In 1880 the population of the United States was about 50 millions—36 millions of them classified by the census as rural and but 14 millions as urban dwellers. In the years since the population not only has trebled but has been so extensively rearranged that in 1955

WILLIAM McC. MARTIN, JR., who graduated from Yale in 1928 has held various positions both in government and with private firms. He became president of the New York Stock Exchange just ten years after graduation. Mr. Martin is currently chairman of the Board of Governors of the Federal Reserve System. He also has held the position of Assistant Secretary of the Treasury and executive director of the International Bank for Reconstruction and Development.

96 millions were classified as urban and only 54 millions as rural dwellers. This enormous growth and transition, which might be termed a peaceful industrial revolution, is the more phenomenal when it is remembered that the 8-hour day, the 5-day week, and paid vacations were as unknown to working men in those days as the washing machine, the automatic refrigerator, and other escapes from drudgery were to their wives. What I think should be emphasized above all is that under our system the vast strides in production—notwithstanding temporary setbacks in depression interludes—have been accompanied by ever-increasing leisure amid unprecedented physical comforts and satisfactions in the life of the overwhelming majority of Americans.

The workers benefit first

It seems to me to be beyond dispute that the working man and his wife—as well as their working daughters—have been the chief beneficiaries of Capitalism's achievements. The reason is simple. Capitalism is first and last an engine of mass production, which necessarily means mass production for use by the mass of mankind, as distinguished from a wealthy few. An economics professor of a New England university illustrated the point by reminding his students that Louis XIV, while he did not have electric lights or a car, for instance, which are among the boons available to the working man, his wife and his daughters today, nevertheless had so much that, for him, little was to be gained from capitalist mass production. Since he was in no hurry, speed of travel was not vital to him; he had plenty of candles and servants to light them. He had silk stockings. So did Queen Elizabeth of England. Mass production could not do much for them, but it could, and today does, provide abundance for the many—the stockings, the electric lights, cotton, rayon, and nylon cloth, shoes, washing machines, and countless other articles that typify the achievements of capitalist production.

The rate and abundance of our material progress is unmatched in all history. Can it be said that the soul of a nation—its spiritual and cultural values—suffer in the long run? Is it true, as the Nazis and the Japanese jingoes believed, that we grow soft in the midst of plenty? It is for today's and coming generations to provide the conclusive answers to such questions.

Steady economic progress is aim

The statistical magnitudes measuring our money supply, our bank deposits, our savings, are correspondingly large—and, of course, our debt structure, notably the Federal debt, and incidentally, the public payroll. But these vast sums, staggering as they are in comparison with other days, need to be seen in proper perspective—against the background of our gross national product and income today as compared with earlier times. Our concern is to maintain steady economic progress—a balanced economy and trade at home and abroad. We rightly perceive that the poison of rampant inflation could destroy ours as it has other economies.

Complacency about an ever-rising public debt, growing deficits, and thus an excessive money supply would, indeed, be a cause for alarm. But the country is far from complacent. Irrespective of political affiliation, there is an overwhelming insistence upon principles of fiscal credit and monetary conduct that have stood the test of centuries and of reason. Much has been written in the past about the restoration of these principles, particularly in the monetary fields, both in our country and in other free nations. It suggests, again, that the "New Capitalism" adapted though it is to changed conditions, is nevertheless fundamentally dependent upon long-established, traditional rules of survival.

The Federal Reserve System was created by Congress as its instrumentality for carrying out, free from extraneous political or private pressures, monetary and credit policies that will contribute to a continuing, stable economic progress. Unbridled inflation, which is the forerunner of ruinous deflation, cannot be averted by monetary and credit measures alone. Fiscal and public debt policies are of first importance—but they, too, cannot succeed unless supplemented by appropriate monetary and credit measures. These are, perhaps, complex matters, but they cannot be brushed aside. The right answers at the right times will, like many crucial decisions of the future, depend in no small degree upon what young men of America learn about Capitalism, whether in new garb or old.

Overseas Investments in Underdeveloped Lands

First U. S. investments overseas were extraction industries like this copper mine in the Andes at Potrerillos, Chile.

DOLLARS: A REWARDING EXPORT

Robert L. Garner

ALMOST three decades have passed since the depression of the 1930's when widespread defaults on foreign government bonds left a bad taste in the mouths of American investors. Throughout the intervening years there was little interest on the part of such investors to place their money overseas. Perhaps it would be useful to review briefly the experience of foreign financing in the 1920's and relate it to the situation now existing.

Following World War I and the subsequent recession of 1921 the United States experienced a great business upsurge. This was accompanied by the greatest volume of financing of all types the country had ever seen, and for the first time American investment bankers entered actively into the promotion and underwriting of foreign securities. Almost all of these securities were bonds of foreign governments or their agencies. Our investment bankers were largely inexperienced in foreign financing and in the scramble for business, and in line with the speculative fever of the times, many of them stimulated loans of excessive amounts and for non-productive purposes. Unfortunately, the bonds were sold widely to unsophisticated investors who were attracted by the high yields. A total of about $7.5 billion of foreign bonds (excluding Canadian issues) were sold in this market in the 1920's. Despite the unsound nature of much of the financing, about two-thirds of the issues were paid on schedule. However, nearly $2.5 billion went into partial or complete default. The subsequent losses affected a large number of investors and the fact that there were also widespread defaults on domestic issues did not prevent the foreign defaults from being given special emphasis. Nor has the fact that in subsequent years a substantial number of these defaults have been cured in whole or in part changed the unpleasant memories.

ROBERT L. GARNER became president of the International Finance Corporation July 24, 1956, after a long career in finance, industry, and government — with the Guaranty Trust Company, General Foods, and the International Bank for Reconstruction and Development.

The picture today

Shifting our view to the present we find that the world of today presents an entirely different picture with regard to American

THE MIDDLE EAST AND AFRICA

Underdeveloped lands with a special appeal are those overlying the world's largest known oil reserves. From left: Cities Service employees load supplies for an exploration trip into southern Arabia; free enterprise pumps gas for Aramco; Standard Oil goes on location in Libya.

SOUTH AMERICA

Variety of profit opportunity awaits the Good Neighbor: here Creole Petroleum builds roads in eastern Venezuela, at left; Alcoa ships bauxite direct from Paramaribo to Point Comfort, Va., right; American money built this Brazilian textile mill, center.

THE FAR EAST

Rubber was the magic that early drew investors to the Far East. The vintage railroad at right hauls bulk latex out of the rain forests of Southeast Asia for shipment to the States.

business and investment from that of the decade following World War I.

The United States has become deeply involved in world affairs. Financing of foreign governments has been organized on a massive scale, first by the U. S. Government and later with the assistance of European governments and their agencies. The World Bank, the International Monetary Fund and the International Finance Corporation represent new types of public international financial institutions. Western Europe has recovered from the war and is moving towards economic integration. The less developed areas throughout the world have joined in the urge for economic growth. American industry, which widely increased its exports in the years following World War II, is now steadily expanding its operations overseas.

In examining the opportunities and problems involved in the movement of U. S. private business and capital, it is useful to consider two different types of capital.

First, there is *business* capital which arises from and is coupled with business operations. It is applied by the businessmen who control it to enterprises which they administer.

Secondly, there is *investment* capital which represents accumulated savings and profits of individuals and institutions which are available for such employment as its owners may select. It seeks investment wherever it can find the most attractive return related to the risks it is prepared to accept.

Both types of capital are necessary to industrial growth.

Extraction industries were first investments

The earlier foreign investments by American business were chiefly in the field of oil and other minerals, with a few large manufacturing companies establishing production in Western Europe and Latin America. Furthermore, with relatively few exceptions, exports comprised a relatively small part of the business of most U. S. companies prior to World War II. However, with the end of hostilities in 1945, American and Canadian exports expanded tremendously. These countries had the only highly developed industrial plants which were undamaged by war. Their products were in universal demand, and American business moved into the export market in a big way. All types of capital goods equipment—power plants, railroad, construction and agricultural equipment, machine tools, trucks—together with consumer goods from automobiles to soap, made up the cargoes of ships moving from American ports. Large sectors of American industry became involved in this export trade.

THE WORLD AROUND

The Ubiquitous American, our best-known export, thrives on the charms of Paris, the beaches of Mexico —leaves millions of dollars behind, to build foreign dollar reserves used in turn to buy from the U. S.

But as the years passed, Western Europe and Japan have come back into production at rates exceeding their prewar levels and have pushed aggressively into overseas markets. The formation of the European Common Market is not only stimulating European production but making this market a more attractive field for American industrial investment. Furthermore, throughout the industrially less developed areas there is an insistent urge to build up their own industries as a part of their economic growth, thus substituting domestic production in many lines for goods formerly imported.

Faced with such conditions, American, European and Japanese industries are making strong competitive plays to establish production in these countries, not only to hold the markets which they have been supplying but to take advantage of the great potential for growth. It is no exaggeration to say that a large proportion of the sizeable industrial companies in the United States, Canada, Western Europe and Japan are initiating or expanding production in the developing areas.

Private capital brings better living

This activity on the part of private enterprise in the industrialized countries is on the whole being met by an increasingly receptive attitude on the part of the developing countries themselves. All of them are faced with demands in excess of their financial and human resources to provide essential governmental services—basic facilities of transport, power, communications, social services, education and health. Increasingly most of the countries are realizing the importance of stimulating private capital and initiative, both foreign and local, if they are to attain the greater productivity and better living which their people are demanding.

This development offers wide opportunities to investment capital in the United States. Such capital does not, of course, have the commercial urge to move abroad that is impelling the industrial businessman. However, in its constant search for the most attractive returns, investment capital has over the past few years been looking increasingly abroad. It is natural that the first move was investment in the leading companies of Western Europe, and over the past few years an increasing number of investment funds, trust accounts and large individual investors have been buyers of shares in the leading European companies. An indication of this growing interest is the listing on the New York Stock Exchange of a number of European share issues. Over the past year or two, however, increasing prices on the European exchanges have carried these shares to levels approximating those of the blue chip American shares. In consequence, therefore, investment capital which is looking for a return materially higher than that available at home is coming to consider the opportunities in the developing areas. The relative shortage of available capital in these areas and the evident risks involved make it possible to obtain returns considerably higher than those available at home.

There are certain fundamentals involved in foreign operations and investment that need to be borne in mind. Essentially the basic elements of business are the same whether at home or abroad. There are the same problems of management, organization, labor, markets, costs, distribution. None of the factors which enter into calculations and appraisals at home can be neglected in considering foreign operations. There are in addition special conditions that need to be given particular attention.

In the first place the traditions, backgrounds, and characteristics of the local people need to be taken into account. The introduction of new enterprises and modern methods will obviously require some alteration in traditional habits, but to introduce innovations with a minimum of disturbance of local sensibilities requires tact and patience. Any stranger coming into a new community will find a more agreeable life if he makes reasonable adjustments to the existing habits and culture and seeks to become a part of the community. This principle applies particularly to a foreign business, and I believe that American business going abroad is becoming increasingly conscious of this fact. Aside from providing jobs, including in many cases responsible executive and technical positions for local people, there is an evident trend towards arranging local participation in ownership. There are still a number of large American companies which insist on 100% ownership of foreign subsidiaries. At the other extreme there are some companies which insist on majority ownership being in local hands. In between, an increasing number are welcoming a minority interest by local businessmen and investors.

A tendency which seems less justifiable is the financing of foreign operations with excessive debt as compared to equity capital. It is quite usual for foreign enterprises to be set up with a much higher debt than would be considered acceptable in this country. Furthermore, particularly because of the widespread use of suppliers' credits, the debt is often concentrated in short maturities. With delays in completing projects, which are the rule rather than the exception, and with the overruns in costs which are accentuated by inflation, heavy debt maturities in the early years often lead to trouble. Under inflationary conditions, there is also continuous need for more and more working capital, with larger amounts of the units of currency required to finance the turnover of a given volume of goods.

There are plenty of problems, but despite them the experience of American industry in its operations abroad has been successful. The proof is in the fact that many large companies experienced in the foreign field are expanding their international activities.

Ordinarily the businessman setting up a foreign operation has an organization to develop his plans and to reasonably provide for the development of his project and conduct of his business abroad. On the other hand, the private investor, even an institutional investor well equipped for domestic investment, has in most cases limited facilities for investigating projects overseas. This is one of the basic problems involved in increasing the flow of private American capital into investment in the developing areas.

A number of organizations, affiliates of commercial banks or groups of investment bankers, have been set up over the past few years to specialize in foreign investment. Experience is being accumulated. My own organization, the International Finance Corporation, organized in 1956, has built up a staff of financial, engineering and accounting personnel which is in position not only to analyze projects in Washington but to go out into the field to make investigations on the spot. Our own staff is supplemented by outside technical and accounting consultants retained for specific jobs. In addition we are fortunate to have access to the well-developed economic resources of the World Bank and the experience of its personnel in the various areas. Retaining the services of local lawyers, we are developing practical procedures for fitting our types of financing into varying local legal systems.

The story of Champion Celulose

A recent investment in Champion Celulose may afford a useful example.

This company was set up as a subsidiary of Champion Paper and Fiber Company of Hamilton, Ohio, to manufacture sulfate paper pulp in the State of Sao Paulo, Brazil. The total cost of the project is about $20 million and the capacity of the plant is about 50,000 tons of pulp annually. This will replace presently imported pulp.

Champion approached IFC to secure $4 mil-

Champion Paper raised seven million in the U. S. to build this Sao Paulo pulp plant—the investment (including the IFC's four million) is represented by unsecured 7% dollar notes, maturing from the 6th to the 10th year. In addition, they carry 5% interest and an option on shares, both contingent on earnings.

lion to supplement their own investment in the company. Their plans, including both technical and financial aspects, were studied by IFC. We retained as advising consultant a pulp expert who made a quick review in Brazil. In cooperation with Champion we worked out arrangements with three private investment institutions in New York to take sub-participations in our investment on the same terms to the extent of $3 million.

IFC did the spade work in appraising and setting up the investment, thus facilitating action by the private investors.

This project was sponsored by a large, experienced American company; therefore the investigation was relatively simple. However, many of the foreign projects which come to IFC and other investors do not have behind them such financial and technical experience, and much more work is required in investigation. In fact, we find that it is frequently essential to take an active role in putting the project in shape, advising the sponsors on the type of engineering and other assistance which is required. Not infrequently we consider it essential that local sponsors bring into the project as a partner some experienced firm from an industrialized country, and we are often able to be of assistance in helping to work out suitable arrangements.

Under existing conditions private investors seem to be more interested in equity type investments than in fixed interest obligations. Rightly, I think, they desire to have a chance to participate in the profit possibilities which are available rather than to depend on a fixed rate of return, even though considerably higher than available at home. Although IFC is prohibited by its charter from investing in either preferred or common stock, our investment pattern combines an obligation with certain equity type features. Normally we make an unsecured loan with a fixed interest rate, one that is moderate by the standards of the international capital market, plus provision for some share in profits or options. Thus our investment ranks in between a combination of short- or medium-term lenders and the shareholders.

This type of investment seems to be viewed with favor by private investors and we believe that it offers a suitable type of financing both for the borrowing company and for investment funds.

Foreign careers have a special appeal

I have tried to outline briefly some of the opportunities and the problems involved for private American business and capital in foreign operations and investment. The foreign field also offers career opportunities for individuals. The substantial expansion of operations overseas has created demand for American personnel in a wide variety of lines to participate in the operation and management of these activities. I find that a considerable number of young men are attracted by the opportunities and challenges of living and working abroad. Perhaps to some of them the prospect seems more glamorous than it will prove to be in reality, because success in this field will require the same qualities of ability and willingness to work hard as at home. Nevertheless, there are elements of pioneering and of participating in the building up of new enterprises that naturally appeal to ambitious youth.

Likewise, there is very limited experience in this country in the foreign investment field. If, as I believe, this is an expanding activity, it offers promise to the individual interested in financial affairs. The best training for this is a sound grounding in the principles of domestic corporate finance and business analysis. On this foundation it is not difficult to acquire additional experience in foreign investment.

Beyond the economic and personal opportunities, I believe that the expansion of American enterprise into the developing countries has a bearing on our country's role and security in the world. Communism and other forms of socialism are making powerful attempts to spread their systems into these developing lands. I am convinced that the best answer to this challenge is the spreading of our type of competitive private enterprise, with its great productivity potential for extending its benefits widely among the people. I consider that it is our most valuable export and that it can bring mutual benefits to us and to those who receive the injections of its vigorous and dynamic force. To the extent that we succeed in spreading this system, we are applying our most effective weapon against the inroads of Communism.

part 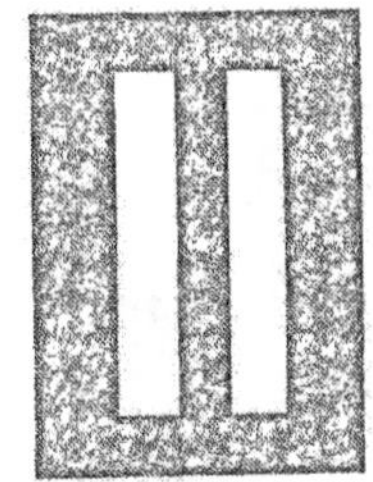

WALL STREET

More than 8,600,000—52% of them women!—own a share in American business today. Here is the mammoth annual meeting of A. T. & T. stockholders, where more than 4000 were in the audience. American Tel's stock is the most widely-held security in the world today.

The People's Capitalism

IT STARTED IN AMERICA

G. Keith Funston

G. KEITH FUNSTON became President of the New York Stock Exchange on September 10, 1951. A Phi Beta Kappa graduate of Trinity College and the Harvard Business School, he served the *War Production Board during World War II* as Special Assistant to Chairman Donald Nelson. He left the presidency of his alma mater, to which he had been elected at the age of 33, to accept his present office.

SOME TIME AGO I learned about a young man named Philip Miller. He lives with his wife and three growing boys in a comfortable home in Aurora, Illinois, where he works as an industrial relations specialist for a modest annual income. At the age of 31, Mr. Miller is a friendly, thoughtful fellow whose pattern of life is much like millions of others.

Yet in at least one way Philip Miller of Aurora is something more. According to age, income, family size, education and geography, he is about as close as you can come to the statistical average new American shareowner —typical of all those who have recently bought shares of the nation's businesses. As such, I found him a symbol of the change our free enterprise system has fashioned in recent years.

Along with millions of other individuals, Philip Miller has clearly defined investment goals. As the father of three growing boys, he wants them to have the sort of college education that he himself was forced to work hard for by holding a full-time job while attending night school.

"If I possibly can, I would like the three boys to be able to get an education with a minimum strain on the family finances," says Miller. "I think the good investments that I make today will help educate the boys tomorrow."

For all his natural optimism, Miller is realistic enough to understand that stock prices may go down as well as up. As a result, before investing in stocks, Miller made sure his family finances were in order. He had cash savings and protection against emergencies.

Miller's realism tempers his approach to investment

"We're investing for the long-term," he explains, "and not for any overnight profits. So why should we worry about the day-to-day ups and downs of the market?" He and his wife check the stock tables in the newspaper occasionally to see how their securities are doing, but they take any change of prices calmly.

In an expanding land whose economic shape is constantly altering, Philip Miller may well dramatize the most impressive change of all.

The tape that covers a nation: reports of Exchange transactions begin here, appear almost instantly on 2500 tickers in 450 cities.

As a brand new shareowner, he and his calm approach illuminate major differences between the present and the past.

There was a time, of course, when only a relative handful of people directly owned the productive resources of a less abundant, less complicated economy. Since that time we have moved closer to a true People's Capitalism in which millions of people everywhere—the

Educating the public is a major activity of the New York Stock Exchange and its member firms. Booklets, motion pictures, advertising are all part of a multi-million dollar annual effort. Here an Exchange guide explains an exhibit—more than 300,000 visitors see the Exchange each year.

great bulk of them in the middle income ranges—own the shares of American business. What's more, the trend toward shareownership is continuing to expand every month.

Nothing casts a light on this healthy growth more than a census of shareowners released recently by the New York Stock Exchange. The shape of our People's Capitalism as it exists these days comes into vivid focus through these findings.

One in eight holds stock

For one thing, publicly held companies are owned directly by 12,490,000 individuals, or one out of every eight adults in the nation. This figure represents an increase of 45 per cent in three years, and a jump of almost 100% since 1952. Between 1956 and 1959, in fact, one hundred thousand new investors a month were added, nearly a million and a third a year, almost four million over the three-year period.

Exciting as these figures may be, however, they are only a part of the picture. Some 100 million people are indirect owners through their investments in insurance companies, pension funds and other institutions which invest their funds in stocks. In one way or another, virtually everyone has an ownership interest in American Business.

While stockholders live in every section of the country, come from every occupational group and every income level, they can be defined in terms of a statistical average. Like Philip Miller of Aurora, Illinois, the average new shareowning capitalist is a Midwesterner in his early thirties who earns somewhere between $5,000 and $10,000 a year.

The growth of shareownership in recent years, of course, raises several crucial questions for the economy. How are investors approaching the market, for example, and are they heeding the necessary cautions? Our studies indicate that most people are in the market for the long-term. They have sound objectives. They are tending to concentrate not on speculative securities but on the blue chip issues, and they are often reinvesting dividends. Besides, they are using cash primarily and relying on only modest amounts of credit.

Wanted: capable people

Under the circumstances, it isn't surprising that America's investment community has more and more hung out the "Help Wanted" sign in an effort to attract capable young people to serve a much broader investing public. Large numbers of qualified men and women must be recruited to work at every level of the securities business.

Job opportunities range from registered representatives employed by Member Firms to deal directly with customers, to the highly skillful technicians who utilize the latest electronic equipment in member firm offices from coast-to-coast. In addition, new fields are opening as the industry expands. Twenty years ago, for example, the securities analyst was something of a novelty; today he is a vital link between the brokerage firm and its research facilities, and the investing public.

In addition, turnover and replacements steadily increase job opportunities. In one recent year we learned that 7,800 individuals had joined the Stock Exchange community, including 550 recent college graduates—a statistic that points up the industry's need to attract more and more qualified men and women.

Young people who have recently taken jobs in the securities business know they are part of an exciting and significant field. They know that the rewards can be ample as well. One study revealed that a group of 30-year-old college-trained men averaged some $9,000 after only five years in the business. What's more, those surveyed expected to double their incomes in five years and to triple them in ten.

Encouraging as investment careers look today, they are likely to be even more promising tomorrow. In a country where mass shareownership is a relatively recent development, future personnel needs are obvious. Now and in the years ahead the securities field will add additional manpower, additional branch offices, additional firms.

Giant electric boards in brokerage offices across the country show trade-by-trade reports on stock transactions.

Educating the public

We recognize, of course, that the growth of shareownership is linked to many factors, including the level of prosperity over the past decade, high personal incomes which could be channeled into investments, a generally rising stock market, a continued fear of inflation and a growing understanding of the investment process. In this last connection, the Exchange's long-range educational program has been crucial and in the years ahead we will continue to inform and educate the public about existing investment opportunities.

In pursuit of that goal much has already been done. A long-range information program was planned to take the investment story directly to the public. We developed a basic theme—"Own Your Share of American Business"—which continues to key our advertising, literature, films and other programs. It is used simultaneously by many of our Member Firms.

Educational advertising is placed in leading newspapers and magazines across the country. In recent years the Exchange has allocated about $1.2 million annually for this effort. Our Member Firms, of course, collectively spend many times this on their own behalf.

In addition, millions of educational booklets are distributed to the public every year. A large volume of material is supplied to the press, radio and television. Our motion pictures are seen annually by more millions over television, at meetings and at lectures. In 85 leading cities, personnel from our Member Firms have formed committees to carry out adult education activities. Educational displays for office windows, fairs and conventions are in steady circulation.

Regular warnings issued

In everything the Exchange does to explain the investment process, we raise warning flags for the public. We point out, for example, that stock investments involve risks, and people must scale their risks to what they can afford. We make it clear that investors should have a steady income, cash savings and other protection for their families. They should get the facts and seek sound advice from a broker whose reputation they can check. Finally, they should avoid rumor-mongers and get-rich-quick artists.

Apart from our informational activities we have helped develop investing techniques that contribute to greater opportunities for many people. Our Monthly Investment Plan has dramatized the idea that a man of average means can invest in the stock of his choice for as little as 45 cents a day. We have encouraged the investment club movement through which groups of 10 or 15 people pool small sums to buy securities.

Our listed companies have done considerable work to broaden the ownership base as well. They have waged their own education programs and encouraged the growth of employee stock plans, some of which call for automatic payroll deductions. Today, more than 1.3 million people invest regularly through these plans.

Looking to the future, it is apparent that the trend towards a still broader ownership base will continue.

The extent of any forthcoming demand that this will place on our community is plainly beyond any accurate predicting. But we do know that in the years since 1945 our economy has expanded materially, experienced brief setbacks and then continued its forward momentum. Shareownership has boomed. Additional millions have considered their first stock investments. The number of shares listed on the Stock Exchange grew from 1.6 billion to about 5.5 billion shares. During this 14-year period, the daily volume on our Exchange was 1.7 million shares.

Thus, if for planning purposes we consider the 1954-58 experience as a rough guide, and if we allow for a continuing favorable pattern of growth, it would appear possible that during the middle of the 1960's we might have a daily average volume of about 4.5 million shares, and a total stock list of perhaps 8.5 billion shares.

In much the same way, continued growth throughout the 1960's could bring, in the 1970's, a daily average share volume of 5.5 to 6 million shares, and a total stock list of something over 11 billion shares.

When I first mentioned these and other figures recently, I was asked how large I thought the American shareowner population might be a decade from now. Again, I know of no sure way to predict the future. But an extension over the years of the increase in shareownership experienced during the past seven years would mean an average net gain of at least 860,000 shareowners per year.

This would give America a shareowning family of about 18 million in the middle 1960's,

and 22 million by around 1970—or 76 per cent more than the present. This significant expansion will surely give new dimension to the concept of a nation of capitalists.

These are, I must stress, by no means predictions. They are, instead, possibilities to be considered as the idea of a People's Capitalism becomes more widespread. And they are possibilities we must consider in our own planning for the future. In our market place in recent years we have moved to add qualified new people, modernize our equipment, and streamline our operations. Studies now underway will undoubtedly suggest additional changes that are necessary in order to serve a still wider public.

There is no question in my mind that the future financing of our industries is tied to the soundness and success with which our educational efforts develop. But even more important, by putting ownership within the reach

Behind this famous facade at the corner of Wall and Broad better than 500 million shares change hands each year. Two thousand people work on or near the floor, almost as long as a football field and 79 feet high. Gallery visitors look down on 18 trading posts, shown at left.

of millions of people, we can exert an enormous influence for good on the growth of the free world.

For this reason, while we are pleased with the results of our own efforts to date, we by no means feel that shareownership has gone as far as it can and should. The idea of mass stockownership among millions of people who can afford the risks is still, perhaps, a new one.

But the future will soon be on us. As more and more Americans of average means soundly invest a part of their earnings in securities, the key to an even broader People's Capitalism will be just what you might expect—qualified men and women within our community who possess the vision, courage and sense of responsibility that will enable them to serve millions of additional investors.

A Brief History of Wall Street

UNDERNEATH THE SPREADING BUTTONWOOD TREE

Harold W. Scott

Twenty-four brokers founded the New York Stock Exchange in 1792, under this tree.

Cows, INDIANS and the English were responsible for naming what is perhaps the best known street in the world—Wall Street.

Some three hundred years ago, a brushwood fence was erected across the tip of Manhattan Island to keep the cows from leaving and the Indians from entering. A decade later the fence was strengthened and backed up by an earthen wall, largely because of fears of an English invasion. This wall ran roughly parallel to what is now Wall Street.

Wall Street was a political capital before it grew to be the nation's financial heart and an international financial capital. The Continental Congress decided to hold its sessions in City Hall, later rebuilt as Federal Hall; and George Washington came to Wall Street in April 1789, to be sworn in as the new nation's first President. He took the oath of office on a balcony of City Hall, across the street from the present New York Stock Exchange.

From his office in what is now 33 Wall, Alexander Hamilton, first Secretary of the Treasury, labored to establish the new republic's credit and enunciated principles of finance which have endured to this day.

It was the First Congress which consolidated the government's debt—largely the cost of fighting the Revolutionary War—by authorizing an issue of $80,000,000 in government stock. New York City merchants and auctioneers began to deal in the government stock, as well as the shares of a few such enterprises as the Bank of the United States, the Bank of North America, and the Bank of New York. The need for a market was obvious even then—for people were reluctant to buy securities unless they knew they could sell them readily.

In 1792, twenty-four of these "Brokers for the Purchase and Sale of Public Stock" drew up an agreement which laid the foundation for the New York Stock Exchange. Their meeting place was on the street, just a few blocks from the present Exchange, under an old buttonwood tree which had escaped the English axes. They traded in stocks and in merchandise—and were not above making a wager on the outcome of political disputes. The following year the brokers moved indoors, to the Tontine Coffee House at the corner of Wall and Water Streets.

1812 war signalled nation's growth

At the turn of the century there were few enterprises large enough to call for public financing. Still, the nation was growing, the West was opening up and trade flourished. Yet it was not until after the War of 1812—which, of course, disrupted commercial activity—that the United States really began to flex its muscles. Successful conclusion of a war with a great power unleashed the energies of a united and strong people. Commercial activity thrived, new enterprises multiplied, speculation was in the air.

The national debt jumped from $45,000,000 in 1812 to $123,000,000 in 1817. Erie Canal bonds were successfully floated and New York City had a direct link with what was then the West. New banks, new marine and fire insurance companies were formed. The states issued bonds to pay for roads and canals.

Money funneled into Wall Street from all over the country—and Wall Street pumped that money into the arteries of trade, commerce and industry.

Trading in securities quickly became an integral part of American financial activity.

Stock brokers, faced with this expansion in their business, decided that formation of a more cohesive organization was a necessity, and in 1817 they drew up the first formal Constitution of the New York Stock and Exchange Board.

The 1817 Constitution provided that the President of the Exchange would call out the names of each stock issue to be traded and the members would then make their bids to buy or offers to sell. For interrupting the President during the call, a member was subject to a fine of six to twenty-five cents. A record of sales was kept and rules governing admission of new members were laid down. Absence from a call was apparently considered a pretty serious affair, for the guilty member—except in the case of sickness—was liable to a fine of 1/16 of a dollar.

From 1817 to 1827 the Board met in various offices in the vicinity of Wall Street. It was not until 1865, and a dozen or so moves in the meantime, that a permanent location was acquired at 10-12 Broad Street, which contained a large part of the trading floor as it is today. An adjoining office building which also contains an extension of the trading floor, known to irreverent members of the Exchange as "The Garage," was erected in 1922.

In the year following adoption of the first Constitution in 1817, the young economy suffered from one of the periodic speculative sprees which intermittently plagued the nation for another century or more. Self-confidence and extravagance were outstanding national characteristics for many decades in American history—characteristics which successfully developed a lusty nation and which also got the country in trouble on more than one occasion. We still have our self-confidence, but youthful extravagance has been replaced by the sense of responsibility which accompanies maturity.

Securities speculation was only mildly in evidence in those days—actually, speculation embraced every phase of the country's commercial life. The temper of the times precluded any long-range view except dynamic optimism —but optimism at times was carried too far.

Rail securities ushered in a new era

Trading in securities on the Exchange gradually increased, but it was not until the advent of railroad stocks in 1830 that a new era in American finance was opened. In August of that year the Mohawk & Hudson Railroad (later a part of the New York Central System) was started and its stock listed on the Exchange, the first railroad to have that distinction. In the next few decades rail lines were laid with prodigious rapidity and the securities of many of the new carriers were traded on the Exchange.

The growth of our rail system, of course, was of tremendous importance to the growth of the country. Possibly even more important was the need for large amounts of capital to construct railroads and the emergence of the corporation as a dominant form of business enterprise.

Rail securities quickly caught the public fancy: bonds, common stock and even preferred stock, the latter first issued about 1836.

Through the years Trinity Church has dominated Wall Street.

In 1837 Wall Street was crushed by financial disaster. Furious speculation in land and securities in 1836 culminated in the Panic of 1837, which threw into bankruptcy some of the strongest banks, financial houses, and business enterprises in the country. The Stock Exchange, incidentally, did business then in a former hayloft because of the great fire of December 1835, which ravaged Wall Street.

The tempo of the nation's business life naturally slowed after 1837 but once again the country showed extraordinary recuperative powers. This was an era when trading and mercantile fortunes were being amassed, when gold was discovered in California, when the telegraph was perfected (later to become one of the most valuable tools of business and finance), and the spectacular speculator made his first appearance in Wall Street.

The DL&W says "no"

It was in these years that the Stock Exchange inaugurated its policy of asking for fiscal information about the companies whose securities were traded on the Exchange. Today, any corporation which wants to list its securities on the Exchange knows that this will involve public disclosure of pertinent fi-

different churches were built: 1696, 1788, 1846. Views here are 1829, 1887, 1926, 1960.

nancial information. But less than 100 years ago the Delaware, Lackawanna & Western Railroad, in response to a request for information from the Exchange, could reply:

"The Delaware, Lackawanna & Western R. R. makes no reports and publishes no statements—and has not done anything of the kind for the last five years."

Contrast that attitude with the views expressed recently by Eugene Holman, Chairman of Standard Oil Company (New Jersey), who said that the development of better products at lower costs is a major social contribution by the corporation. He added:

"But I think that the American people today expect more than that of companies—large or small. I think they believe we have a duty to be actively concerned about the whole society in which we operate. I believe that a large company especially has a duty to its shareholders to think continually of the general welfare, not only to avoid actions contrary to public interest, but to take positive, constructive actions for the common good."

Text continued on page 50

World War I Liberty Bonds made millions of Americans into owners of securities for the first time. From this base developed the nation-wide interest which built the 20's boom.

THERE ONCE WAS A WALL

Wall Street began as a brushwood fence 300 years ago, a fence later strengthened into an earthen wall. In the early days of the Republic, New York was the governmental *and* financial capital of the new nation. The Treasury, shown right, was located in a miasmic Potomac swamp—but the money was in New York.

Federal Hall, originally New York's City Hall, once included both a jail and a fire house. It was rebuilt when the Continental Congress decided to hold its sessions there, and in 1879 General Washington became president on its balcony.

"Ye Olde Mint," America's first, was established in 1792 in Philadelphia through the efforts of Washington, Jefferson, and Hamilton. It remained an independent government department until it became a Treasury bureau in 1873.

The first Merchant's Exchange, home of the New York Stock Exchange from the mid-1820's till December 16-17, 1837, when it was destroyed in the Great Fire. The fire, visible for 100 miles, burned for days, destroyed 17 blocks. The Exchange is shown burning in the contemporary print (right).

Trading rooms in less frenetic times: left, the Merchants' Room of the second Merchant's Exchange, where members gathered twice daily to hear the list of securities and transactions called out. Right is the interior of the 12 Broad Street building, where—for less than two hours!—75 members assembled on an average day (2000 people are on the floor today).

The Tontine Coffee House in 1800 was the home of the Exchange. At the corner of Wall and Water, it served for 24 years.

"Stephen Girard's Bank": the first Bank of the United States, in Philadelphia, 1818.

Nineteenth Century traders were housed in this imposing edifice, the second Merchant's Exchange, from 1842 to 1854. In 1865 a permanent home at 12 Broad Street was bought (right); today's 21-story building stands on this land.

A giant step forward was the first stock ticker, installed in 1867.

Panic! Saturday, September 20, 1873.

The well-upholstered investor checked his portfolio in plush comfort in the 1870's. Fortunes were made and lost in rails, as builders fought across the continent.

Trading on the Curb took a special stamina. From left: the market before 1900, as it appeared when at the corner of William and Beaver Streets (Delmonico's portico is in the right background). After the Curb moved to Broad Street phone clerks worked from windows, ate on the run. At right is the historic "last day" of the outdoor Curb, June 25, 1921.

J. P. Morgan Sr. and *President Taft emerge* from Fifth Avenue's fashionable St. Thomas Church on a wintry day in 1910.

A few minutes before noon, September 16, 1920, a horse-drawn wagon pulled up to the curb before the Sub-Treasury Building, across from the granite edifice housing the Morgan bank. Moments later the wagon disintegrated with a roar heard for miles—a wall of flame shot into open windows six floors up, burning people seated at desks. Even more destructive were 1000s of iron fragments, later found to be parts of sash-weights, which exploded in a deadly rain. Hundreds were injured, 38 dead, property damage ran to $2½ million. The horse and wagon simply disappeared; one shoe remained, but the blacksmith who made it was never found and the mystery of "who" and "why" remains unsolved.

HAROLD W. SCOTT, former chairman of the Board of Governors of the New York Stock Exchange. He is today a member of the Exchange and a partner in the investment banking firm of Dean Witter & Co. Mr. Scott attended Princeton University.

Continued from page 46

A few years later, in 1869, the Exchange adopted another rule of profound significance. Prior to then it was not unusual for a company to issue stock secretly as an aid to manipulation. The Exchange decided that the shares of all active stocks must be registered at some satisfactory agency in order that the public would know how many shares were outstanding. Erie Railroad thought so poorly of this innovation that the road refused to comply and its shares were removed from the list. A rival exchange known as the Erie Board was formed, but in a few months Erie capitulated and its stock was back on the Big Board.

New war renewed growth

The Civil War opened the modern era in American finance. New fortunes had been accumulated during the War, the country had a rail net that was soon to link the East and Far West, the rebuilding of the South was undertaken and the West opened up, and the corporation was refined to the point where the nation's first billion-dollar enterprise—U. S. Steel Corporation—was formed at the turn of the century. The industrial revolution was pounding away at high speed.

In 1860 a little more than $1,000,000,000 was invested in manufacturing; in less than 50 years the total had increased to more than $12,000,000,000. In 1860 there were some 1,500,000 industrial wage earners employed in the United States; less than 50 years later there were 5,500,000. During that same period, the value of manufactured products increased 15 times to $15,000,000,000.

Before the nineteenth century ended America led the world in the quantity and value of her manufactured products.

It was an era of intense speculation—and magnificent accomplishment.

The driving power behind this period of empire building were men whose names today are legendary—Jay Cooke, Vanderbilt, Carnegie, Rockefeller, Morgan, Hill, Harriman. They were often bitterly attacked for their methods—and often with justice—but they were great builders and great administrators, men with the creative imagination to build America's industrial might.

The philosophy that guided John D. Rockefeller in the creation of Standard Oil Company was probably shared by most of the early trust builders. It was believed simply that competition was inefficient and wasteful—and competition was destroyed with surgical precision. They recognized the value of integrating production, processing, transportation, and marketing. Similar thinking guided the formation of other trusts—the Harvester Trust, the Sugar Trust, the Tobacco Trust, the Steamship Trust, even an Ice Trust. Monopoly in those days was regarded as just good business sense.

Most portentous: the Sherman Act

Then in 1891 the Congress passed what one observer has described as "probably the most portentous single legislative act in the history

TODAY...

of American capitalism: the passage of the Sherman Act against monopolies and combinations in restraint of trade."

Today, of course, competition in the United States is an accepted fact of economic life.

Wall Street was the hub of all these activities—Wall Street writhing in the despair of Black Friday, 1869, when speculation in gold touched off a monumental panic; Wall Street pledging its resources to save the credit of the United States Government; Wall Street, where an English lawyer pyramided a handful of cheap mining shares into a $13,000,000 fortune; Wall Street providing the money to build a nation.

The pulse of Wall Street was the New York Stock Exchange, mirroring the nation's business tempo, the hopes and fears of speculators and investors, providing the market place without which the flood of securities which financed growth could never have been sold.

Some highlights in Stock Exchange history in that period included: 1863, when the name "New York Stock Exchange" was adopted; 1868, when memberships were made saleable; 1869, when a new constitution was adopted; 1871, when the call market was replaced by the continuous auction market; 1879, when the first telephones were installed in the Exchange; 1886, when a day's volume topped 1,000,000 shares for the first time; 1892, when the Exchange established the right to select the telegraph company or companies which would distribute its quotations.

Control of the ticker quotation system carried a great deal more importance than appears at first glance. For decades the Stock Exchange fought the "bucket-shops"—alleged brokerage firms whose main function in life was to fleece the public. Access to Stock Exchange quotations was essential to the operation of the "bucket-shop", so the Exchange removed tickers and wires from fraudulent nonmember concerns all over the country. Some of these firms had even obtained a license from the State in which they were operating. Today, thanks to this control, the "bucket-shop" is extinct in the United States.

In the past fifty years Wall Street and the Stock Exchange have weathered two wars, the biggest bull market and the worst depression in our history, Congressional investigations, Federal regulations, and taxation.

Wall Street and the Exchange, though, are still doing business today, still financing American industry, still providing a public market place where the securities of the nation's leading corporations are bought and sold fairly, honestly, and efficiently.

Wall Street has outlived the abuses which reached a climax in 1929. The Stock Exchange and its members—self-regulated more meticulously than any other business group—have never enjoyed greater public esteem.

The old wall that once formed a barricade across the tip of Manhattan Island has long since disappeared and Wall Street itself is no longer bounded by Trinity Church and the East River bulkheads.

Today Wall Street extends into every Main Street in the country, for it is Wall Street and the Stock Exchange which enable millions and millions of American families and individuals to own their share in the industrial might which keeps this nation strong and free.

...AND TOMORROW?

MURRAY SHIELDS is a partner in MacKay-Shields Associates, Inc., and president of Management Economics, Inc. He also serves as trustee of the Bowery Savings Bank and the National Industrial Conference Board. Formerly, he was vice-president and economist for the Bank of the Manhattan Company and Irving Trust Co.

The Economist in Wall Street

THE NEW INFLUENTIAL

Murray Shields

ECONOMICS IS an essential tool for and part of the basic operating apparatus of almost every phase of the financial community's activities. It pervades Wall Street's thinking to a far greater degree than is the case in any other business or financial center of the country. Its role in investment programming, for borrowers and investors alike, has increased substantially in the past decade. And it has come into active use in the long-range planning and short-range budgeting of all major financial institutions.

The "woods" of Wall Street are full of highly-placed individuals who may not now carry the title of professional economist, but who are nonetheless highly perceptive observers of the domestic and international scene and highly sophisticated students of the basic economics of the money markets, of international finance, of government fiscal affairs, of the bond and stock markets, and of markets, prices and profits for industry as a whole, as well as for all of our important individual industries.

The fact that in many cases professional economists have been elected to positions of administrative responsibility in some of our major financial institutions gives testimony to the new important role economists are playing in the life of our financial community.

The financial community also has access to, and actively makes use of, the analysis and research done by many independent, professional economists and economic consulting agencies.

Furthermore, the quality of the professional economic analysis and research done by the commercial banks, insurance companies, pension funds, open-end mutual funds, investment banks, stock exchange houses and consulting firms has increased immensely, as has the size of the economic staffs devoted to such work at the professional level.

Contributing factors outlined

Several factors have contributed to the increased use of economic analysis in our financial community:

1. The sheer magnitude of *the problem of selecting individual issues* in markets that comprise the stocks and bonds of thousands of individual companies: this problem makes it essential that economic analysis be used to focus the techniques of security analysis on areas where they can be intensive enough to be effective.

2. *Our domestic economy is now so complex* that its behavior patterns are undergoing significant change. The response of parts of the economy to movements in general business display unconventional trends. For example, our booms and our recessions tend to "roll" from industry to industry and from area to area, which makes it difficult to time the peaks and bottoms of the business cycle and to use the cycle in formulating investment strategy. Inflation moves from one part of the commod-

ity and security price structure to another. The business cycle has been modified by the changing distribution of consumer incomes, by the automatic stabilizers, and by the role of government in the expenditure stream, with the result that the cycle has magnified effects on some industries while others display counter-cyclical tendencies. In this environment economic analysis of such factors has become prerequisite to successful investment programming.

3. *Communication and transportation progress* is making our economy increasingly dependent on and, in fact, part of the international economy—with business and finance becoming internationalized at a very rapid rate. Therefore, the economic analysis of conditions, trends and prospects in the major commercial countries of the West has become indispensable to investment programming, not only because investment markets abroad provide attractive media for the employment of funds, but because international factors—gold, balance-of-payments trends, relative costs of production, the activities of international financial institutions, etc.—have come to have a vitally important bearing on the prospects for our own economy as a whole and for many individual industries and companies.

4. *The new era of technological revolution*, supported by roughly $10 billion of private and governmental outlays for research and development, affects—adversely or favorably—the growth patterns of every industry in the land. Analysis of the general and particular impacts of the new and massive factor of planned innovation involves the use of the most advanced economic and statistical tools.

5. *The role of government in our economy* has expanded enormously—not only because government expenditures dominate a larger and larger part of the flow of incomes, but also because government administrative, legislative and regulatory agencies now exercise powers which deflect the growth and profit patterns of so many individual industries and areas. Economic analysis of the highest competence is now essential if the business, banking and investment communities are to make adequate allowance for the new role of government.

6. *The sheer growth of our major financial and investment institutions* calls for highly imaginative use of economic analysis. It is commonly agreed that our investment markets are becoming more and more "institutionalized." The end of that process clearly is not yet in sight. What is clear is the fact that institutions of such heroic size can and must base their policies on the most careful analysis of the outlook for our economy as a whole, on intensive analysis of the economic factors which affect the relative attractiveness of fixed income and equity securities, and on the economic impact of changes in the economic climate on individiual sectors of our economy.

7. *Inflation* is now a built-in factor in our way of life, because of the powers granted to organized labor and because of the widely-accepted notion that government deficit expenditures are necessary to and contribute to growth. Such spending, it is contended, must be used to prevent unemployment, and must be brought to the assistance of any area or industry which is dissatisfied with its lot and possesses sufficient power to tap the public till. The impact on investment of this new factor is inevitably immense. But the process of inflation is not continuous: its timing varies, as does its effect on various facets of the economy; and its form changes dramatically and rapidly. It is not surprising, therefore, that economic analysis of this vital factor, its origin, its speed and its effects has now become generally regarded as a necessary base for investment programming.

From the general to the specific

In such a dynamically changing environment, there is quite naturally a new tendency for investment management to argue from the economic "general" to the investment "specific." The end result is the same, i.e., the selection of specific issues. But there is a new tendency to get there by a route which involves much broader and much more intensive economic analysis.

This economist, whose experiences in Wall Street covers a bit more than a quarter of a century, is convinced that in the decade ahead, the role of the professional economist in the financial institutions of our country will continue to expand and that the influence of the economists who counsel with our great financial institutions will increase—to the good of everyone concerned.

Wall Street:
Myth and Reality

THE INVESTMENT BANKER— A BULBOUS PRINCE OF PRIVILEGE?

John M. Schiff

THE POWER OF "Wall Street" is one of the most persistent myths in American life. There is a fallacious belief that most of the financial strength and much of the political power controlling the destinies of our nation, its industries and its people, are concentrated in the few square blocks of New York's Wall Street district. Those of us who are part of this financial community know how far this myth is from reality. We know that the commercial and investment bankers, the brokers, and the other financial institutions lack cohesion and unanimity, they speak as individuals rather than collectively, and as individuals they are by no means capable of wielding a fraction of the vast powers erroneously attributed to them under the generic term of "Wall Street."

The "Wall Street bankers" legend is an old one which has been exploited for generations

The "banker legend" probably began in the titanic political struggle between President Jackson (left) and banker Nicholas Biddle (opposite page), with the Bank of the United States as prize. Two such banks existed; one from 1791 to 1811, the other from 1816 to 1836. Congress chartered the second for 20 years and watched it grow strong in Whig politics while it gained a firm grip over the nation's banking system. Although the Bank's friends were powerful enough to pass the re-charter through Congress in 1832, Jackson—determined to crush it—vetoed the bill and the Bank expired. The Democrats' cartoon shows Jackson (center) "doctoring Mother Bank" while Biddle holds the patient's head.

by demagogic pretenders of political reform. Long before the repercussions against Wall Street and the bankers, which followed the 1929 market crash, Andrew Jackson, our seventh president, tossed the banker legend into the political arena in his epic struggle with Nicholas Biddle over the destinies of The Bank of the United States. Jackson's reelection in 1832, following his veto of the Bank's charter, was interpreted as a mandate to destroy the Bank. Under Jackson's prodding, the government withdrew its funds on deposit and re-deposited these funds in certain favored State banks. The young Republic's central banking system no longer existed, nor, for much longer, did The Bank of the United States, which expired in 1836. The Panic of 1837 followed. Perhaps, this free-for-all between Jackson and the early nineteenth century bankers paved the way for the cartoons which later appeared and are used to this day, which depict the banker as a bulbous, over-fed prince of privilege, silk-hatted, frock-coated, smoking a Churchillian-sized cigar and labeled "Wall Street."

Popular fancies, however exaggerated, generally have some basis in fact. The "Wall Street" myth is no exception. In the early days of our history, most of our capital was concentrated in eastern seaboard cities—New York, Boston and Philadelphia—and the bankers of that era had considerably more influence in our affairs than they exert today. Their power resulted from being strategically located at the gateway to America at a time when England and the Continent were the primary sources of investment capital. There was very limited capital available on the east coast and the small amount that we possessed was largely in the hands of scattered individuals and was derived from real estate, agriculture, and trade. It was not until after the Civil War that fortunes amassed in manufacturing made any appreciable difference to our growing economy.

Our land and natural resources were rich; but there was a great need of money and manpower for their development. The pressing shortage of tools, wagons, cattle, warehousing, sources of credit, manufacturing capacity, and other facilities essential to a productive economy limited a country straining to expand. The West was waiting to be opened to the vast flow of immigration. There was a surplus of labor in many parts of Europe and the more venturesome citizens saw in our vigorous young country opportunities for a new and profitable life. The cry of many returning Civil War veterans from both North and South was: "Go West!" Capital was lacking to open up the vast lands west of the Alleghenies, and the bankers of our leading trading cities turned

to the European lenders who supplied much of the money so greatly needed.

The east coast bankers channeled European capital into American enterprise. The wealth of Europe had been accumulating for generations, and in its older culture, society was ordered, risk opportunities were few, and there was a surplus of capital. During this era, world trade further added to Europe's bounty in the form of earnings remitted from investments overseas. Interest rates on funds loaned in Europe were low contrasted to funds loaned in America, and as a result of this yield differential their bankers saw in our budding economy opportunities for investment. Here the larger risks and shortage of venture capital meant a higher return than could be obtained on the Continent or in England.

The new American industrialist, hard pressed for risk money, had neither the time nor the qualifications to canvass Europe in search of investors. Conversely, the European lender was not sufficiently familiar with our new country to search for likely enterprises in which to invest his money. Both relied on the bankers, who joined the flow of European capital to the trickle of American capital, and these essential funds made it possible to develop the railroads, steamships, and communications which were the first steps toward tying together our rapidly expanding nation. Thousands of miles of rails were to cross and crisscross the continent; soon the produce of our fertile lands would be harvested, the forests lumbered, minerals and ores extracted and transported to market. Mills and factories were to be erected in the East, South and Midwest. In providing this necessary capital the American bankers performed a requisite function and their integrity, prudence, and financial knowledge proved their ability to serve—and in so serving to profit.

Speculations brought chaos

The era of investment in young industries was accompanied by fits of speculative fever, which had their inevitable aftermaths in chaos and depression. The savings of thousands were wiped out during the recurrent panics of the 1800's and the Panic of 1907, as artificially created and maintained security prices collapsed. Hatred and despair welled up in the people and much of their feeling was vented against the "bankers." The term "Wall Street bankers," according to the loose definition of those days, included promoters, or market manipulators, who all too frequently profited during periods of widespread misfortune. Overlooked were the bankers whose services were dedicated to their profession and whose performance fulfilled the highest standards of business ethics. Forgotten for the moment were the monuments to their efforts—the railroads, the steel mills, the mines. Constructive work had been done and for the most part the funds had been honestly invested. Despite these sporadic setbacks, the dynamism of our country could not be denied and soon after each depression we started an upward cycle. The inherent vigor of our growing economy reasserted itself and our productivity and standard of living once again resumed their upward course.

The turn of the century brought a new function of the banker to the fore. In the era of merger and consolidation which marked a maturing economy, the banker, through his control of capital, was in a position to bring together competing entities into larger and more efficient productive units. Bankers at that time

JOHN M. SCHIFF, a partner of the investment banking firm of Kuhn, Loeb & Co., graduated from Yale in 1925 and received his M.A. from Oxford University in 1927. He has been with Kuhn, Loeb & Co. since 1929 and is a director of a number of corporations.

Depositors caught in the Panic of 1907 beseige the teller's window—to withdraw their funds before the rumored collapse.

were quick to recognize the economies of vertical integration and the stabilizing effect of diversification. Through their efforts many companies were able to consolidate, and this period probably represents the high point in the influence of the "Wall Street bankers." By the advent of World War I new forces were coming into being which challenged the prestige of the bankers and minimized the significance of the capital at their command.

In the early part of the twentieth century the United States changed from an importer to an exporter of capital. So rapid had been our growth and so productive our economy, that we were generating savings more than sufficient to finance our own expansion. Europe, meanwhile, through a series of tragic misfortunes, was to dissipate her wealth and become dependent upon us for help.

Liberty Bonds introduced securities to millions

The Liberty Loan drives of World War I had a far-reaching effect on our procedures for distributing securities. The purchase of a Liberty Bond became a patriotic duty, and millions of our citizens were thereby for the first time introduced to security ownership. Following the Liberty Loan drives of 1917-19 the American public was educated to invest at a time when income taxes, as compared to our present rates, were relatively low and interest rates relatively high, with the result that individuals were attracted to the retail purchase of corporate bonds, which provided an acceptable return on the money invested. This understanding continued after the war and has had a beneficial effect, since it has spread into the equity markets and has enlarged the public ownership of corporations, thus making it possible to gather the savings of millions to finance corporate expansion.

World War I ended, bringing distress and ruin in Europe. In our country it brought unrestrained speculation in securities and real estate. The resultant financial collapse of 1929 and the depression of the 1930's brought an era of "reform" legislation once again aimed at Wall Street—the "whipping boy." While many of the reforms were desirable and reflected merely the adoption into legislation of the practices of the reputable investment banking firms, the punitive nature of the legislation seriously dislocated established methods of security distribution. More than a decade of adjustment was required before the capital markets were functioning smoothly again. By then World War II had broken out and the responsibility for financing the war effort and the subsequent rehabilitation was taken over by the government. But even prior to this takeover, Wall Street had yielded much of its pre-eminence in monetary affairs to Washington.

Under the several Roosevelt administrations we tended both politically and economically towards a stronger central government which was emphasized by government financing of relief and public work projects during the early and middle 1930's. In those years the management of the public debt became the dominant fiscal activity and the securities markets became sensitive to decisions made in Washington. Despite the change in administration, management of the Federal debt and the inflationary or deflationary implications of the Federal budget continue to affect and at

The fortress home of a nineteenth century bank: the National Park Bank built this main-office at 214 Broadway in lower Manhattan in 1893, when its assets made it the largest bank in the U. S. The ornate and forbidding interior featured murals depicting commerce, industry, and agriculture.

times to dominate our securities markets.

Another factor diminishing the power of the bankers has been the growth of corporate wealth. As our larger corporations grew in size and in capitalization, their reliance on the bankers lessened. In many instances, such corporations have been able partially to finance their expansion programs from retained earnings and depreciation, and their trips to the public market have been rare. However, in the postwar period, despite their tremendous growth in assets, General Motors, Westinghouse, Allied Chemical, United States Steel, Bethlehem Steel, among many other giant corporations, have found it necessary to come to the public market with offerings once again underwritten by investment bankers.

The "institutional investor" now pre-eminent

The rise of the "institutional investor," more than any other post-war development, has come to characterize today's investment market—they are now the pre-eminent factor in our securities market. The institutionalization of the people's savings in insurance companies, in pension and welfare funds, in investment trusts (both open and closed end), and the substantial wealth in trust accounts have had a direct bearing on investment banking procedures. These great repositories represent the savings of millions upon millions of individuals and their growth can be largely ascribed to the desire of the Amercan public to provide personal security against illness, old age, and misfortunes. Exemption of private placements from the Securities Act of 1933 eliminated the costly and laborious necessity of registering security offerings not involving a public sale. This gave further impetus to the financial importance of these institutional investors who increasingly became substantial buyers of securities placed privately. By 1938, the annual rate of private placements had already reached a volume of $800,000,000. By 1958, approximately $3,712,000,000 of securities were sold privately to institutional investors to provide the funds for industrial or business expansion, the construction of utility plants, natural gas transmission lines, oil pipe lines, and for other corporate purposes.

In negotiating a private placement the dollar risk of the investment banker is nil. In this type of transaction, he is no longer a principal and performs essentially a professional task. He is the servant of both the borrower and the lender. His function is that of a service organization whose expert knowledge of the security markets enables him to serve the issuing company and the lender in creating a security best suited to both.

The risk function of investment banking basically divides into (1) the negotiated purchase of various types of underwritten securities, which are offered publicly, for industrial and other types of clients whose business affairs are not subject to regulatory authorities,

Liberty Bonds in World War I first made ownership of securities meaningful—and patriotic—to millions of Americans. Here's a window display for the fourth Liberty Loan.

and (2) competitive bidding which is imposed on certain public utility and railroad companies by regulatory bodies. This requirement was put into effect by the Securities and Exchange Commission in 1941 for the utility holding companies under its jurisdiction. The Interstate Commerce Commission in 1944 made competitive bidding compulsory for any railroad debt financing aggregating over $1,000,000. It has seriously limited the ability of the issuing corporation's management to create variations in the conventional types of securities which could produce important economies in the raising of capital. At the same time it makes impossible private placement, except in unusual circumstances, and it deprives the issuer of investment banking assistance in the creation and timing of a security issuance. Competitive bidding thus limits the banker's function to market risk and distribution.

Persistence of the myth of "Wall Street" is probably based in part on ignorance and has undergone little change over the years. This myth does not acknowledge the affirmative contributions of New York's financial district to our economy. The economic employment of savings is as essential to production as machine tools, or the physical labor of men, the acumen of management, or even the flow of electrical current. Without capital, production cannot be continued, inventories carried, nor wages paid. In bringing together those who have savings to invest with public authorities and business enterprises requiring capital, the investment community, wherever it be located, fulfills a definite need in our free country.

A concept too convenient to change

Unfortunately, headlines are not made by the constructive aspects of the banking business, since the investment of capital is not a spectacular endeavor; rather, headlines are made by those rare and unusual events which attract public fancy—notices of fortunes quickly acquired, battles for corporate control, financial collapse, and those few occurrences of misfeasance. These are the types of items that nourish the popular myth and it is not likely that the American public will soon be disabused of one of the most widespread and fervently held notions in its folklore. The "Wall Street bankers" legend is too convenient a concept in political agitation to be abandoned; it is the handy whipping boy upon which the rabble-rousers blame the country's economic troubles. "Wall Street" has been sold to the public as being synonymous with power, privilege, and concentrated wealth. The cities on the eastern seaboard other than New York also have their financial districts. Chicago has its LaSalle Street, San Francisco its Montgomery Street, and there are financial sections in Dallas, Detroit, Los Angeles, St. Louis, and Pittsburgh, as well as in many other cities. All of them are of vital importance in supplying the capital requirements of this country, yet none of these cities, streets, or financial districts have the apocryphal stigma of "Wall Street." If the future follows the past, any financial failure of great magnitude, from whatever point of the compass, will probably be blamed on the "Wall Street bankers."

Fortunately, the satisfaction which comes to those who constructively employ their energies in the investment field in New York are many,

Railroads went to the money market for billions to finance their cross-country growth.

and popular misconceptions do not dissuade them from pursuing their very essential functions. It might be well to remember that the American banker is a necessary conduit through which a large part of the people's savings flow into productive assets, and it is these savings that make possible the strength of our American free enterprise system.

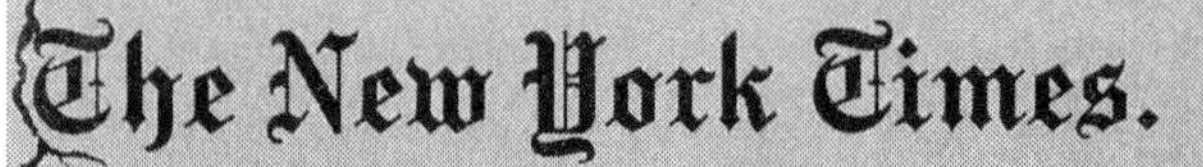

Copyright, 1929, by The New York Times Company.

NEW YORK, WEDNESDAY, OCTOBER 30, 1929.

TWO CENTS

THE WEATHER

STOCKS COLLAPSE IN 16,410,030-SHARE DAY, BUT RALLY AT CLOSE CHEERS BROKERS; BANKERS OPTIMISTIC, TO CONTINUE AID

KAHN REFUSES POST IN SENATE CAMPAIGN; CALLS CHOICE UNWISE

He Writes to Moses to Withhold His Name for Treasurer Due to 'Divided Reception.'

WAS RELUCTANT, HE SAYS

Recalls He Told Senator of His Stand, but Yielded as a Duty to His Party.

HOLDS VIEWS CONFIRMED

Declares He Is a Wall St. Man but a Liberal in Politics—Friends See Him Put in False Light.

Newark Man, 4 Feet 10, Says He Was Smallest in A. E. F.

MISSING AIRLINER BROUGHT IN SAFELY

Pilot Lands Western Express Ship at Albuquerque After Being Forced Down.

WOULD NOT RISK STORM

LEADERS SEE FEAR WANING

Point to 'Lifting Spells' in Trading as Sign of Buying Activity.

GROUP MEETS TWICE IN DAY

But Resources Are Unable to Stem Selling Tide—Lamont Reassures Investors.

HOPE SEEN IN MARGIN CUTS

Banks Reduce Requirements to 25 Per Cent—Sentiment in Wall St. More Cheerful.

240 Issues Lose $15,894,818,894 in Month; Slump in Full Exchange List Vastly Larger

CLOSING RALLY VIGOROUS

Leading Issues Regain From 4 to 14 Points in 15 Minutes.

INVESTMENT TRUSTS BUY

Large Blocks Thrown on Market at Opening Start Third Break of Week.

BIG TRADERS HARDEST HIT

Bankers Believe Liquidation Now Has Run Its Course and Advise Purchases.

Anxious investors throng the steps of the Sub-Treasury Building across the street from the New York Stock Exchange, during the market break on Tuesday, October 29, 1929, which wiped out thousands of life savings and plunged the nation into its worst depression. The New York Times headline records the historic day.

The Historical Role of the S.E.C.

BLACK TUESDAY'S WONDROUS AFTERMATH

Edward N. Gadsby

THE YOUNG MAN who was fascinated in the 1920's and early 1930's by the mechanics of the capital market was faced with at least one less complexity than is the college graduate of today. At that time, he was not required to contemplate any substantial governmental regulation of his putative business. There were rules of the game, surely, but they were in large measure inchoate, based more on custom, experience and the law merchant than on any well-defined code of behavior. It was a more carefree existence, perhaps, than that of the banker, broker, investment technician or speculator of today. It might even be characterized as more colorful.

The Wall Street man of today is no longer a free agent, privileged to adopt such code of business ethics as he may be persuaded is for his own immediate profit. A series of Congressional enactments effectively circumscribes his freedom in this area, and he must perform his allotted functions with a weather eye out at all times to the limits so prescribed. This legislation may have dissipated some of the freebooting atmosphere of prior years, but it is a fair statement that it has established a more intelligent, more orderly, more purposeful and a socially more significant securities market. I cannot help feeling that the participant in Wall Street can today be properly proud of his business affiliations, where there might have been a question some years ago.

A quarter-century has gone by since the original five Commissioners of the Securities and Exchange Commission held their first meeting in Washington on July 2, 1934, and elected the Honorable Joseph P. Kennedy as their chairman. It was their responsibility and privilege to administer the then one-year-old Securities Act of 1933 (the so-called "truth in securities" law) and the Securities Exchange Act of 1934, and thereby to chart the early courses of an entirely new venture in Federal regulation in the field of economic activities. Within the next few years after the creation of the Commission, four additional statutes* dealing with securities and finance were enacted into law and entrusted to the SEC for administration. This complex of legislation, popularly referred to as the Federal securities acts, comprises principally the area of the Commission's competence and jurisdiction. In addition, the Commission has certain advisory functions to the Federal courts in corporate reorganization proceedings under Chapter X of the National Bankruptcy Act.

A quarter-century of improved conditions

To review the experiences and activities of the SEC under these statutes during the past quarter-century would be a monumental task consuming reams of paper, requiring myriads of tinder-dry statistics of little significance here. They are contained in its annual reports over the years, and much of the more meaningful material is being adequately compiled and covered elsewhere. To reflect upon the difference between the conditions in the securities markets as they existed in the pre-SEC days, and as they developed under Federal legislation and presently exist, may serve to show how the Federal securities acts function and may in some measure permit an appraisal of their effectiveness in protecting the interests of investors and the public.

Every student and practitioner in the field of business and finance, every new Commissioner and every staff member of the SEC must of necessity be to some degree a student of financial history; and one of his most important tasks is to evaluate the modern scheme in terms of the situation as it existed in the Twenties and as it has evolved in the 25 years of the existence of the SEC.

At the outset, in comparing our present day markets with those of the roaring Twenties, it should be made perfectly clear that under the Federal securities acts the SEC has no statutory responsibility bearing directly upon general market price levels as such, or the prices of individual securities. In fact, the Commission's powers are generally the antithesis of price regulation. When the prices do advance or retreat, the Commission is directed only to see that they do so free of the sinister influences which in earlier days caused distress and tragedy in countless homes and business establishments.

The evils of pool operations

Prior to 1934, many of the operations in the exchange markets could hardly be described as being in the public interest. No one could be sure that prices in these markets bore any relation to values or reflected the impersonal forces of supply and demand. What was more serious, the exchange rules and customs were not designed to produce any such results. In

EDWARD N. GADSBY, a Phi Beta Kappa graduate of Amherst College in 1923, was appointed an S.E.C. Commissioner and the board's Chairman in August, 1957. He earned his law degree in 1928, while working as an engineer for A. T. & T., and since then has practiced law in New York and Boston, and also lectured at Suffolk University.

*Public Utility Holding Company Act of 1935, Trust Indenture Act of 1939, Investment Company Act of 1940 and the Investment Advisers Act of 1940.

Symbol of a nation in distress: the applesellers on New York corners during the early Depression years.

fact, it is now clear that many highly artificial forces were at work. For example, during 1929 the prices of over 100 stocks on the New York Stock Exchange were subjected to manipulation by massive pool operations. In the classic situation, the operators of such a pool would arrange for a source of supply of a security, usually through options, and then by concerted group action create activity and interest in the stock in order to unload the syndicate holdings at a profit upon the public which had been attracted by the activity. Floor traders and specialists roamed freely and without supervision on the floors of the exchanges and participated without restriction in pool operations. Bear raiders periodically barraged the market with short sales in order to accentuate price declines. Listing requirements were minimal and the data given in listing applications were indifferently investigated. Administration of the exchanges was lax; their rules apparently ignored or even contemplated the existence of manipulative activities.

In the intervening years, the major exchanges at least have come to realize that they are institutions vested with a public interest. They are obviously acutely aware of the danger to which they would be subject if the public were to suffer serious loss due to improper functioning of the exchanges as institutions or due to improper conduct by exchange members. They understand that the destruction of confidence of investors in the integrity of the securities markets which would follow such a contingency would be disastrous to our national economy and to the financial community of which they are a part. As a result of this awareness, they have specified procedures and adopted rules to guard against abuses. For instance, they have adopted rules restricting the activities of floor traders and specialists; listing requirements have been made more rigid, and periodic certified financial reports have been required; and excessive trading by members has been restricted. In addition, under the Securities Exchange Act, manipulative pool operations are prohibited, as are wash sales, the dissemination of false and misleading information, and other devices for rigging the market. Rules adopted by the Commission have taken the sting out of short selling.

In the over-the-counter market, the National Association of Securities Dealers has become a powerful force for the establishment and maintenance of standards of good business conduct. Membership in the organization carries with it very valuable privileges in the over-the-counter market and in the underwriting business. It exercises a discipline

"Drawn . . . by the vision of castles in Spain, margin customers assumed (over-extended) positions . . . the impact of a relatively small decline in prices under these circumstances was disastrous . . ."

over its members which is no empty gesture. Members may be, and are, fined for misconduct, and suspended or expelled for cause, and are subject to rules adopted to promote fair competition and to protect the public from unfair practices.

In the second place, the bull market of the Twenties involved the use of large volumes of credit to finance speculative activities. Call money rates in 1929 were as high as 20 per cent and credit poured into the stock market from all over the country. Brokers' loans rose from $1.9 billion in 1922 to a peak of $8.5 billion in October 1929. Industrial corporations even found it profitable to issue securities in order to raise funds destined to be thrown into the call market. The machinery for supplying credit for securities transactions (in which process banks supplied funds to brokers, brokers carried their customers and gave back their customers' collateral to the banks) was driven at a dizzying clip by the mirage of quick, easy and riskless wealth. Speculators ignored the fact that the yield of the securities purchased on margin was far less than the interest on their debit balances with their brokers. There were no limits save the prudence of the broker, which was sometimes debatable, to the amount of margin that was required of a speculator. The expectations of capital gains overshadowed the present economics of the transaction. Drawn into the market by the vision of castles in Spain, margin customers assumed positions to protect which they had insufficient liquid resources. The impact of a relatively small decline in prices under these circumstances was disastrous. Sales on margin calls depressed prices, causing more calls and more selling pressure. It was not a pretty sight, nor was there any control over it under the then existing exchange practices.

Speculation today demands ready cash

Under the Securities Exchange Act of 1934, this machinery for creating stock market credit is subject to strict regulation through margin requirements established by the Federal Reserve Board. Ever since the adoption of the Act and at the present time, cash requirements so established largely prevent the use of credit to support a speculative orgy. Brokers' loans at present in a far larger market run to about $3 billion. There is no longer any serious danger that a surge of cumulative margin calls will force liquidations and accelerate declines. Speculation must now be largely financed through ready money rather than credit, and if the customer does not have substantial cash in his jeans he cannot join in the party.

In the third place, there was a time when an underwriter about to offer a new issue for sale to the public could get and issue a statement of financial condition of the issuing company only if and when the management chose to release one. The press could then find out about a company and its operations only what the company chose to divulge. The affairs of corporate management (such as their ownership of securities, their compensation and transactions between management and their companies and affiliates) were withheld from stockholder or public scrutiny. In those literally dark ages, information supplied by an underwriter or an issuer was not susceptible of any reasonable verification simply because no one could be compelled to tell the whole truth. Furthermore, when a new issue of securities was to be sold it broke on the market with an instantaneous force. No time was allowed for investors, analysts or salesmen to study what little financial data might be released. There was intense pressure to sell the securities at once.

In today's market and under the securities acts, no significant industrial, commercial or utility financing can take place until all important aspects of the company and of the proposed transactions are laid open to leisurely public scrutiny. All but a few of the important publicly held corporations are required promptly to file with the exchanges or with the Commission or both, and thereby to make available to the public a report of every major business event which will materially affect its balance sheet.

There is no way to measure the direct and indirect effect of the various provisions of the securities acts which direct that the truth, and all of it, be told to investors and to the public. Many a deal has died aborning or has been hastily snatched back and reformed, solely because its proponents came to realize that they were going to have to submit the full and true story to public scrutiny and analysis; and this they were unwilling to do. Many an issue was eventually realistically priced only because the story which the law requires to be told would have made it impossible to sell the issue at an inflated price.

Operations without independent audits

As a fourth consideration, there was a day when an issuing company could and, like as not, did bring out a new issue without subjecting its books to the audit of an independent accountant. Also then, even though management did condescend to employ an accountant, the issuer was under no obligation to follow his recommendations. The results may be read in the reports of the various investigations as the consequence of which the securities acts were passed. In many instances, the financial statements upon the basis of which the public was asked to advance its savings were replete with concealment, double talk and downright falsification; and when management deigned to publish earnings statements and annual reports, it was a fair bet that the truth was not in them.

Things are quite different today. The securities acts now require the production of adequate financial statements and insist that these statements be certified by an independent public accountant. This, probably more than any other single influence, has revolutionized business accounting and reporting. These provisions gave the accountants an essential voice and authority in corporate matters. The American Institute of Certified Public Accountants has accepted the responsibility thus thrust upon it, and has introduced and enforced high-minded concepts of independence, proper accounting practices and sound accounting principles. The issuer can no longer safely ignore the advice and recommendations of the accountant. No more can he forthwith discharge the honest accountant and consult another in the hope that some fundamental problem can be avoided by different accounting treatment. Sound accounting principles have been evolved by the profession and accepted as standards which must be followed by its members. These procedures and policies have produced a quality of financial reporting and a sense of public responsibility not excelled anywhere in the world, and have made it improbable that economic reverses will result in uncovering any substantial inherent weakness in corporate finances.

As another consideration to be taken into account in comparing present day markets with those of 30 or so years ago, there are other disciplines now operative in the financial market which are of major significance, though largely unknown to the public generally. Important among such vehicles are some of the trade organizations. Contrary to the general impression, these groups were not formed and do not exist for the sole purpose of holding periodic conventions, the expenses of which are deductible items on corporate earnings statements. In large measure, these are sincere organizations of skilled technicians who are deeply interested in pooling their experience and knowledge. Some of the principal groups with which the SEC is in continual contact are the American Society of Corporate Secretaries, the Controllers Institute of America, the National Federation of Financial Analyst Societies, the American Management Association, the Investment Bankers Association and the National Association of Investment Companies.

Here, as elsewhere in the relations of the SEC with the people who operate under its jurisdiction, points of view may and often do differ; but also here, as elsewhere, there has generally been an informed and reasonable attempt to adjust industry practices and standards so that they may be consistent with the interests of investors and the public. With the blessing of the SEC, there has throughout the years been a vast improvement in corporate reports to stockholders, in stockholder relations, in the quality of the proxy material submitted to security holders, in the honesty of the sales literature used by investment companies, in sound accounting practices, in clear exposition of corporate policy, and in the creation of an atmosphere conducive to warm investor reception of American securities as investments and American industrial corporations as sound economic institutions. The open discussions in forums sponsored by organizations such as the above are the very antithesis of the organized deception and deceit which at one time accompanied the fantastic operations of the securities markets.

Publicity helps ensure compliance with the law.

The S.E.C. is housed in a war-built "temporary" building in Washington, where the Commissioners meet in a plain room on the second floor. Approximately half the agency's employees are located here, the rest scattered in regional and branch offices.

The SEC wields many a big stick

A sixth notable facet of the modern market hinges on the existing persuasive deterrents to violations of the securities laws. Their presence in the statutes, and the activities of the Commission and of the courts in applying them, have for many years served to impose upon the deliberate wrongdoer and the irresponsible adventurer some important sanctions in case of misconduct. The result has been to take out of the present market a number of morally or financially unreliable operators in securities, and to expose to severe penalties those who may be tempted to make hay in any kind of a disorganized market.

The Securities Act contains civil liability provisions which place personal responsibility on management for acts which individuals at one time might have safely assumed would be concealed behind the corporate shield. The statutes permit civil actions in such cases which are not subject to the jurisdictional limitations of the State courts. Sellers of securities are now exposed to actions unknown or most difficult to maintain under the common law. The touter has not the freedom he once had to practice his art. When the insider gains some secret information and seeks to take personal advantage of it by purchase or sale of his corporation's securities, he must disclose the transaction. Confession thus made is under some conditions an invitation for a stockholder to bring suit to recover any profit for the benefit of the corporation.

All the securities acts provide for criminal liabilities which have been resorted to on many an occasion to incarcerate the fraud and the cheat.

But more effective than any of these sanc-

Regulatory responsibilities include the activities on all the nation's exchanges. Here phone clerks at the American Stock Exchange receive and transmit orders to the brokers on the floor; hand signals are unchanged from the days when the Exchange operated outdoors.

tions is probably the power given to the Commission to investigate, to publicize, and to comment upon actions and practices in various types of administrative proceedings. The power to suspend the right to sell an issue of securities, to revoke the right of a broker-dealer to engage in business, to suspend or revoke the registration of a security on an exchange, to suspend trading in a listed security, to apply for an injunction against prohibited conduct: all these powers place in the hands of the Federal Government a strict control which never before existed. However, after all, these and the other regulatory provisions are residual powers and remedies. It should be remembered that informal disciplines which reflect an intelligent self-control in the very large preponderance of cases render direct government intervention unnecessary.

A "rough justice" eventuates

Of course, in administering the Federal securities acts the Commission does have a multitude of difficulties and problems. Nor are the securities acts examples of flawless legislation. In fact, the Commission is currently engaged in a program contemplating extensive amendments to them. Also, the Commission cannot always be sure that every security transaction is effected without any deceit and after full and frank disclosure. In the very nature of things only a sort of rough justice can eventuate even under all the safeguards which have been described. Nevertheless, it is clear that the situation today is essentially different from that of twenty-five or thirty years ago, and what was true then is by no means necessarily true now.

The history of the enactment of the securities laws—and of their fearless and effective enforcement for twenty-five years—is of vital interest to the embryonic financier. He will, as I have said, be in daily contact with this legislation. The development of concepts and the delineation of jurisdiction over the past twenty-five years, as they have evolved in the concrete applications of the law to actual business life, is an enthralling study, though it may be more so to the legal specialist than to the layman. It is most certainly true that it requires a rather high degree of ability properly to analyze a given business venture in the light of the securities laws. As a corollary, it is perhaps pertinent to say that the constant application of these resourceful minds to business problems serves to keep the SEC from any noticeable tendency to complacency. The imagination and ingenuity utilized in framing financial deals seem almost boundless, and can be effectively kept within even reasonable limits only by exercise of the most ceaseless and unremitting diligence by those whose duty it is to administer the securities acts.

At any rate, the securities business has become eminently respectable within the framework of this legislation. Wall Street performs an indispensable function in our economic world, a function which is becoming more important every day. With the growth of corporate business, with the growth of American enterprise, the securities business becomes more complex, more subtle, more sophisticated. To play a part in such a business and to grow up in it should be looked upon as a privilege and a challenge to the capabilities of the new graduate.

THE FUNNY SIDE OF FINANCE

"Crazy, Man!!"

"Hello, Merrill Lynch, Pierce, Fenner and Smith? This is Carleton Richardson Henderson the third, over at Batten, Barton, Durstine, and Osborn. Hello, are you still there . . . Hello. Hello!"

"All this financial chit-chat is Greek to little ol' me. Do you intend to avoid the after-acquired clause through creation of a subsidiary company or by consolidation?"

"Anybody seen that fifty thousand in ones lying around?"

"I was hoping you could suggest a highly speculative stock that's never failed to pay a dividend."

Reprinted from THE WALL STREET JOURNAL

The end of a long day

Differences in Investment Firms

A ROAD MAP OF WALL STREET

William D. Kerr

THROUGH THE YEARS, an air of mystery has shrouded Wall Street, at least to the casual observer. Programs of enlightenment more recently have lifted this veil to some extent. The purpose of this volume is to further this better understanding of the Wall Street machinery and function, which in essence is completely devoid of mystery.

Such mystery as there is in Wall Street lies in the markets. No one knows even from day to day exactly what the market has in store. Many forecasts are made. Huge sums of money are invested in stocks and bonds each day in the belief that the action taken will prove beneficial to the person or institution making the purchase. But there is no certainty, and probably there never will be.

Other than that, the basic operation of Wall Street by the many individuals and concerns involved can be readily outlined. I shall attempt to catalog briefly the principal activities of the member firms of the Investment Bankers Association of America. These member firms generate the preponderance of securities' dealings in Wall Street. The activities cover a wide range of functions with each firm participating in one, several or all. The primary difference between firms is largely determined by the variety of the capacities and the fields in which each acts. Also, amounts of capital employed will differ substantially, ranging from a modest minimum of $50,000 to figures in excess of $40,000,000.

The Constitution of our Association suggests that the investment banker shall devote himself to serving both buyers and sellers of securities in such a manner that the necessary funds for the operation and expansion of business activities and for the carrying on of public functions may be provided. Thus the investment banker would make a contribution to the increase in national wealth and to its wide diffusion. These objectives are to be approached in a spirit of mutual cooperation with a dedication to high standards of service, adequate self-regulation and support of appropriate legislation. Against this uniform backdrop, the scope of the member firms varies from a single function, such as a specialist in United States Treasury obligations, to a multiple operation wherein almost every activity is practiced.

Most IBA members belong to other organizations which are useful to them in the conduct of their businesses. Important are:

♦ THE NATIONAL ASSOCIATION OF SECURITIES DEALERS, which, through its staff and volunteers from the member firms, formulates rules and regulations of proper business conduct and governs the enforcement thereof. In trading securities with fellow members, a member of NASD is entitled to advantageous terms in the form of discounts or concessions allowed from the prices at which such securities are offered to non-members, including the general public.

♦ THE NEW YORK STOCK EXCHANGE, THE AMERICAN STOCK EXCHANGE, THE MIDWEST STOCK EXCHANGE AND OTHER REGIONAL EXCHANGES, which afford to their members the privilege of acting as brokers, at prescribed rates of commission, for non-members in the purchase or sale of such stocks and bonds as are listed for trade on each Exchange. Strict codes of ethical trading practices govern the members of each Exchange. In most firms the business conducted through a membership on one or all of the principal Exchanges is a most important source of revenue.

♦ THE ASSOCIATION OF STOCK EXCHANGE FIRMS, which acts as a liaison group between its members and the Stock Exchanges in formulating the most efficient and adequate procedures possible consistent with the varied interests of the members. The Association also helps members improve service to their customers, and is constantly in touch with Federal and State legislators concerning the industry.

The benefits provided by membership in these organizations, plus the proven managerial talents of the partners and officers of the firms, place at the disposal of the personnel of the investment banking industry all information needed to make an intelligent and satisfactory selection of various operating functions.

The breadth of any firm's activities will be the result of the preferences of the individuals in the firm. These preferences may vary from single specialization to a virtual jack-of-all-trades attitude.

Activity of investment bankers in securities is conducted by four broad types—traders, brokers, dealers, and underwriters. A firm or an individual in a firm may wear all four hats simultaneously in a series of transactions conducted with different clients. In any given transaction the capacity in which a firm is acting must be fully disclosed to the client. No individual or firm may be both broker and dealer, or both agent and principal, in the same transaction.

♦ TRADERS usually perform at a professional level (that is, they buy from and sell to other traders, dealers or financial institutions). Their contact with the general public is only occasional. For the most part they act for their own account as principals, although agency transactions are frequent. The preponderance of trading is done in the over-the-counter (unlisted) market, although some traders are active in securities listed on the Stock Exchanges. Many traders acquire unlisted securities in anticipation of turning them over to others in their own organization for resale to the public on a dealer, or principal, basis. The trader provides the important function of giving body to the market. Through him a large volume of business can be handled without causing undue price fluctuations, for he will often buy or sell as principal for his own account without having an immediate offsetting trade in prospect.

♦ The BROKER functions in both listed and unlisted markets. On the Stock Exchanges the member broker accepts orders given to him by other members and executes them for a fee

Corporate stocks provide "prodigious" business for investment houses. A. T. & T. stock is probably America's most popular; and when Ford first sold shares to the public, it was front-page news nationwide.

which is a fraction of the full commission, or he accepts orders from non-members, including the general public, and executes them for the full commission set by the Exchange. In unlisted markets he acts for a variety of clients, both individuals, institutions and corporations. He buys or sells upon instruction and exercises due diligence in finding the most favorable prices obtainable. Often the broker will spend a considerable part of his commission in communications, telegrams and telephone calls, in the effort to locate the best bid or offer. Many of the over-the-counter orders given to a broker originate through representatives of the firm who are soliciting this type of business. The broker always acts as an agent rather than as a principal.

♦ DEALERS act largely for their own account, making purchases from and sales to customers as principals. The securities they deal in may cover the whole category of stocks and bonds available in the over-the-counter market and occasionally those listed on the Exchanges as well. (A dealer who is a member of an Exchange must obtain the special permission of the Exchange to deal as principal in a security listed thereon. Often permission is refused when the Exchange judges that the transaction can be satisfactorily consummated in a normal manner.) Acting as a dealer in present-day markets is as broad a function as can be imagined from the standpoint of the types of customers and the variety of securities handled. A dealer invariably acts as a principal. His profit arises from his ability to sell at retail to customers the securities he has purchased. The mark-up may not exceed 5%. The profit is less than this permissive maximum in most instances.

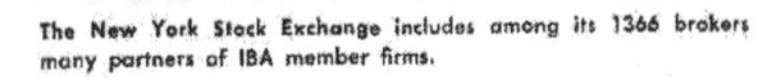

The New York Stock Exchange includes among its 1366 brokers many partners of IBA member firms.

The American Stock Exchange identifies its 499 regular members with white badges and a traditional linen office coat.

♦ The UNDERWRITER is actually a dealer performing a specialized function. He negotiates with the seller the terms under which securities are to be purchased and reoffered for sale.

The "products" of the market place

What are the principal types of securities? How are they marketed?

♦ UNITED STATES TREASURY OBLIGATIONS are offered by the Treasury, through the Federal Reserve System as fiscal agent, on terms set by it after proper consideration of all factors, especially the market climate. Any class of investor is eligible to subscribe, although certain conditions or limitations are frequently imposed. Allotments against subscriptions are made in due course. While there is no underwriting involved, nor any compensation paid to dealers in the distributive process, the opinion of investment bankers is often considered when arranging the offering terms. Once issues are allotted and outstanding, trading is largely in the hands of the commercial banks and the government bond specialists whose customers are principally other banks, corporations, insurance companies and pension funds. Commercial banks do a substantial volume in relatively small amounts with individuals, most of whom are depositors in the bank. Investment bankers who specialize in trading government bonds are few in number. However, virtually all investment bankers are vitally interested in the government bond market and are equipped to render expert customer service in this area. Trading profits are extremely small per unit.

United States Government Agencies, such as the Federal Intermediate Credit Banks, the Federal Land Banks, the Federal National Mortgage Association and the Federal Home Loan Banks offer their obligations by the same method employed by the Treasury, except that each has its own fiscal agent. Trading in the outstanding issues is largely conducted by the same parties as are interested in Treasury obligations.

♦ STATE AND MUNICIPAL BONDS carry interest exempt from personal income and corporation taxes. This attraction, plus the inherent value of the pledge of *ad valorem* taxes, makes this type of obligation desirable to many individuals, as well as a wide range of institutional investors. Resultingly, investment bankers in all categories engage actively in the tax-exempt bond business. Virtually all issues are offered at competitive bidding only. The purchase of some sizeable issues are negotiated by an underwriting group of many members. Also, some small, obscure issues which would attract only limited notice are negotiated by specialists in this type of procedure. From a daily profit standpoint this segment of the securities business is very important to the investment banker, although the exposure to inventory losses when prices move lower is substantial.

♦ CORPORATE BONDS account for a significant volume of business to the investment banker. Commercial banks are not permitted to deal in these securities except as brokers for the account of customers. Investment bankers of all other types actively engage in underwriting, dealing, trading and brokering corporate bonds.

WILLIAM D. KERR
is a partner of Wertheim & Co., and served as 1958-1959 president of the Investment Bankers Association of America. He received a B.A. from the University of Chicago in 1925.

♦ CORPORATE STOCKS, particularly common stocks, are probably the most important single type of securities handled by the investment banker.

The volume of trade in common stocks on the Exchanges and in the over-the-counter markets is prodigious. On the Exchanges the activity is in the hands of members of the Exchange who are serving almost exclusively as brokers. In the over-the-counter market, most investment bankers, during the course of a day's business, will act as underwriters, then as dealers or traders, again as brokers as circumstances may require. Every class of investor, from the individual to the large insurance company, participates in corporate stock investment.

The securities business in Wall Street is pretty much the elementary process of bringing a buyer and seller together through an intermediary—today's investment banking firm is a well-integrated entity, ready to act as underwriter, dealer, broker or trader as required, dealing daily with an assortment of customers whose preferences in the aggregate cover the entire field of investment securities. He has specialized knowledge and experience on a broad front. He must provide expert advice and efficient service in order to attract and hold clients. The investment banker is a professional man in the finest sense.

part 

INVESTMENT BANKING

THE INVESTMENT BANKER: "INVOLVED, PIVOTALLY

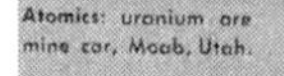

Atomics: uranium ore mine car, Moab, Utah.

Gas: building seismic profiles of the promising geologic structures of Western Canada.

Oil: a Jersey Standard tanker lies in New York's North River, riding light and empty, ready to clear for sea.

Investment Banking—an Appraisal

THE FULCRUM OF THE FREE WORLD'S ECONOMY

Robert Lehman

THE AVERAGE BUSINESSMAN, strange as it may seem to us, knows very little about investment banking. To him it is simply part of that vast, roaring, mysterious world of stocks and bonds and the stock exchanges—a strange world, located in New York City, south of City Hall, somewhere around Wall Street, in which a rather monolithic-looking group of individuals and firms appears to be involved in matters of high finance. Their involvement in such matters is rather vague and mysterious—and apparently deep. The firms themselves, however, are without shape; there is no distinction between them in terms of investment banking, or commercial banking, or brokerage. They fuse into one fantastic whole—a world of money in which people imagine that everyone gets rich without working very hard.

The image is highly inaccurate, of course. It is also unfortunate, as it possesses none of the real drama of truth. Investment banking, in fact, has all the aspects of drama—drama day by day, full of conflict, highly competitive, compelling, and absorbing. To the investment banking professional, the business stands alone as a way of life offering more fulfillment, more rewards of every kind, than any other ever could.

Star on a giant stage

The reason for this is simple: it is that the investment banker today functions at the fulcrum of the free world's economy; he performs an indispensable role, a starring role, in the gigantic complex play of business, industry, and government. The part is demanding; it requires energy and enthusiasm and in the performance of it a man must employ all of his capabilities, all of his intellectual

EVERY MAJOR INDUSTRY OF OUR AGE..."

Aviation: a 707 jet approaches the Atlanta, Georgia terminal.

Pipelines: Texas crews add feeders to the national net.

Toll roads: the New York Thruway, biggest of all.

Chemicals: recovery towers, Fortier, La.

capacities. The investment banker loves it, not in spite of the fact that it demands so much, but because it does.

Investment banking covers a tremendous range. Fundamentally and historically, the profession is concerned with providing long-term capital to industry and government. Years ago, investment bankers raised the money to finance the first railroad and industrial enterprises; more recently they raised the money to finance the spiderweb of oil and gas pipelines that now run the length and breadth of our land. When a manufacturing company starts expanding; when a public utility decides to enlarge its generating capacity; when a city needs new schools, or a state elects to pay its veterans a bonus; when a turnpike authority agrees to build a new toll highway, or a bridge or tunnel—the chances are much more than good that the given corporate or governmental unit will turn to an investment banker for help. Each of these diverse projects requires capital in large amounts and few corporate or governmental bodies have available that kind of money for capital expenditures.

"Craftsman and artist"

So this—the raising of capital, the financing of growth—is the basic function, and this, indeed, involves great craft and art. In our sophisticated world the investment banker may work alone, although he usually enlists other bankers in a syndicate. In either case, he first works closely with the issuer and advises on the type of financing required—whether debt, equity or a convertible type security. He then may arrange for the private placement of the security with an institutional investor, an insurance company or a pension fund, if this seems to fit the client's requirements; or if a public offering seems desirable he either singly or in a syndicate with other investment bankers purchases (underwrites) the securities from the issuer and sells it publicly to investors.

He has many other functions, too. He gives financial and industrial advice to corporations; he handles capital transactions in foreign lands; he deals in arbitrage and securities. He employs lawyers, economists, tax experts, salesmen, accountants, accounting machines; he specializes in studies of most of the industries of the world. He is, in short, or should be an expert, knowing business in its broad scope and depth as few men do—a qualified master of the industrial chessboard of our time.

As he is an expert, as his stage is broad and his role vital, so his responsibilities, too, are heavy. He is responsible to industry, to government, to the public, to himself. If he is

Railroads grew, financed from the beginning by investment bankers. Here, the Northern Pacific builds across the Great Plains.

to be respected, he has hard tasks to perform. His financial advice—to corporations, to government, to the public—may carry great weight and influence and therefore he must fashion it as impeccably as he can, utilizing all his knowledge, experience, and training in the markets of the world.

Mr. Indispensable

Today, there is hardly a phase of industry in which the investment banker does not participate actively at some time or other in his career. In his routine function he may maintain extensive and elaborate facilities through which investors may purchase or sell securities, but that is only a small and obvious part of what he does. In his work as financial advisor to corporations, he also often plays a pivotal role in corporate mergers and acquisitions—and it is not uncommon for him to negotiate personally for the principals in the deal. More and more in recent years he has been investing his own capital in situations that appear favorable, and thus has assisted in the growth of smaller corporations. The variety of his tasks is infinite. He has been involved, pivotally, in every major and most minor industries of our age, ranging from automobiles and retail chains and aviation through oils and chemicals to electronics, atomics, and polymers, among many others.

In the pages that follow, various specialized functions of the modern investment banker are discussed in specific detail by others in their respective fields. I hope I have conveyed the sense that investment banking is an enormous field, a constructive field, a challenging field, full of variety, vital, fascinating, and absorbing. As I have said, it demands a lot, but it returns a lot in terms both of true satisfaction and remuneration. It is a field that embraces the whole economy. Its successful men have not been geniuses (although we have had them, too), but men of experience and balanced judgment and common sense, who have worked hard and have brought enthusiasm and energy to their jobs.

In my opinion, the investment banker occupies a very special niche in our great free capital markets, which are so largely responsible for the growth of our nation. Public participation, in the final analysis, has brought that growth about, and the investment banker has helped to serve the public in its expanding role as owner. He is the man through whom the corporations and the municipalities have issued their securities; he is the man who makes the securities available to the investing public.

ROBERT LEHMAN is a partner in the New York investment banking firm of Lehman Brothers and president of the Lehman Corporation. He serves as director for many major concerns; vice president, the Metropolitan Museum of Art; member, Council of Foreign Relations.

A Scientific Approach to Business Problems

MODERN VENTURE CAPITALISM

John Hay Whitney

A CENTURY HAS gone by since Karl Marx tolled the bell for our capitalist economy, but it is growing more robust all the time. So much so that Communist caricaturists ought to start substituting a crew haircut for the silk hat they have been tacking on that old devil, Capitalism, for years.

Fresh breezes are blowing in American business. New enterprises are coming into being; new products and new services are being made available; new concepts of social responsibility are being practiced. We are moving toward ever-higher standards of living for our own people and toward intensified American assistance in the material advancement of our neighbors in the remotest corners of the world.

A free society means more for everyone

We are demonstrating that free industry and free labor, cooperating in a free society, can generate more prosperity, more security, and more happiness for everyone than is possible under any system in which all the decisions are made by a little clique of supermen. We are doing it by keeping our economy dynamic. When new methods of manufacture or finance become necessary to insure that there will be no break in the growth of our productive power, we have both the will and the resourcefulness to develop them.

In this flexibility lies the chief explanation for the ability of our economic system to bring the products of technological change so quickly to flower. It is a flexibility that extends through every industrial process, from the extraction of raw materials to the delivery of finished goods.

But there is little room for flexibility on the industrial front if there is no flexibility in our financial institutions. The world may beat a path to the door of the man with a better mousetrap, but he cannot go into mass production. The more complex the product and the less aware the world is of how much it is missing by not having it, the harder it will be for the originator to finance his brain child.

This is the area in which venture capital is needed, and it is in this area that some of our most interesting forward steps have been taken in the last few years. The words "venture capital" have a challenging and exciting ring. They summon up a picture of pioneering in new and unexplored regions of industry. There is even, I fear, an overtone of speculative recklessness about the term. The excitement and the pioneering are there; the recklessness is not. Indeed, nothing could be more distant from the operating approach of the modern venture capital organization. A little explanation may supply perspective on what such an organization does and what it does not do.

The concept of venture capital is not new. The shoemaker who made sandals in the market place of ancient Rome was essentially a venture capitalist; but it was not until the Industrial Revolution, with its requirements for much more substantial plant investment, that venture capital in the modern sense took root and began to grow.

The years from the Civil War to the end of the Nineteenth Century represented the most feverish period of venture capital activity in America's history. Railroads, public utilities, steel mills, and factories sprouted up in an unprecedented era of industrial expansion. Unrestrained by taxes or other government curbs, many of the earlier capitalists organized giant corporations and spread their investments into one new venture after another.

The enterprises created in that period have continued their vigor and growth. They have vastly expanded their plant facilities and branched out into a limitless range of new products and services. By the fruitful reinvestment of their earnings, they have made a major contribution to the development of our nation.

But the dynamism of our economy cannot be maintained solely by having the big get bigger. There must be an economic climate in which the individual entrepreneur can grow and in which the prospective entrepreneur can

"Unrestrained by taxes or other government curbs . . ." Rugged men of vision and courage built America—men like Andrew Carnegie, who began as an immigrant "bobbin boy" in 1848, built his fortunes through dozens of acquisitions and mergers till by 1875 Carnegie Brothers & Co. merged with Henry Frick's Frick Coke Company to make the Carnegie Steel Co. In 1901 the Scot sold to Morgan's U. S. Steel for $250 millions and retired. Frick bought control of the coke industry through purchases made in the Panic of 1873, grew powerful through "dealing uncompromisingly with labor," retired to build the renowned Frick Collection of art masterpieces, valued at better than $40,000,000.

Keystone of their empire was the Homestead plant in the Monongahela Valley, where on July 6, 1892 the company brought in 200 Pinkertons to break an historic strike on its 143rd day, with a battle in which 7 were killed, more than 20 wounded. The entire Pennsylvania militia was needed to restore order. Charles M. Schwab was general manager at Homestead in 1892; he rose to become president of the merged U. S. Steel Corporation and later chairman of Bethlehem Steel's Board.

James J. Hill built the Great Northern and Northern Pacific systems, to tie Chicago to the West. Brokers watched wide-eyed as bankers J. Pierpont Morgan, George F. Baker (donor in later years of the Harvard Business School), Anthony J. Drexel (he built the Drexel Institute in Philadelphia) fought for power and control of America's expanding industrial empires.

Homestead, July 6, 1892

Drexel, Schwab

Frick

Hill

Baker

Carnegie

make a start. It is in this area that the venture capitalist has his role—one which cannot be played by the large company, the commercial bank, or the institutional investor.

Established financial institutions, concerned with the careful husbanding of other people's money, are restrained, both by law and by their own proper caution, from investments that entail any substantial element of risk. Even the investment banker finds most proposals for new business unsuited to public placement and therefore, beyond his field of interest.

This leaves the individual investor, who is, and I hope will continue to be, an important source of venture capital for new enterprises. He is particularly helpful in connection with the smallest of small businesses. The corner grocery store, the filling station, the neighborhood tailor shop—numerically the great majority of our new ventures—are started on the savings of the owner and what he can borrow from his relatives, neighbors and friends.

New business born in this manner is healthy for the economy, the community, and often for the sponsors. However, a new industrial enterprise requiring more substantial funds with which to start or to spread its wings may look less hopefully to the individual investor for the needed assistance. The required sums are likely to be much larger, the investigation more intricate, and the degree of risk incalculably greater. Moreover, the investor's problems do not stop once the investment has been made. The amount of essential follow-up is likely to increase in proportion to the complexity of managing a more ramified business. Putting this type of venture capital to work wisely and keeping it at work effectively is not a spare-time job for an individual. It is a full-time job for an organization.

Specialists in an exciting new field

Today a handful of new venture capital organizations are engaged in an experiment that may prove of inestimable benefit to our industrial society. There is nothing altruistic or philanthropic about this experiment; it is being run on a hardheaded investment basis. But it gives promise of unlocking endless doors of industrial development for the enrichment of all Americans.

JOHN H. WHITNEY, senior partner of J. H. Whitney & Co., is now the American Ambassador to The Court of St. James. He graduated from Yale in 1926 and attended Oxford University in 1927. Mr. Whitney is a well-known experimental financier and philanthropist. This article originally appeared in "Wall Street 1955".

What these investment firms are trying to do is to create, through trial and error, a mechanism which will make available to new or struggling small companies financial assistance; and enable such companies to acquire all the tools and facilities of professional scientific management. This is something more than the mere supplying of money. It embodies the active investigation and supervision by an organization made up of specialists in the techniques of modern industrial management, research and development, factory organization, production, marketing, and all the other aspects of successful commercial operation.

Today, taxes, legislation, and restrictive regulations complicate the development of new enterprises. The businessman needs more than a sound, basic idea to assure solvency and success. Tax laws have become an integral part of all policy thinking and planning. Other legal considerations press in on the man struggling to get his business off the ground. He must have expert technical and professional assistance. Capital alone is not enough.

That is why the modern venture capital firm does not confine itself to the thorough investigation required to determine whether an investment should be made. It is equally concerned with active supervision of its investment in the enterprise until the project is safely launched.

The whole operation must be on a basis as scientific as that of any research laboratory

FROM LITTLE ACORNS...

General Electric's Schenectady, N. Y., Research Labs began in this barn in 1900. Charles Steinmetz, the great electrical theoretician, started with one assistant; today 1200 people work at the facility.

The independently-owned service station developed at the turn of the century. Mid-century models are almost always affiliated with major companies, which grew to dominate the field after Rockefeller set the competitive pattern with the formation of the first Standard Oil Company in 1881.

The first "Great 5¢ Store," modeled here, opened in Utica, N. Y., in 1880 with an inventory worth $315. Woolworth's now has 102,000 stockholders, 9,703,600 shares outstanding, 2,160 stores and more than a half-billion in assets.

in chemistry, physics, or biology. Experts are needed to guide the firm in passing on investment opportunities and in supervising them after the investments have been made. It would be foolish, however, to suggest that the ultimate in diligence or in technical competence could guarantee a profitable outcome for every venture.

No one can determine the potential demand for a new product with total assurance. No one can foresee all the problems that will arise in making and marketing it. Most difficult of all is the evaluation of the people on whom the success of the project is likely to depend. The best business can be wrecked by bad management, and we will never be able to devise a trustworthy measuring rod for human fallibility.

Every firm in the venture capital field has had its successes and its failures. The investment of venture capital as practiced in these firms is still a test operation. It is too early to appraise the results with finality, but I am convinced that we are making headway toward a function of great usefulness both to business and to society.

A Negotiated Underwriting

"FIRST BOSTON INVITES . . ."

William B. Chappell

WEBSTER DEFINES the word "negotiate" as "To have dealing with a view to coming to terms upon some matter." Thus, in the investment banking business, a negotiated security offering is one in which the issuer selects the firm or firms to manage a particular security underwriting, in contrast to the sealed public bidding method in which the issuer sells his securities to that firm or firms offering the highest price. The purpose of this article is not to defend the merits of either method (both common in the investment banking field), but to attempt to show by successive steps just how an investment banking firm places an issue of securities on the market by means of what is commonly referred to as the "negotiated route."

Perhaps the simplest way to illustrate this method will be to take a particular example and follow it through from the time it is first conceived until it ends as a certificate in the portfolio of an investment buyer.

Financing decision

In the spring of 1954, the Aluminum Company of America, following the advice of its Finance Committee, entered into conversations with The First Boston Corporation relative to the issuance of debentures to pay off large amounts of outstanding bank loans, which had been incurred in their expansion program designed to increase the output of aluminum facilities in this country. Building new plants for the production of aluminum is a costly process, and huge sums are needed in this particular industry to meet the ever-increasing demands for this metal. Consequently, at this time, following a series of conversations and studies between the Company and their investment banker to whom they had gone for advice and counsel, it was decided to proceed with the issuance and "public sale" of one hundred millions of debentures.

Why "public sale"? Because the issuer wished to effect a broad distribution of these debentures, providing investment funds all over the country with the opportunity of purchasing them. (As opposed to this method, corporations often do their financing by the "direct sale" route, where the securities to be sold are offered either directly by the issuer or by an investment banker, acting as the issuer's agent, to a limited number of institutional purchasers. The "direct sale" method entails no filing of a Registration Statement with the Securities and Exchange Commission, and once sold, securities rarely return to the market for re-sale.) We are concerned here,

WILLIAM B. CHAPPELL is director, vice president and syndicate manager of The First Boston Corporation. He graduated from Yale in 1927.

for illustrative purposes, with the "public sale" method.

"A Small Army . . ." was needed to prepare the Alcoa offering. Company headquarters in Pittsburgh's Triangle was the scene of much of the detail work.

Following the determination of the size and provisions of the issue of debentures, financial men from the Aluminum Company and their investment banker proceeded with the preparation of a Registration Statement, a document listing in full detail the complete financial set-up of the Company, its operations, schedules of plant facilities, past financial history—in short, everything needed to set forth in complete detail the entire operation of the Company.

A small army—legal counsel, public accountants, financial men from the Company and from the investment banker —were needed to compile and prepare this important document, to insure that any investor studying the published statement would be afforded "full disclosure," as called for under the law.

Upon its completion, the Registration Statement is then filed with the Securities and Exchange Commission in Washington where it undergoes its twenty-day "incubation" period, giving the Commission the opportunity to study and later to comment upon the material as set forth. The Commission does not approve or disapprove of the security or pass upon the accuracy or adequacy of the Registration Statement. However, both the issuer and the underwriters are subject to very serious liabilities, both criminal and civil, for misstatements of fact or omission of material facts in the Registration Statement. Hence the great care and responsibilities involved in its preparation and use.

Formation of syndicate

While all this was taking place, the investment banker, having been chosen to manage this very large and important undertaking, was making use of his personnel and facilities to proceed with an orderly and carefully mapped-out program. As no one investment banker would wish to underwrite alone an issue of securities totaling one hundred million dollars, the Syndicate Manager was called into conference by the head of his firm and told to prepare a list of firms to be invited to participate as account members.

The preparation of such a list requires very specialized knowledge of firms in the investment banking field from Maine to California —the amount of capital they have, their ability to place securities properly, their background and reputation. In the issue under discussion, for instance, a firm with capital funds of less than one hundred thousand dollars would not have been asked to undertake an underwriting committment of one million dollars—and vice versa.

Also, as the issuer and the investment banker were anxious to obtain as broad a list of purchasers as possible, firms from practically every state in the nation were included as underwriters. A firm in Boston, no matter how large, would not list among its clients a church or labor union pension fund in Milwaukee, hence the need when composing an underwriting group to select the best and strongest investment banking firms in every important financial center in the United States.

By forming a wide geographical group, the manager—who alone has the responsibility of bringing to a successful conclusion a particular security offering—not only spreads the risks of the underwriting but ensures the broadest possible distribution of the securities. This in turn will carry out the wishes of the issuing company, which having determined to sell its securities via the "public route" is quite understandably anxious to find widely diversified acceptance from security buyers. In the aggregate, the twenty-five thousand or fifty thousand bond buyer is just as important as the large insurance company which buys in the millions.

Once the list of underwriting firms had been prepared and approved by all concerned, including the issuer, and at about the time the Registration Statement was filed, formal invitations to participate in the Alcoa loan were issued by telephone and telegraph, as follows:

"Aluminum Company of America will file May 20 a Registration Statement covering $100,000,000 Sinking Fund Debentures due 1979 to be offered publicly.

"The Debentures will be entitled to a Sinking Fund sufficient to retire $4,150,000 in each of the years 1956 through 1978 or 95.45% of the issue prior to maturity.

"It is expected underwriters will sign on June 8th—with interest rate, price and underwriting compensation to be determined just prior to signing.

"We will charge a management fee.

"We are pleased to offer you an underwriting interest of approximately $ ....

"Please advise immediately if you wish to accept in principle.

"THE FIRST BOSTON CORPORATION."

Quality of security

Acceptance of corporate securities by buyers is based in part on the "ratings" given to debt securities by such statistical firms as Moody's and Standard & Poor's. These agencies rate new securities (from a top of *triple A* down to *C*); and since some investment funds cannot purchase securities under a certain rating, the investment banker performs an important function in helping the issuer to present pertinent data to the rating agencies; and generally calls on them with company financial people to answer questions about the issue.

With the filing of the Registration Statement and the formation of the underwriting group, there ensues a period of twenty days before the Registration Statement becomes effective and the securities may be offered formally to the public. The investment banker is not idle, however: during this period he presents all the facts of the issue in question

Alcoa's expansion plans required financing of massive new facilities to meet the exploding post-war demand for aluminum. Sheet aluminum sheathing for buildings has come into wide use: the Pittsburgh Hilton used 350,000 pounds, anodized to a gold color, for the new hotel's curtain walls. To produce sheet products, Alcoa operates this 106-inch hot rolling mill—one of the world's largest—in Davenport, Iowa (bottom, left).

Other new developments demanding immense amounts of the lightweight metal are forged airframe members such as this 3,000-pound section for the Martin SeaMaster jet; and gargantuan castings—here's sixteen tons that form a single mold, to produce huge Goodyear tires for earth-moving equipment.

to his prospective purchasers by means of a preliminary or "red-herring" prospectus filed with the Commission. The analyst is also busy answering inquiries and questions from all parts of the investment world. Meetings, with talks by the chief officers of the issuing company, attended by the members of the underwriting groups, are held in various financial centers and information is disseminated as widely as possible to all prospective purchasers.

Under the terms of the Securities Act, no offering may be made by any securities dealers until the Registration becomes effective; but by this time the manager of an underwriting group on a negotiated offering has a pretty definite idea as to what the reception should be to the offering. He has received many "indications of interest" from the large list of possible purchasers—insurance companies (both life, casualty and fire), banks, pension funds, savings institutions, trustees of charitable funds and estates, and many others. He has also been in frequent contact with the member firms of his underwriting group—in the case of the Aluminum Company of America debenture issue, there were one hundred and seventy-six—who have indicated their own individual "indications of interest" as received from their prospective clients.

Formation of selling group

Besides the members of the underwriting (or banking) group there are many other securities dealers in the country who will wish to participate in this public offering—they are what is referred to as "selling group" members, and while they do not participate as underwriters, they are allotted securities by the manager at a concession less than the gross underwriting "spread." Each underwriter gives up proportionately to the amount of securities which the manager sets aside for securities allotted to the "selling group." These added members who aid in the distribution of a security issue play an important function in the distribution of an important issue and assist the manager in trying to conclude a particular piece of business successfully.

Just prior to the time that the Registration Statement becomes effective, the question of the offering price and the underwriting compensation become of paramount importance. The manager of the underwriting group, who must correlate all known factors in arriving at a decision, carefully sounds out the character of the market through talking with both his own salespeople and also his major fellow underwriters.

He then presents to the financial officers of the issuing corporation his conclusions as to (1) offering price; and (2) the underwriting compensation to be paid by the issuer to the underwriters. The matter is discussed freely and openly, and if no real differences of opinion arise, the terms are presented to the board of directors of the issuing company, and the business between the seller and buyer has been negotiated. (In the Aluminum issue, the "waiting" or "incubation" period had seen a slowly rising bond market, which meant that the Alcoa securities could be priced for slightly lower "yield" than had been unofficially estimated at the time the business was initiated.)

The pricing of a large issue of securities is a highly important function of the manager—if he prices them too cheaply he is not giving sound financial advice to the issuing corporation, which may be somewhat embarrassed and subject to criticism should the security rise sharply in the public markets following the offering. Conversely, should he price them too high, the purchasers, who are aware of markets, will tend to "stay away in droves," leaving the underwriters with large unsold balances on their hands; and the issuing company simultaneously will be somewhat taken aback to learn that their issue has had a poor market reception.

This means hairline decisions—especially when markets are nervous and apprehensive—for the manager is of course anxious to prove his worth and knowledge of securities markets and distribution, and to end with a satisfied customer. In a negotiated underwriting the manager has the confidence and trust of the issuer, and is free at all times to review and discuss every phase of the undertaking; for if he falls down on his job, the chances are that the next time the issuer comes to market he will choose someone else to handle his affairs! Therefore the relationship between an investment banker and his client is carried on at the highest level and between the two there exists the most implicit confidence and trust. This relationship takes place continually and not only at the time of a new security offering, for it becomes the responsibility of the investment banker to keep abreast of affairs pertaining to his client, and in turn to keep security dealers and others informed.

We now move into the final stage of the offering—that stage when all the members of the underwriting group assemble at the office of the manager to sign the underwriting agreements, which commits each member to take up and pay for his share of the securities at some prescribed time. These agreements are fully binding upon the members, and become effective when all necessary documents have been cleared by the Securities and Exchange Commission.

Public offering

Let's take a look at what happened on the day when the huge issue of Aluminum debentures were placed on the market. The offering price was set (for a 3% debenture due in 1979) at 100%, and underwriters paid 99% for the debentures. This underwriting compensation or "spread" was $10 per $1,000 debenture. Each of the underwriters paid to the manager a certain portion of this, in payment for his services as rendered, known as a "management fee." Members of the selling group received a concession of $5 from the public offering price, which left $3.50 as the underwriters' gross profit. Certain expenses such as advertising, transfer taxes and legal fees were likewise deducted from this gross profit. Of course, each underwriter gave up only a small portion of his total underwriting to the selling group, so that he retained the gross spread on the greater amount of his debentures, less the management fee.

The issue was successful from every angle, and the manager was able to announce within a short time that the offering had been oversubscribed and the subscription books closed. This is the ultimate aim of a manager of a security flotation, and brings much satisfaction after many weeks of intensive work.

It may be of interest to point out the type of purchasers of this issue and how broadly they were distributed. There were 3,858 separate transactions, and the largest number of these sales were in the $6,000 to $10,000 sale category. Sales were effected in 44 states, demonstrating the wide coverage obtained by the 176 underwriters and 189 members of the selling group.

Life insurance companies accounted for approximately 15% of the purchases, fire and casualty companies 1.5%. fraternal orders 5.5%, savings banks 11.2%, banks (for own account and accounts of others) 39%, pension funds 23%, corporations 1.4%, investment trusts 0.4%, individuals 2.2%, and miscellaneous sales 1.3%.

A 101-member syndicate managed by the Chase Manhattan Bank here discusses preliminary scales before arriving at a final interest cost on a $15,200,000 Commonwealth of Puerto Rico municipal bond issue.

This shows the functioning of the investment banking machinery at its best; the example used happened to be one particularly large in size, but many are smaller, some few are larger. Negotiated underwritings cover the entire field of common stocks, bank and insurance stocks, preferred stocks, and exchange offerings for industrial companies, utility companies, railroads—in short, all industry. Also, negotiated underwritings are used in the securities offerings of certain quasi-governmental instrumentalities, and for some municipal revenue authorities, which recently have figured so prominently in the financing of the huge toll highway systems, built and building.

The investment banker serves a vital role as supplier of capital to those wishing to raise funds—his efforts are central to the successful financing—and growth—of American industry.

KENSINGTON GATE.

The Role of "Municipals"

AFLOAT, ASHORE, AWING

Walter H. Steel

STATE AND municipal bonds perhaps more than any other form of financing demonstrate democratic government acting through its elected or appointed state and local officials and free enterprise, as typified by investment banking, working together to create, improve and maintain the standard of living to which we are now accustomed. No other form of financing affects so many people, nor is there a citizen or taxpayer throughout the nation who is not in some way and in some degree responsible for the creation and discharge of debt for these essential purposes. One has but to pause and observe to see all around concrete evidence of the result of this combined effort.

In 1958 about \$7½ billion in par value of

Most of the greatest bridges in America were financed through municipal revenue bonds, with the structures designed to be self-liquidating through user tolls. World's longest single span is the Golden Gate suspension crossing, 4,200', built in 1937.

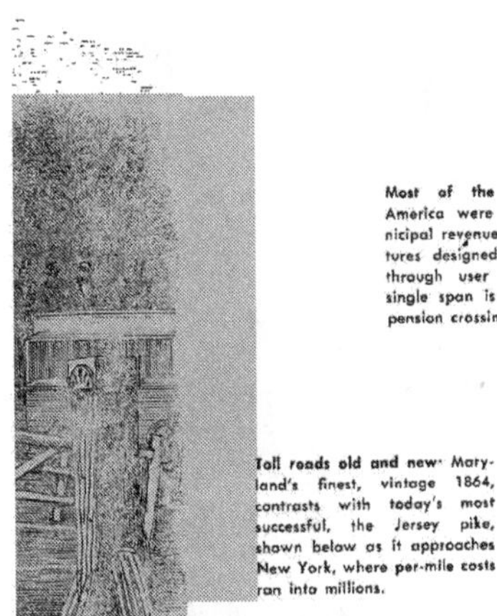

Toll roads old and new: Maryland's finest, vintage 1864, contrasts with today's most successful, the Jersey pike, shown below as it approaches New York, where per-mile costs ran into millions.

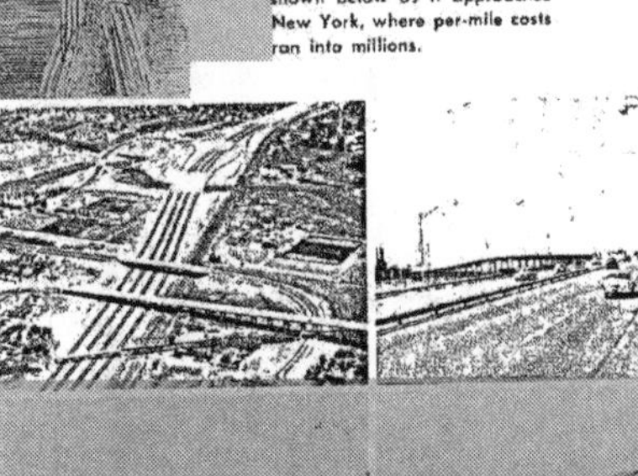

Longest U. S. plate-girder bridge (below) spans the Quinnipiac River for the Connecticut Turnpike.

Nation's greatest cantilever bridges the Mississippi for the New Orleans Bridge Authority.

More than four miles of steel cross Chesapeake Bay. Opened in 1953, tolls began at $1.40 per car.

long term State and municipal bonds were distributed by the investment banking industry. The proceeds of this financing were employed in the acquisition, construction or maintenance of a host of facilities vital to our American way of life. These facilities include: schools, highways, bridges, electric light and power, water, airports and many others. The term "municipal bonds" as used herein includes all debt obligations issued by States, territorial possessions, all political subdivisions (cities, counties, townships, school and other special districts), as well as Authorities, Commissions or other public agencies.

A pattern of continuing growth

The volume of over $7 billion was recorded in 1958, the highest to date in the long history of State and municipal debt issuance and—in light of volume in previous years—is an accurate measure of the growth of this type of financing. In 1946, the first year following World War II, the volume was short of $1 billion. Since then it has increased almost steadily and prospects are that it will continue to grow. In fact, one authority has predicted that by 1965 the annual issuance of municipal securities will approximate $15 billion.

Many factors account for this growth in volume. The increase in the number of school-age children creates an enormous demand for schools. Add to the population growth factor the changing pattern of living, the shift from city to suburb and the vast amount of housing and industrial construction springing up throughout the countryside, and it is not difficult to realize that in addition to schools, water, sewage, highways, flood control, lighting and a host of other necessities must be provided for.

To provide funds in the substantial amounts required for so many and varied purposes, municipal financing must be of a character to generate strong appeal to a wide variety of investors. These investors include individuals, trusts, estates, casualty and life insurance companies, commercial and savings banks, corporate funds, public funds and others. The basic features that have established such an appeal and have made municipal bonds attractive to these varied groups may be summarized as follows:

1. SECURITY—Full faith and credit obligations of States, cities and other municipalities are generally considered second only to United States Government obligations. The history of such securities as far as safety of principal and prompt payment of interest is concerned amply justifies such a position. Municipal revenue bonds, while outstanding in much smaller volume, have also established a splendid record in this respect.

General obligation bonds support major construction projects not necessarily self-liquidating. Such projects include giant free roads (here, Los Angeles' famed downtown Freeways) and port modernization and development.

2. MARKETABILITY—With only one or two exceptions municipal bonds are not traded on securities exchanges. However, active over-the-counter markets exist for most bonds, and the investor finds little or no

difficulty in liquidating holdings when desired. Many such markets are specialized as to type, while others are purely local. Whatever the type or location, the investor, with the aid of a well-informed investment banker or a bank bond department, can quickly find a market for almost any municipal general obligation or revenue security.

3. DIVERSIFICATION—Serial as well as term maturities enable the investor to maintain an orderly run-off of principal over almost any desired period. Further, the varied purposes for which bonds are issued and the wide geographical sources from which they emanate enable broad diversification in these respects. It should be noted that trusts and other investment laws of the several States vary in specified investment qualifications, thus further emphasizing the extreme adaptability of municipals as an investment medium.

4. TAX-EXEMPTION—Interest on all municipal bonds is exempt from Federal income taxes, under present laws. This feature alone, of course, is of considerable appeal in these times of high Federal income taxation. In addition to exemption from Federal income tax, the interest on municipal bonds is usually exempt from State income taxes in the State of issuance and almost all States accord personal property tax-exemption to issues within the State. This latter exemption is of considerable importance in some States, such as Pennsylvania, where a millage tax is levied on security holdings.

Municipals fit two general categories

All municipal bonds for purposes of this discussion may be grouped into either of two very broad categories. These are "general obligation bonds" and "revenue bonds." The first category embraces, as the name implies, all bonds secured by the full faith, credit and taxing power of the municipality. The nature of the tax in the case of such bonds may be "limited" as to the extent of the tax to be levied for payment of principal and interest, or it may be "unlimited" as to such extent. Obviously, "unlimited" tax bonds are a preferred risk and command higher prices in the market.

The second category will include (again, for present purposes) bonds payable from a special tax (gasoline tax, for instance) and housing authorities. Most popularly, the term "revenue" covers bonds issued to provide a facility such as a toll bridge or highway, airport, water, power—for the use of which fees, tolls, or other charges are assessed. Such facilities are sometimes aptly called "user pay facilities," meaning that the cost is borne solely by the user and in direct proportion to the extent of the use.

Revenue bonds popular favorites

Financing through the medium of revenue bonds has become increasingly popular in the period following World War II. The greatest ratio of this type of debt to total municipal volume occurred in 1954 when almost half of that year's total municipal volume of nearly $7 billion was recorded.

Municipal debt is authorized by the issuing body through various procedures depending upon applicable Constitutional and statutory provisions. In many instances a vote of the people is necessary; in others special legislative authorization is needed; while, in some cases, the Constitution or enabling act is sufficiently

WALTER H. STEEL, a general partner of Drexel and Co., is also chairman of the National Municipal Securities Committee and a member of the Board of Governors of the Investment Bankers Association of America. He is a graduate of the University of Chicago School of Business.

broad to cover issuance of debt for specified purposes merely through action of the governing body.

The Constitutions of many States limit the amount of debt that may be outstanding at any one time and/or the purposes for which such may be issued. In such cases, it is necessary to amend the Constitution (sometimes a prolonged procedure) before issuance of debt obligations not previously permitted. Many of the large veteran's-bonus bond issues that followed World War II and the Korean conflict were possible only after Constitutional amendments were effected.

Authorities, Commissions, and other special Agencies are created by the States' Legislatures and are by such legislation authorized to issue bonds for the specific purposes for which the entity was created. Such special agency may be inter-State, as in the case of a river crossing or port involving more than one State. The Port of New York Authority is an outstanding example of such inter-State cooperation. In addition to specific legislative authorization, bond issuance by an Authority or Commission is further governed by the terms of the Trust Indenture or Bond Resolution.

Because of the complexity of laws, court decisions and instruments such as Trust Indentures, attorneys especially versed in the field and referred to as "Bond Counsel" are retained to advise the issuer as to compliance with the Constitution, laws, etc. Such "Bond Counsel" also upon delivery of the bonds issues a statement known as a "Legal Opinion," which is delivered to the purchaser of the bonds. Such opinion recites the basic legal facts of issuance and concludes with an unqualified statement to the effect that the bonds in question have been legally authorized and issued and constitute a valid and binding obligation of the issuer.

The Lincoln Tunnel, opened in the mid-30's, today is the world's only three-tube vehicular tunnel, carries millions to . . .

Marketing by competitive bidding

Once the issuance of debt is authorized, the marketing machinery is moved into action. The majority of issues, especially in the general obligation category, are sold through competitive bidding. Advertisements inviting bids at a stated time and place are run in financial publications, and more detailed information is mailed to prospective bidders. The advertisement and supplemental data describe the issue, give pertinent financial information and set forth the terms of bidding. Since most municipal issues are serial maturities (a portion of the issue matures annually over a given period of years), the best bid is usually determined on the basis of "lowest net interest cost." Such interest cost, while somewhat complicated mathematically, may be said to be that interest rate or combination of rates which over the life of the issue results in the smallest number of dollars being paid in the form of interest.

Large revenue issues are customarily sold

RK AUTHORITY

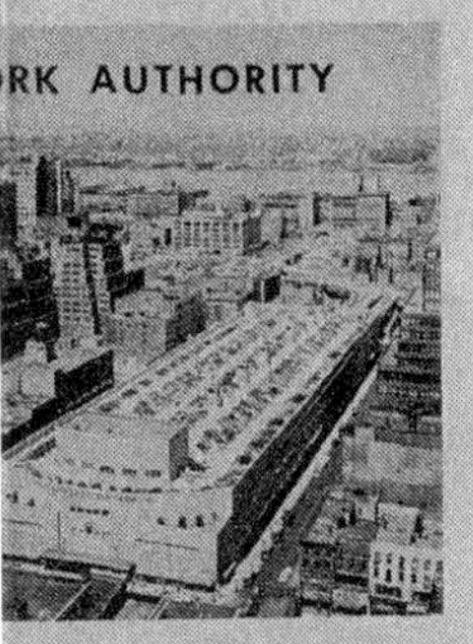

. . . Manhattan's P. A. Bus Terminal, located at the New York end of the great tunnel.

"An outstanding example of inter-State cooperation," the Port Authority was established April 13, 1921 by legislative act. Its revenue-backed bonds, among the nation's most popular, have developed and supported 38 major regional facilities, including the port's giant airfields: Newark (left), where today's terminal is designed for quick change to just another jet hangar—when demand forces a bigger building; La Guardia, now being rebuilt for $56 million, to service 36 planes simultaneously, park 5000 cars; Idlewild, tomorrow's world—colored fountains front a tower with Univac, 55 radios, air and ground radar so powerful it can spot a tricycle a mile away.

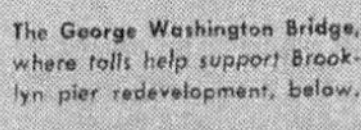

The George Washington Bridge, where *tolls help support* Brooklyn pier redevelopment, below.

through negotiation. The issuer selects his principal underwriters (consisting of one or more investment banking firms) who, in conjunction with engineers, bond counsel, accountants and others, assist the issuer in the development of an issue. The principal underwriters also organize an underwriting group and at the proper time submit a purchase proposal.

In an effort to avoid oversimplification, it would perhaps be in order to elaborate a bit on the function of the investment banker in the marketing procedure touched on above. An organization of personnel specially trained for the purpose is essential. Such personnel includes those familiar with the technical aspects of municipal finance, such as compilation and analysis of financial statements, mathematics, Trust Indentures (in the case of revenue bonds), legal procedures, syndicate organization, sales work, and perhaps most important, market judgment. It is not uncommon in the case of large revenue issues for as much as two or more years to elapse between authorization and marketing.

Syndicates create market

In the case of issues sold through competitive bidding, syndicates or "groups" are formed under the leadership of one or more banks or investment banking houses. These leaders are known as "managers" or "heads." They have the responsibility not only of group organization but of obtaining and supplying all members of the group with information necessary to consider the bonds in question. The managers conduct price meetings where the bid and reoffering terms are agreed upon and submit the bid proposal at the time and place designated. Upon purchase of the issue, the managers have the further responsibility of maintaining all records of the undertaking, placing advertisements, preparing offering circulars or prospectuses, arranging for loans and payment and accepting delivery on behalf of the group—as well as accounting for and disbursing profits (or collecting losses) among the participants of the syndicate. Group formation is accomplished with an eye towards underwriting strength (capital) and distributing abilities (selling). The extent of participation as between members varies depending upon those factors. The participants with the largest interest are known as "majors" and the smallest as "minors."

In the case of negotiated issues, syndicate formation may be more nearly ideal from the standpoint of basic factors because the managers (or principal underwriters) are in a position to be much more deliberate and selective in their efforts to form a group strong both as to underwriting and distributing ability.

Pricing—complex and variable

Pricing municipal bonds is perhaps more complex than in the case of corporate securities. This is because of the many gradations of security even by the same issuer, preference for name and location and the serial nature of the majority of issues. A further factor is the absence of quotations and listings of exchange transactions on the bulk of serial issues so that close comparison with outstanding similar securities is impossible. Variations in pricing because of gradations in security are typified by different prices on "limited" and "unlimited" tax bonds of the same issuer at the same time. Differences based on preference for name and location is perhaps best illustrated by the price differentials existing between various bond issues of Federal Public Housing Authorities. In these instances the bondholder's security is in all cases essentially the participation of the Federal Government, which applies equally in all cases. Yet prices between local authorities will vary pretty much as they do between general obligation issues of the same name.

Supply and demand and prices

Municipal securities, like other forms of indebtedness, will fluctuate price-wise in reflection of money conditions—general economic developments in a given area, and, of course, destruction by fire, flood, earthquake or other large scale disaster. The factor of supply and demand will also cause reaction, price-wise, in municipals as in other securities.

Generally, it should be noted that the differential between municipal and corporate security prices of comparable quality reflect the value of Federal income tax-exemption. Municipal bond prices, except for term issues, are generally expressed in terms of yield, and the investor to whom tax-exemption is important measures the difference in price by calculating the yield advantage. For example—under Federal tax laws and rates in effect in 1958, an individual whose taxable income was subject to the 50% tax bracket had to find taxable investment yield of 7%, to equal the tax-exempt yield of 3.50%.

As to the differential in terms of cost to the issuer, a recent study of average interest rates indicated that corporate issuers of "A" and "AA" rated securities paid slightly over 1% more than did municipal issuers of like rated securities.

It is hoped that the reader of this article will appreciate that in the space allowed it is impossible to go deeply into any phase of the subject of municipals. The foregoing is a summary of some of the more important factors present in the origination and distribution of such securities. The Investment Bankers Association of America has recently published an excellent handbook on the subject under the title of "Fundamentals of Municipal Bonds." It is highly recommended to anyone desiring more complete information on this important phase of our financial society.

Development Underwriting

THE STORY OF AMERICAN-SAINT GOBAIN

Craig Severance

AMONG OTHER functions performed by investment bankers is raising capital for business expansion and development. Research can lead to new products; new markets may be opening; opportunities through acquisitions may be available—all, provided that adequate capital can be obtained. This is an interesting, and sometimes risky, area of finance. It can be rewarding not only in terms of tangible compensation but in the personal satisfaction of achievement.

Companies in the promotional stage are not usually sufficiently advanced to justify the services of an investment banker. As a rule they are privately financed, at least until they are established and have a record of accomplishment. Once this has been achieved, financing of further expansion may be of interest.

The banker must, of course, marshal facts to support his financial programs for the financing of new developments; but intangibles are also considerably important. There is a premium on that rare and elusive quality known as judgment: The more the investment banker knows about the industry and business of the prospective issuer, the better he can provide sound advice and recommendations as to financing plans and type of securities to be offered. This knowledge also aids in selling the securities, whether by private placement or by distribution to the public.

What makes a "blue chip" blue?

The question is frequently asked: "What assets, tangible or intangible, should a company have in order to attract the best terms of financing?" It is not easy to provide a satisfactory answer to this question because of the many factors involved that require appraisal. However, let's take as an example a "blue chip" company meeting the optimum requirements. Such a company should be well established, in sound financial condition, with a good record of sales and earnings, and under experienced and competent management.

♦ *Current assets:* As to the financial condition, a quality growing industrial company should plan to attain, on completion of the financing, "quick" current assets (cash, government securities and accounts receivable) at least equal to its total current liabilities. It should have a ratio of total current assets (quick assets plus inventories) to current liabilities of 2½- or 3-to-1, depending on the type of industry and the rate of inventory turnover. The company should provide through its financing program sufficient new cash which, together with its operating cash flow, is adequate to pay for contemplated capital improvements and to augment working capital to support the prospective larger volume of business. Cash flow is generally deemed to be the sum of net profits plus depreciation, amortization and interest charges.

♦ *Funded debt:* Funded debt should be held well within the ability of the company to service interest and repayment charges. Opinions as to the safe limit of funded debt for an industrial company range from one-quarter to one-half of total invested capital. As one investment banker put it: "The amount of debt depends on whether you want to eat well or sleep well." Be this as it may, interest and amortization payments on the debt, existing and to be created, should be covered by cash flow with sufficient margin so there can be no reasonable doubt as to ability to meet these payments in the event of a decline in earnings.

Funded debt takes different forms: term bank loans, long term bonds or debentures, subordinated debt, and "capital" notes, among others. The kind of funded debt will depend on the nature of the business, conditions prevailing in the money and securities markets, and the particular circumstances and requirements of the issuing company. Short term debt should, as a general practice, be cleaned up once a year.

What it takes for favorable financing

In order to attract favorable terms of financing, the issuing company should have a record of sales and earnings over a convincing period. It is preferable that the earnings record be free of wide fluctuations from year to year. It is helpful if the company has demonstrated its ability to earn profits and cover its charges during times of adverse economic conditions. A steady upward trend in sales and earnings is of importance in connection with equity financing—or financing carrying equity privileges, such as conversion or options.

CRAIG SEVERANCE joined F. Eberstadt & Co., Inc., on graduation from Princeton in 1936. He became a partner in 1955, and was named a director of Chemical Fund, Inc., in 1957. He served in the Navy during the Second World War.

The issuing company's business should have or look towards a fair degree of diversification both as to products and markets. It is important to have a well-directed, trained research organization with a record of accomplishment of new and improved products and processes.

These are some of the factors that should attract favorable terms in financing and illustrate those that investors like to see. Few companies will possess all of the virtues just described. If a company possesses only some of them, it still may be possible to arrange financing on mutually satisfactory terms that will provide the funds needed to carry out the expansion program and add materially to future sales and earnings.

Tailor-made financing: American-Saint Gobain

An unusual example of a tailor-made financing program is American-Saint Gobain Corporation's, in which a total of $53,000,000 recently was raised to construct a plant to enable it to enter the plate glass business. The company was the result of the merger of the publicly-owned American Window Glass Company of Pittsburgh and the privately French-owned Blue Ridge Glass Company located at Kingsport, Tennessee. Prior to the new financing, it had a net worth of $14,100,000 and long term debt of $3,950,000. Its earnings in 1957 and 1958 had suffered from the construction and general business slowdown.

Compagnie de Saint-Gobain, an outstanding French chemical and glass company which has produced plate glass in France since 1665, had for some time been eyeing the expanding and profitable plate glass market in the United States. This market was being served by two manufacturers and, in the opinion of the French and American managements, there was room for a third. Anticipating that some day such a move might be made, Saint-Gobain had founded and over the years had acquired stock ownership of the Blue Ridge Glass Company, a manufacturer of rolled glass.

In the meantime another company, American Window Glass Company, was also considering entering the plate glass business. However, both the American and the French groups were concerned at the magnitude of the investment. The American company lacked the technological ability and skills required to manufacture plate glass. The French company needed an established distribution and management organization in this country.

Conversations were held between the two companies and after extensive negotiations a plan of merger was agreed upon.

The first step was to form the new company, American-Saint Gobain Corporation, which was incorporated in 1956. In May 1958, this company acquired through merger the business and assets of American Window Glass and Blue Ridge. Under a Memorandum of Understanding Saint-Gobain of France agreed, subject to the approval of the French Government, to invest $10,000,000 in the new company when the merger became effective and as a part of the program to build a plate glass plant in the United States. This included an option to Saint-Gobain to purchase 275,000 shares of common stock of American-Saint Gobain at book or $20 per share, whichever was less.

A plan of financing was then worked out with F. Eberstadt & Co. to obtain the additional funds for the program. This resulted, after many modifications (due to changing money markets and economic conditions here and abroad), in American-Saint Gobain taking the following steps:

1. Obtaining from financial institutions a commitment to buy First Mortgage Bonds with warrants to purchase authorized but unissued shares of common stock of the company.
2. Offering to the common stockholders of the company rights to purchase convertible subordinated debentures and additional shares of common stock by means of an underwritten "rights offering."
3. Saint-Gobain (France) agreeing to exercise its 275,000 share option in time to become a holder of record for the stockholders' subscription rights, then to take up its proportionate share of subordinated convertible debentures and of the additional shares of common stock. As a result of the improving European and French economy, Saint-Gobain was able to put more than $10,000,000 into the project and, in fact, invested $13,814,780 of its money in the securities of American-Saint Gobain.

How to do it

There are two general methods of offering securities to the public. In the first instance, the managing underwriter forms an underwriting group of investment banking firms which agrees to make a public offering of the securities issued by the company and to purchase any not bought by the public. Normally, a part of each underwriter's commitment is held back by the managing underwriter and offered to the public through a "selling group." This group consists of investment dealers, other than the underwriters, who have customers interested in the securities. Dealers in the selling group have no contractual obligation to purchase the securities from the company. They take and pay only for securities on acceptance of allotments by the managing underwriter.

A second method of public distribution is a "rights" offering. This was the method employed in the American-Saint Gobain financing. The company gives its existing stockholders the prior opportunity during a limited period to purchase the securities at a price normally below the market. This is achieved by issuing "rights" to stockholders. These rights are usually transferable and negotiable. Stockholders may sell their rights on the open market if they do not elect to exercise them and subscribe to the offering. To assure itself that all the securities will be sold, the company usually has the rights offering underwritten by a group of investment bankers, which agrees to buy any securities not purchased by the stockholders.

The underwriting group, acting through its manager, may offer the securities, or "lay off" as it is termed, to the public other than stockholders on a when-issued basis during the subscription period. A lay off book of interest is built up by the managing underwriter, consisting of the indicated buying interest of members of the group or other investment dealers not included in the group. The managing underwriter then purchases at its discretion, in the open market or privately from large holders, rights against which it can lay off stock or other securities as the case may be. At the end of the period, any unsubscribed securities that have not been laid off are taken up by the underwriting group and offered to the public. If the offering has been successful the amount taken up is usually small, in which case the managing underwriter may make one or more retail sales, or "group sales," for the account of the underwriting group.

During the spring of 1959 negotiations were commenced resulting in an agreement for the sale to an insurance company of up to $33,000,000 of 6% First Mortgage Bonds, plus Warrants to purchase 200,000 shares of Common Stock. This commitment was contingent upon the consummation of the sale of an issue of convertible subordinated debentures and of additional common stock.

Registration Statement filed

A Registration Statement was filed with the Securities and Exchange Commission late in June covering an offering of $11,172,600 Subordinated Debentures due 1983 (convertible until November 1, 1971) and 268,141 shares of Common Stock. Since Saint-Gobain had agreed to exercise its option to purchase 275,000 shares of stock and to subscribe to its proportion of debentures and additional shares on all shares held by it, the managing underwriter formed an underwriting group to underwrite the difference between the total offering filed with the Securities and Exchange Commission and the number of debentures and shares of common stock to which Saint-Gobain was obligated to subscribe. This amounted to $4,772,600 of Debentures and 114,541 shares of Common Stock.

Saint-Gobain was well known in Europe, but it was not a familiar name in the United States. Therefore, participating underwriters were approached, among others, who had the reputation in this country of being knowledgeable of affairs abroad. An underwriting group of sixteen such firms was formed.

Preliminary prospectuses were sent to a broad list of investment dealers in those states where it was expected that the issues would be qualified, along with a letter setting forth the offering schedule and inviting indications of interest in the common stock, should there be lay offs. In addition, representatives of the managing underwriter called on dealers in the major cities of the United States to explain the financing and the company's program. About a week before the offering, a due diligence meeting for the underwriters was arranged by the managing underwriter in New York, which officials of Saint-Gobain, American-Saint Gobain, attorneys and accountants attended. During this meeting the underwriters had an opportunity to review the prospectus and ask management questions about the program.

The "lay off" book shows coast-to-coast interest

By the time the Registration Statement was scheduled to become effective, a lay off book had been built up indicating a substantial interest in shares of common stock and debentures on the part of investment dealers from coast to coast, practically assuring the success of the offering. The subscription price was determined to be the same as the Saint-Gobain option price (book value). After the close of the market on the date the Registration Statement became effective, Saint-Gobain in accordance with its agreement exercised its option to purchase 275,000 shares of American-Saint Gobain common stock at book value of $17.30 per share. The record date was fixed as the close of business that day and the offering commenced with the mailing of non-transferable rights for the convertible debentures and transferable rights for the common stock.

During the subscription period, which ex-

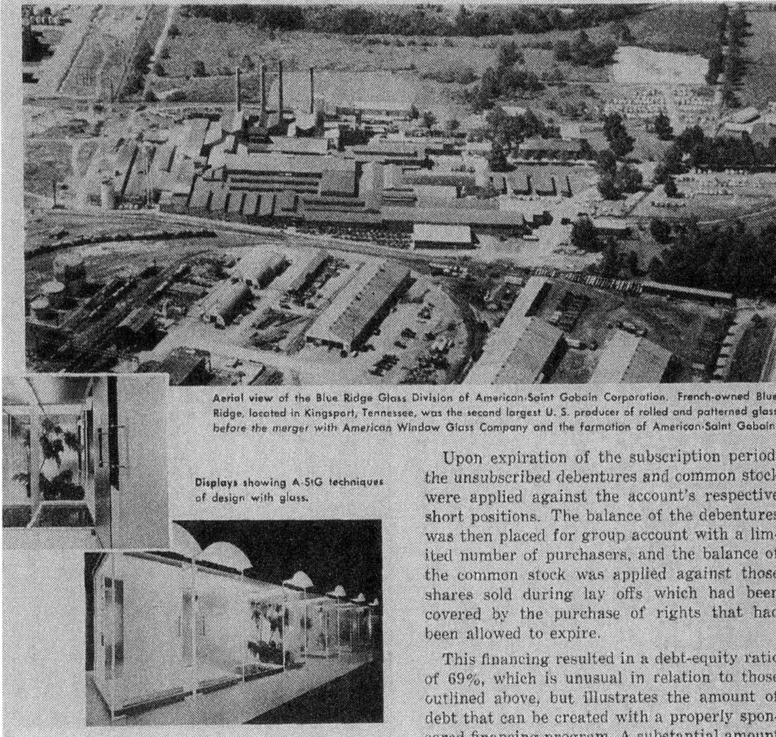

Aerial view of the Blue Ridge Glass Division of American-Saint Gobain Corporation. French-owned Blue Ridge, located in Kingsport, Tennessee, was the second largest U. S. producer of rolled and patterned glass before the merger with American Window Glass Company and the formation of American-Saint Gobain.

Displays showing A-StG techniques of design with glass.

pired 15 days after the offering commenced, the Subscription Agent daily advised the managing underwriter of the amount of debentures and shares of common stock for which subscriptions had been received. There were four lay offs of common stock. A short position in the common stock was maintained for the account of the Underwriting Group. This enabled the group to take up rights offered to it and to reduce its liability during the subscription period. In addition, a block of debentures was sold for group account on a when-issued basis. Since the rights to subscribe to debentures were non-transferable and thus could not be acquired, the underwriting account also ran a short position in debentures.

Upon expiration of the subscription period, the unsubscribed debentures and common stock were applied against the account's respective short positions. The balance of the debentures was then placed for group account with a limited number of purchasers, and the balance of the common stock was applied against those shares sold during lay offs which had been covered by the purchase of rights that had been allowed to expire.

This financing resulted in a debt-equity ratio of 69%, which is unusual in relation to those outlined above, but illustrates the amount of debt that can be created with a properly sponsored financing program. A substantial amount of this debt is subordinated and convertible into equity. Thus, the senior funded debt is less than 50% of the aggregate equity and subordinated debt.

The program employed a number of different techniques, any one of which can be used to raise capital for an expanding company:

1. A joint undertaking to form a new company. A merger is the same type of vehicle.
2. Partial financing by one or more of the parent companies.
3. A private placement of senior securities with a financial institution.
4. A registered offering to the public of one or more classes of securities through the offering of rights to stockholders.

What makes a "blue chip"? A company "well established, in sound financial condition," avers author Severance, "with a good record of sales and earnings, and under experienced and competent management." Standard Oil of New Jersey is recognized as an outstandnig example.

What price success?

In analyzing these steps, certain factors stand out which are important for the successful financing of a company in its growth and development period.

♦ *Financial planning was undertaken at an early stage.* The expansion of a company, particularly through the construction of a new plant to accomplish a new project, is not done overnight. Plans must be made to complete construction, to build up to full commercial operation, and to market the new products, based upon forecasts of the company's ability to create demand or to exploit existing or expected demand for the products. Often projects seem to run about three years from commencement to completion; but this three-year period is usually preceded by months, and sometimes years, of anticipatory planning. It is during this period that financial questions should be resolved as clearly as possible.

Investment bankers were called in as early as 1956 in connection with the American-Saint Gobain financing programs. Subsequently they spent considerable time observing the operations of American Window Glass and Blue Ridge Glass in this country and the plate glass operations of Saint-Gobain in France, Germany and Italy.

They were able to work from the start with both French and American managements and to see through their eyes the future of the business, the prospects of success, and the necessary financial requirements. In addition, they could gauge the further financial needs which the company's success might demand. The assistance of experienced professional advisors when plans are in a formative state often saves a great deal of time, effort and money. Full use can be made of various financial techniques and sources of capital.

♦ *Forward commitments were covered well in advance.* Through the private arrangement with an institutional investor for a commitment of $33,000,000, American-Saint Gobain will be permitted to take down funds, as needed, at several closings over a period of three years to cover construction costs of the new plant.

In addition, the company made arrangements to proceed with its public financing immediately. This brings up the question of timing. A good rule to follow is to finance WHEN YOU CAN—when prospects are good and market conditions are favorable, and WELL BEFORE NECESSITY FORCES THE ISSUE.

The new company, American-Saint Gobain, was well sponsored. Saint-Gobain was known throughout the world for its skill in manufacturing technique, know-how and quality of products, and backed up its own judgment by committing itself to invest substantial funds. The American management was well regarded and had an established flat glass business in this country. The financial backers of the enterprise consisted of a recognized institutional investor and a group of experienced investment banking firms.

The American-Saint Gobain financing is given in detail to point out some of the methods that can be employed to raise funds for a company embarking on a new development. Such a program can be complex, requires time and careful preparation. Each step must be dovetailed with the others. Above all, it requires experience, ingenuity and judgment on the part of the investment banker.

Wall Street keeps on growing . . . UP

The Chase Manhattan Bank's new head office is the largest building to go up in the financial district since the 20's and the largest new building in New York City since the RCA Building in Radio City was completed in 1933.

Ground was broken on January 28, 1957; "topping out" (completion of top-floor steelwork), shown at right, was September 9, 1959.

Strong men, steel beams, and thin air: workmen complete framework 800′ high.

15,000 more people will work in the financial district when the building is filled to its 813-foot roof. The architects planned a 2½-acre pedestrian concourse and open plaza.

COMPETITIVE BIDDING FOR CORPORATE DEBT SECURITIES

Albert B. Hager Jr. Mr. Hager graduated from the University of Pennsylvania in 1927. He entered the employ of Halsey, Stuart & Co., Inc., in 1929 and is currently Vice President and Director of the same firm.

TODAY THE predominant method of publicly marketing public utility and railroad debt securities (bonds, notes and debentures) is by open competitive bids from underwriters pursuant to invitation by the issuer. The alternate method is by direct negotiation between the issuing company and the underwriters or their representative. The practice of competitive bidding for such debt securities has become so widespread that the other method of sale is now the exception rather than the rule. In the field of railroad debt securities the Interstate Commerce Commission, since 1926, has insisted, with certain exceptions, upon competitive bidding in the sale of equipment trust certificates. Similarly, the Commission in 1930 required competitive bidding with respect to an issue of bonds of a terminal company (Indianapolis Union Railway Company). Finally, in 1943, the Commission on its own motion undertook the consideration of requiring competitive bidding with respect to the sale of railroad debt securities issued under Section 20a of the Interstate Commerce Act. The Commission conducted hearings, received numerous briefs, wrote a long and careful memorandum and reached the conclusion that competitive bidding, with certain exceptions, should be required. As a result, competitive bidding is today the accepted method employed for marketing equipment trust certificates, terminal issues and debt securities of railroads.

Massachusetts was a pioneer in the field of competitive bidding for public utility securities. Since 1870 its statutes have required that capital stock of gas and electric companies, not taken by shareholders pursuant to their preemptive rights, be disposed of through competitive bidding and in 1919 a statute was adopted requiring that bonds of gas and electric companies be disposed of through competitive bidding. In 1950 the Massachusetts law was further broadened so that at the present time competitive bidding, with certain exceptions, is now required not only for bonds but also for long-term notes, debentures or other evidences of indebtedness issued by gas and electric companies.

The big impetus to competitive bidding in the public utility field, however, came from the Securities and Exchange Commission which, on April 8, 1941, promulgated its Rule U-50 under the Public Utility Holding Company Act of 1935. This rule requires, with certain defined exceptions, publicly invited sealed written proposals for the purchase or underwriting of securities of or owned by a registered holding company or subsidiary company thereof.

In addition, several other states, which regulate the issuance of public utility securities, have by rule or policy followed the practice of generally requiring competitive bidding. Notable among these are California where in January 1946 the Railroad Commission (now the Public Utilities Commission) issued a memorandum, amended in 1953, which requires public utilities to invite, publicly, written sealed bids for the purchase of their debt securities, with certain exceptions. Most of the publicly offered debt securities (except for smaller issues, and a few convertible debenture issues) of public utility companies in New York State, since 1944, have been sold by the competitive bidding method. Others who have a competitive bidding requirement, by rule or policy, include Georgia, New Jersey (except for small issues), New Hampshire and the District of Columbia.

In addition to those required by law or commission rule or policy to sell their securities at competitive bidding, there are numerous public utility companies which have selected the competitive bidding method of sale although under no requirement to do so. These include some companies formerly subject to SEC Rule U-50 but now exempted from such regulation (by virtue of the fact that they have ceased to be a registered holding company or subsidiary thereof). While certain of its subsidiaries are subject to competitive bidding requirements in a few states, it is a significant fact that, since 1941, American Telephone and Telegraph Company and Bell System companies have sold at competitive bidding 89 bond and debenture issues aggregating over six and one-quarter billions of dollars principal amount. American Telephone and Telegraph Company, although under no requirement to do so, has elected to sell by competitive bidding its own debenture issues in an amount aggregating over two and one-half billions of dollars and ranging in principal amount from $90,000,000 to five issues of $250,000,000 for each of which two large nation-wide underwriting groups submitted bids.

The following tabulation shows the division between competitive and negotiated issues for the total principal amount of public utility and railroad debt securities (exclusive of equipment trust certificates and issues under $2,000,000 principal amount) publicly offered during the years 1941 through 1958. In the public utility category, in addition to electric and gas companies, there are included telephone companies and natural gas pipeline companies. Many of the companies in this category are not required to sell their securities by competitive bidding.

	Amount (in millions)	*Per Cent*
PUBLIC UTILITIES		
Competitive	$23,895	89.0
Negotiated	2,957	11.0
TOTAL	$26,852	100.0
RAILROADS		
Competitive	$ 3,571	94.5
Negotiated	208	5.5
TOTAL	$ 3,779	100.0

Because competitive bidding for public utility and railroad debt securities is so widespread it is of interest to outline the procedures generally employed in this practice.

The initial step taken by the prospective underwriters of an issue is the formation of bidding accounts (groups of underwriting firms which severally will participate in making a bid). Unless the size of the issue is small it is probable that anyone who wishes to submit a bid will wish to do so in association with other underwriters. This step is taken promptly when it is known that the financing is in the offing. Information as to the financing plans of a particular company comes from a number of sources. Underwriting firms may gain this knowledge through personal contact with company officials, through news items, reports that competing firms are forming bidding accounts or perhaps through the official invitation requesting bids.

It is generally the larger firms, with adequate personnel and the capacity to assume relatively large underwriting commitments, which form and act as managers of corporate bidding accounts. The number of accounts that may be formed to bid for a particular issue will depend primarily on the size and the quality of the issue in question. Likewise, the current condition of the market may influence the number of bidders. For the debenture issues of American Telephone and Telegraph Company ranging from $125,000,000 to $250,000,000 principal amount there have been two large competing groups in each instance and three groups have competed for Pacific Gas and Electric Company issues as large as $80,000,000 whereas one utility issue of $4,500,000 attracted 16 bids.

Let us suppose that an underwriting firm hears of a prospective bond issue and decides it wishes to form a bidding account. Naturally, each managing firm wishes to form as strong an account as is feasible. In selecting the firms to be invited into the account the manager gives consideration to such factors as underwriting capital, ability to sell or distribute bonds of the type in question, market judgment and willingness to assume underwriting risks. If this managing firm had previously managed an account which had bid on a prior issue of the company in question it naturally would endeavor to form a new bidding account including firms which were associated with it on the previous issue. If the current issue is of an amount comparable to the previous one the problem is then relatively simple. However, if the amount to be sold differs materially from the previous issue it may be necessary to reduce or increase the size of the account. On a few occasions where the size of the new issue of a particular company represents a substantial increase over a preceding issue there may be mergers of certain bidding accounts where the managers may act jointly or a bidding account may be absorbed into one of the others.

The practice of bidding competitively for public utility and railroad debt issues has been established so long that most utilities and railroads at some time have sold securities by competitive bidding. In instances where a company sells its securities through competitive bidding for the first time, a firm which desires to form and manage a bidding account must compete with others which have the same objective. Thus, it behooves a prospective manager to extend invitations to the firms it wishes to have associated with it as promptly as possible upon receipt of knowledge of the new issue. Likewise, a firm which wishes to join an account to be managed by another, promptly should seek a place in a bidding account of its choosing.

The procedure from this point on is substantially as follows. When the bidding papers are made available by the issuing company the manager of an account obtains a supply thereof. These generally consist of copies of the invitation to bid, statement of terms and conditions of bids, the form of bid and proposed purchase contract, the indenture, preliminary legal opinions and "blue sky" memorandum, preliminary prospectus, etc. These documents are, in turn, distributed to the various members of the bidding account.

After the members of the competing accounts have had an opportunity to study the various documents there is generally a so-called "due diligence" or information meeting. This meeting is conducted by the issuing company and affords members of all the prospective bidding accounts the opportunity of securing additional or clarifying information from the issuer's executives, lawyers, accountants and technical experts. Meanwhile, there may be steps taken by the issuer or others to stimulate interest in the forthcoming issue. Along this line some companies, especially railroads, arrange inspection trips over their properties. Those invited on these trips include representatives of the various bidding groups, important prospective purchasers and the services which assign ratings to securities. These trips afford the interested parties an opportunity to inspect the issuer's properties, become personally acquainted with its management and to evaluate its operations and prospects. Likewise, executives of issuers sometimes make personal calls on underwriters and important prospective buyers of their securities in order to develop interest in the new issue. Also, on some occasions there are arranged other meetings where the company officials may address prospective bidders and, sometimes, prospective purchasers.

Prior to price discussions the Managers and the members of the bidding accounts make thorough surveys of buyers likely to be interested in purchasing the issue. This affords bidders the opportunity to assess the extent of the interest in the issue and aids them in forming an opinion as the price at which the issue can be sold. Subsequently the Managers of the bidding accounts arrange the so-called "Price Meetings" which are customarily two in number. The Preliminary Price Meeting is generally held the business day preceding the day of bidding. The Final Price Meeting is customarily held on the bidding date and is the meeting at which the bid to be submitted by the account is finally determined.

Practices may differ among individual underwriting firms but, in general, it is believed that most firms which act as managers of bidding accounts follow procedures with respect to Price Meetings similar to those employed by the author's firm. Accordingly, the following is a description of the usual Price Meeting procedure.

Prior to the Preliminary Price Meeting of the bidding account there is a meeting of certain key personnel of the Manager (the firm which has organized and is managing the bidding account) including the heads of its Sales, Syndicate, Trading and Buying Departments. At this meeting there is a discussion of the current condition of the bond market, after which the Sales Department reports its findings as to the extent of interest on the part of prospective buyers. Following this, each individual present gives his views as to the market worth of the bonds.

At the Preliminary Price Meeting the Manager will discuss the condition of the bond market and significant features of the issuing company and the bonds which it is issuing. This is followed by the Manager's report as to the extent of institutional interest in the issue with specific mention of certain large institutions which may have an interest. Although not as extensively as the Manager, many individual account members make their own surveys of sales interest and if they have any information differing from or in addition to the Manager's report they have an opportunity to express themselves at this time. The concluding feature of the Preliminary Price Meeting is the expression of price views of the various firms represented.

The Final Price Meeting is generally scheduled by the Manager for as short a time before the hour for receipt of bids as will permit adequate discussion for determining the bid and allow for the completion of the paper work incident thereto. Another reason for scheduling this meeting for as late as feasible is that to do so affords members all possible time to secure the latest information on market conditions and sales interest. Because some accounts, particularly on an issue of large amount, consist of many members it is not always practicable to allow each and every members to participate in the discussions at the Final Price Meeting. In such cases, the determination of the final bid, etc., is vested in a so-called Price Committee which consists of firms having participations down to a certain minimum amount as pre-established by the Manager. It has become a fairly general custom to permit account members not on the Price Committee also to attend the Final Price Meeting if they wish. Such members do not partake in the discussions but each of them present is given the opportunity to declare whether or not he wishes to withdraw from the account if he does not wish to commit at the price decided upon by the Price Committee. If an account member finds it inconvenient or impossible to attend the Final Price Meeting such member may exercise the prerogative of filing with the Manager a price limit. This must be done by a certain designated hour in advance of the Final Price Meeting and indicates the maximum price which the account member is willing to bid for the bonds and that at any higher bid such member no longer has a commitment to participate in the bid.

Prior to the Final Price Meeting there is a meeting of the same key personnel of the Manager. At this meeting the reports of institutional interest in the bonds are again reviewed and individual price views expressed. At the conclusion of this meeting decision is made as to what the Manager will recommend to the Price Committee as a bid and offering price and what maximum commitment or participation the Manager is willing to take on this basis.

At the Final Price Meeting the Manager reviews the interest in the issue and then gives its price recommendations to the Price Committee. Each member of the Committee is polled to determine the extent to which the Committee members are willing to make the bid suggested. Usually some are willing and some are not and perhaps certain of those who want to make the bid also will desire to absorb some of the slack (participations of those firms who indicate they will withdraw from the account at the price level suggested). If it is found not feasible to achieve a bid at the level first recommended by the Manager, attempts are made at different prices until agreement on a bid is obtained. While the Manager makes the initial recommendation to the Price Committee, in some instances, other members of the Price Committee hold generally higher views than those initially expressed by the Manager and thus a bid higher than the Manager recommended is achieved. After determining the bid the Price Committee also decides the proposed price at which the bonds will be offered initially and the discounts to be allowed to dealers.

At the conclusion of the Final Price Meeting the Manager must quickly complete the necessary paper work in connection with executing the bid form and see that the bid is submitted in proper form at the place and by the time designated for the opening of the bids.

Competitive bidding has grown to be accepted by so many public utility and railroad companies, as well as regulatory authorities, that the great bulk of the debt securities of such companies are now sold by this method.

The trading room of C. J. Devine & Co., dealer in government securities, is a nerve center of the New York money market. The electric quote board (background) registers price changes by flashing signals—the books in front of each trader show their position (the amount held long or short) in the securities in which they specialize. Nineteen salesmen—four shown, left —sit facing the traders, ready to answer phones.

Operations of a Government Bond Dealer Firm

MONEY-CHANGING FOR UNCLE SAM

C. J. Devine

GOVERNMENT SECURITY DEALERS perform a variety of operations, all of which serve to implement their principal functions of bringing buyers and sellers together, and of creating and maintaining markets in all U. S. Government and Governmental Agency securities, under favorable or adverse conditions.

The amounts of securities outstanding, $183 billion* of marketable Treasury obligations and $7.5 billion of Governmental Agencies' issues, demand detailed knowledge of market factors and make imperative the need for a specialized type of operation. This is especially true when it is realized that a dealer must be prepared to buy and sell securities, at prices he quotes, in amounts compatible with his size and the condition of the market. He is not a broker—he buys and sells for his own account.

Reasons for the small number of firms in this field are several, but by far the most important is the requisite for expert and special talent necessary to operate successfully in what is perhaps the business with the smallest profit margin, in relation to volume, of any in the world. Although substantial capital is a consideration, this is secondary to the requirement for the specialized knowledge which can be acquired only by long years of experience.

Dealers charge no commissions or fees. They depend on trading profits for their earnings: the spread between bid and offering prices may range from a few hundred dollars down to only a few dollars per million on the principal amount traded.

Practically all trading in Government securities occurs in the over-the-counter market. Each dealer makes his own quotations, and he can provide the best market only if he has the most complete information with respect to the activities of all investors and has considered the effects of all the influences operating in the market. As a result, the facilities for the prompt transmission of information are among the most important of the physical requirements necessary for efficient operation.

A typical dealer organization will maintain its principal office in New York, at which place traders make their markets. It will have its own private wires connecting its branch offices in the important financial centers throughout the country, enabling the firm to communicate with banking and other institutional investors on a nationwide basis. The trader seldom talks to customers himself, but obtains information about current market operations from them through a well trained and highly competent staff of "contact men" located in New York and in branch offices.

The role of the contact man

The contact man is the main link between the buyers or sellers of Governments and the trader. He channels the inquiries and orders to the trader, and is interested in servicing the accounts for which he is responsible to the best of his ability. The more information he can gain with respect to his customers' investment requirements and contemplated portfolio adjustments, the more appropriate will be his recommendations and the greater will be his contribution to the trader's fund of market knowledge. By these same talks with customers, the contact man also continually adds to his own store of information and understanding which he can utilize to assist his customers in their investment problems and in the timely resolution of these problems.

Another unit in a dealer firm is the research staff whose primary duty is to keep the traders and contact men informed generally about current facts and to supply data about past and estimated future price relationships of the various combinations of issues. They supply customers (directly or through the contact men) with expert advice and often with a complete portfolio analysis. This detailed evaluation of a customer's investment position generally includes recommendations based on such factors as earnings requirements, deposit distribution, tax problems, liquidity and other operating ratios pertinent to the institution. The research staff's specialized knowledge is always available for discussion with investment committees, boards of directors and other similar groups where the broader aspects of the market are considered, or where particular problems relating to the investment of funds for various periods of time require the assistance of skilled counsel.

The cashier's department represents still another important unit in the dealer organization, and is responsible for the physical delivery of the securities bought or sold by the trading department. Particular transac-

C. J. DEVINE

He organized his own firm in 1933 to specialize in U. S. Government obligations, following experience with C. F. Childs & Co. In 1958 Mr. Devine established the Institute of Finance at N.Y.U., to study the money market, and related matters.

tions may present unusual delivery problems and, here again, an intimate knowledge of the complex factors involved are prerequisite to a successful operation. It is also the function of the cashier's department to arrange for the financing of the dealer's inventory. This calls for a particularly specialized knowledge as to the location and sources of available funds. Generally, the major portion of a dealer's operations is financed through loans from New York City banks. When, however, funds are more readily available at out-of-town banks, advantage is taken of this fact. At other times, large corporations may hold excess funds for temporary periods, in which event a dealer will utilize these sources.

While the various units of a dealer organization are interdependent, the trading department is of paramount importance, for it is the trader who determines the bid and offered prices of the issues for which he is responsible and the limits to which his quotations will apply. The effective trader is possessed of unusual qualities not ordinarily found in combination. He has an almost infallible memory and a keen sensitivity to impressions. While seldom talking with customers, he is the repository of inquiries, orders and exchange propositions which come from within and without his organization. His mind must be capable of synthesizing all this information and reflecting it in his bid and asked quotations. He must render a decision instantly—with no time for deliberate and lengthy consultation, since most transactions in an active market are executed "on the wire."

While the trader must of necessity be a student of the money market, his approach must be realistic as well as academic. The academic expert on money market conditions may not be an effective trader, as he is apt to be guided in his trading actions by carefully considered factors which might affect the market weeks or months hence. A successful trader in Governments must give much greater weight to the actual flow of orders and inquiries occurring within the hour or day.

Specialization within a giant market

The number of issues and the amounts of each issue outstanding require the active participation of at least four traders and their assistants in a typical large Government dealer firm. There are 83 separate issues of U. S. Treasury obligations in which markets must be maintained, with individual issues outstanding in substantial amounts up to $11.2 billion.* In addition, the 53 separate Governmental Agencies' issues which are traded are outstanding in the amount of approximately $7.5 billion. In order to perfect the specialized character of the business, various segments of the market (by type or maturity) are assigned to individual traders. Thus, in a typical dealer firm one trader will be concerned with short-term Governments, another with those of intermediate maturity, and a third with longer-term issues. Trading in Agency issues will be the responsibility of a fourth trader. These maturity or type groupings appeal to various investor classes and may, at times, react differently to market influences.

Apart from satisfying customers' desires to sell or buy, the trader must constantly keep in mind the existing price relationships between various combinations of issues in order not to acquire an abnormal supply of bonds which appear to be high-priced in the market, nor to deplete his inventory of an issue which appears to be currently undervalued. It is in situations of this kind that his specialized training and knowledge prove to be of particular value, for they will open avenues of operation which will permit him to maintain a two-way market and to minimize price fluctuations which otherwise might result.

The large Government bond dealer, operating with his nation-wide network of branch offices, contributes substantially to the economic life of the country as he performs his many functions and services. At the assumption of considerable risk, he assists in the underwriting and distribution of the marketable debt of the United States, and helps to even out maladjustments in the distribution of reserve balances. In his daily talks with officials of the Federal Reserve System, he reflects the changing conditions of the market as they occur and implements the System's credit policies. In addition, he is a reservoir of specialized information and advice for his customers for whom his ultimate purpose is to provide a ready market in Government securities at the least possible cost.

*As of September 30, 1959.

part

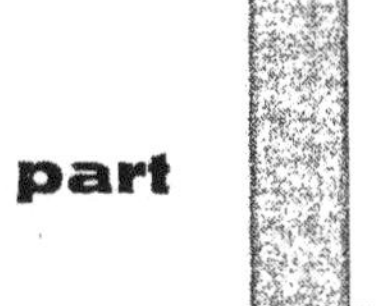

ANALYSIS AND EVALUATION OF SECURITIES

Security Analysis as a Career

THE MEDICINE MEN OF LOWER MANHATTAN

Benjamin Graham

DURING THE forty-odd years that the writer has worked in Wall Street the position of the security analyst has undergone significant changes. In 1914 the term itself was virtually unknown. The larger brokerage firms had information departments, tended by "statisticians" who put together the available financial data and wrote up quite superficial analyses of stocks and bonds. Their work was severely limited by two conditions: the absence of adequate information regarding most securities, and the related emphasis on purely speculative and even manipulative influences, especially in the area of common stocks. Thus the would-be analyst usually lacked the factual material necessary for a competent job, and even when he had it his work was subject to unwholesome influences both from without and within himself.

On the other hand, the early pioneer in the field had some advantages. By determined digging or by shrewd detective work he could often uncover important facts not generally known—such as the original amount of "water" (intangible assets) in the capital of the United States Steel Corporation or the true earnings of the Consolidated Gas (now Edison) system. More broadly, he could develop new approaches to investment theory and practice—at times with boomerang effects. It was some scholarly security analysts, for example, who demonstrated to a sceptical world that representative common stocks had shown a much better long-term investment performance than high-grade bonds. This truth was soon distorted to give a psuedo-scientific basis for the wild stock market of the late 1920's. The resultant collapse and economic disorganization gave security analysis itself a setback from which it took some years to recover.

Spectacular recent progress

But in the last two decades security analysis has made continuous and even spectacular

BENJAMIN GRAHAM graduated Phi Beta Kappa from Columbia in 1914. Prior to retirement, he was president and director of the Graham-Newman Corporation and a general partner of Newman & Graham. He is considered an outstanding security analyst and has written many books on finance.

progress. At present there are some 6,000 recognized analysts, belonging to 22 local societies, which are leagued in a National Federation. They have a highly respected publication, "The Analysts Journal;" they stage elaborate annual conventions and numerous regional meetings. After some hesitation, they appear to be moving definitively towards a professional status.

What has caused this rapid growth? Probably a number of factors:

- the great improvement in the quantity and reliability of corporate data, largely due to the SEC legislation.
- the rise in the financial strength of publicly held corporations, and the higher investment standing of their securities.
- the unquestionable subordination of speculative to investment interest in Wall Street —aided in good part by the more favorable tax status of "long-term capital gains."
- the increasing emphasis on technology in the world of business, calling for more and more expert knowledge in appraising prospects and values.

Security analysts tour the General Electric electronics laboratory in Syracuse, New York. Such on-the-scene reviews help answer specific questions about the company.

Functions of the security analyst

The characteristic job of an analyst is to select suitable securities for a given investor. He may also advise switching from one issue to another, or outright sale because of high price or impaired quality. He may work for a variety of employers: a brokerage firm, an investment banking house, investment counsel, a financial news service or an investment advisory service (sometimes combined); an investment fund; a bank or trust company; an insurance company; a private investor; or even just for himself. He may specialize in a single field—e.g., U. S. Government, municipal, or corporate bonds; public utilities, railroads, chemicals, electronics. As a top man in an underwriting house, his important function may be to determine the proper provisions for a new security issue and the price at which it may be successfully syndicated and sold to the public.

Whatever his employment, a good security analyst requires both broad and intensive knowledge. He must understand general economics, business and financial practices, the behavior of the security markets, accounting methods and technicalities, much corporation law, and all the important tax regulations affecting business and security transactions. He needs a knowledge of human nature—especially the non-economic motivations that often govern the actions of people in the stock market, corporate managements, and security holders. He has to be enough of a scientist to keep up with the numerous important technological developments that are affecting both individual securities and the general economy.

The security analyst deals with stock prices in two different and somewhat contradictory ways. On the one hand, the current price should be an integral part of every investment decision. Any security, no matter how sound and promising the company, may conceivably be selling too high for sound investment; conversely, even though the picture is unfavorable, the price may still be so low as to make the security a better purchase than sale. In these formulations, the analyst is acting as a critic of the market level. Consciously or by implication, he is comparing the current price with his independent concept of the proper value—a range, rather than a single figure—and he is ready to set his own judgment in opposition to the multi-jurored verdict of the market place.

But the analyst has to live with and from the security markets. He must be circumspect rather than quixotic in his disagreements, and be just as ready for irrational as for logical movements in prices. For this reason nearly every security analyst has at least a trace of the stock market analyst in his make-up, and many follow one calling as seriously as the other. Does the endeavor to forecast price movements assist or handicap security analysis? The controversy over this question has been raging for a long time, and shows no sign of ever being settled.

The medicine men

To understand both the possibilities and the limitations of the analyst's work it is useful to compare it with that of the medical man. The doctor has a lot of professional training and skill; he does valuable and necessary work; yet there are serious gaps in his knowledge, and many areas where medical science must give place to a more mysterious *art* of medicine. Security analysis today undoubtedly has less science, more art, and a higher admixture of "educated guesswork" than the other, much older discipline. But like the doctor, the competent analyst starts with the advantage of knowing more than his clients; on the whole—if not in every case—he should be able to do better for them than they would do for themselves.

The medical man deals with patients, with diseases, and with drugs or other means of cure. Our analyst deals with investors (including certain types of speculators) and with securities. The analogy suggests the amusing thought that a poor or disappointing security corresponds to an illness on the part of its owner, while choice of a satisfactory security corresponds to a successful cure. Security analysis lags far behind medicine in the collection and systematic study of case histories. It knows much less than it should of how various theories and techniques for the evaluation and selection of securities have worked out in many applications. Until the serious work done by our numerous senior analysts is itself collated and carefully analyzed, our endeavors will lack the broad foundation needed for a soundly scientific discipline. This deficiency is a challenge to the security analysts of the future; it is pleasant to think that some readers of this article may possibly contribute to that cause.

In recent years the analyst has grown to resemble the physician in one further respect—the increasing attention he is giving to the fruits of research as they show themselves in new scientific and technological developments. The position and prospects of many companies have been affected radically by the advent and rapid growth of aviation, plastics and other synthetics, electronics, etc. Now the security

Analysts specialize in many fields . . .

Chemicals Rails Electronics

analyst must struggle hopefully with all the implications of the dawning atomic age.

The imperfections of security analysis grow mainly out of the uncertain relationship between the past and the future. Each investment decision must look to the future for its vindication, yet most of the analyst's studies are directed to or at least grow out of past records. Broadly speaking, the analyst takes past performance as a rough guide to future expectation—subject, however, to whatever allowance for changing conditions is suggested by his knowledge, his judgment, and even his imagination. There is sufficient ambiguity about all this to explain the extraordinary differences in the methods used by individual practitioners, and in the conclusions they reach about the merits of specific securities at a given time.

Steel Oil Atomics Aviation

Two schools of thought

It may not be inaccurate to declare that there are currently two distinct schools of thought in security analysis—the one emphasizing mainly the *qualitative*, the other emphasizing chiefly the *quantitative* factors in investment. The first seeks most of all for the "good companies," with promising futures. The second lays most stress in finding a calculable "margin of safety"—typically in the form of value substantially higher than market price. The reason these two viewpoints are generally in conflict is that in most instances the shares of promising companies sell at relatively high prices while, conversely, undervalued issues are generally found in concerns and industries with doubtful prospects.

Thus every analyst agrees that General Electric is a great company with a highly promising future. But do these considerations justify the valuation of more than $7 billion for the business which the stock market placed on it in the recent past—nearly four times as high as in 1952? Should the investor be warned by the fact that the price of General Electric fell from 95 in 1930 to only 8½ in 1932 and from 65 in 1937 to 28 in 1938? Or is this past history basically irrelevant to the conditions of 1959? There is room here for a variety of viewpoints among experienced security analysts.

The standard method of evaluating a common stock consists of estimating future earnings and dividends, and applying to these a multiplier or capitalization rate which reflects the company's quality and long-term prospects. A simple enough formula—but, unfortunately, the future earnings are largely a matter of guesswork and the correct capitalization rate is largely a matter of opinion. In both aspects the analyst can employ a good deal of knowledge and skill, but he is never on the solid, comfortable ground of the physical sciences. As a consequence, the analyst's judgment is necessarily influenced to some degree by the surrounding psychology, as expressed in the level and activity of the stock market itself. Instead of prescribing standards of value for the public, he too often finds himself taking his own standards from the public—like the famous politician who exclaimed, "I have to follow them, because I am their leader."

SAMPLE CONSOLIDATED BALANCE SHEET

ASSETS		
CURRENT ASSETS:		
Cash		$ 749,077
Accounts receivable:		
Customers	$ 653,020	
Other	71,787	
Total	$ 724,807	
Less allowance for possible losses	10,000	714,807
Inventories — Finished goods, work in process, materials, and supplies (partly pledged) (Notes 1 and 3)		5,439,314
Total current assets		$6,903,198
PROPERTY, PLANT, AND EQUIPMENT, at cost:		
Land	$ 43,423	
Plant and equipment	3,296,580	
Total	$3,340,003	
Less accumulated depreciation	1,150,454	
Property, plant and equipment—net		2,189,549
DEFERRED CHARGES:		
Unamortized patents, research and development	$ 41,604	
Other—unexpired insurance, etc.	58,090	
Total deferred charges		99,694
TOTAL		$9,192,441

LIABILITIES		
CURRENT LIABILITIES:		
Accounts payable		$ 380,985
Current maturities of long-term debt		247,047
Federal and State income taxes		1,348,111
Accrued expenses		68,152
Total current liabilities		$2,044,295
LONG-TERM DEBT:		
Mortgage payable, 4% (less current maturities, $60,380, included above) (Note 2)	$ 214,542	
Notes payable, 4% (less current maturities, $186,667, included above) (Note 3)	373,333	
Total long-term debt		587,875
RESERVE—Deferred income tax (Note 4)		17,000
STOCKHOLDERS' EQUITY:		
Common stock—authorized, 800,000 shares, par value $1 each; outstanding, 468,440 shares	$ 468,440	
Surplus:		
Paid-in	4,153,926	
Earned (since January 1, 1945) (Note 3)	1,920,905	
Total stockholders' equity		6,543,271
TOTAL		$9,192,441

A balance sheet: the analyst's best friend.

The very difficulties of the security analyst's job give it much of its fascination. If everybody could agree on the value of each security, Wall Street would become a mighty uninteresting place. The analyst functions in a sort of limbo between scientific predictability on the one hand and mere guesswork on the other. His task is to arrive at a useful synthesis of knowledge and uncertainty. Since there are a countless number of different securities, and since it is important to investors that each of them be evaluated with intelligence and judgment, the security analyst has become an indispensable part of the machinery of finance.

Nor is it fair to our profession to leave the reader with the idea that the security analyst is merely a more expert guesser of the financial future than the lay investor. There are wide areas in the field of securities in which the analyst's work can attain a high measure of dependability. This is true typically in the selection of safe bonds and preferred stocks, where the objective is to find so much present protection that the uncertainties of the future may be disregarded. Even in the riskier domain of common stocks the analyst may strive for an approximation to mathematical reliability by combining the principles of "margin of safety" and diversification. To some extent the growing acceptance of *formula* approaches to investment—in particular that of "dollar-cost averaging" over a period of years—parallels these endeavors of the security analyst to minimize the role of prediction in his work.

Security analysis is not yet a full-fledged profession, but it will be. It offers great opportunities to the capable young man. Also, it has much to gain in its own development from the contributions that can be made to it by the flexible and open-minded thinking that is the hallmark of successful academic training. The security analyst leads an interesting life. He learns not one business but a thousand. He is called on constantly to adapt the experience of the past to new and unprecedented situations. He can look forward to meeting many people of importance, and to much travel not unmixed with entertainment. And the financial rewards are fully commensurate with his abilities.

KENNETH WARD, who graduated from Yale in 1921, is also a graduate of the Columbia Business School. He became a general partner of Hayden, Stone & Co. in 1950, and is a member of the New York Security Analyst Society.

Some Basic Factors Affecting Stock Prices

HINDSIGHT WOULD MAKE US RICH

Kenneth Ward

As all of us know, our own school team will command our loyalty and devotion, win, lose, or draw, and even when we know that an occasional rival seems certain to beat us, we stick with our team regardless of the outcome. Such is not the case when one goes into the stock market to make a purchase. Here, our sole objective is to decide in advance which side is going to win and then join that side. If, after we have made a decision in favor of a certain security or a group of securities, we find that the other side is likely to win, we promptly change to that side.

We are all excellent as Monday morning quarterbacks, but to call the winning plays while the game is in progress is a lot more difficult. So it is with the stock market. Our hindsight would make us rich in a short time, but unfortunately the investor or the forecaster must base his decisions on what he thinks lies ahead. While successful investing and forecasting can never be an exact science, there are a number of factors which can be weighed and certain tools which can be used that greatly reduce our margin of error.

Perhaps the foremost factor which must be considered is the constantly changing psychology of the stock market. While I believe it is safe and true to state that although 75% of the fluctuation in stock prices is caused by changing fundamentals such as earnings, dividends, and book value, the other 25% usually reflects not only company reports or news, but also sharp, sudden changes in public sentiment. The mass action of people, as reflected in their changing moods, is one reason why statistics and economic figures often lead us astray.

Market movement a marriage of sense and sentiment

I have found over the years that economists, in forecasting business, have always been more bearish than others; and that in forecasting the stock market investment analysts have always been more bullish. They usually expect the market to sell higher than business justifies. What it all boils down to is that the majority of us is too optimistic at times and at other times too pessimistic. We are a nation of extremists. We wait for some of the clouds of uncertainty to clear up before we invest and when they are all cleared it is usually too late. For by that time the market has generally discounted the favorable event. The trick is to endeavor to measure these psychological moods, and time their various changes.

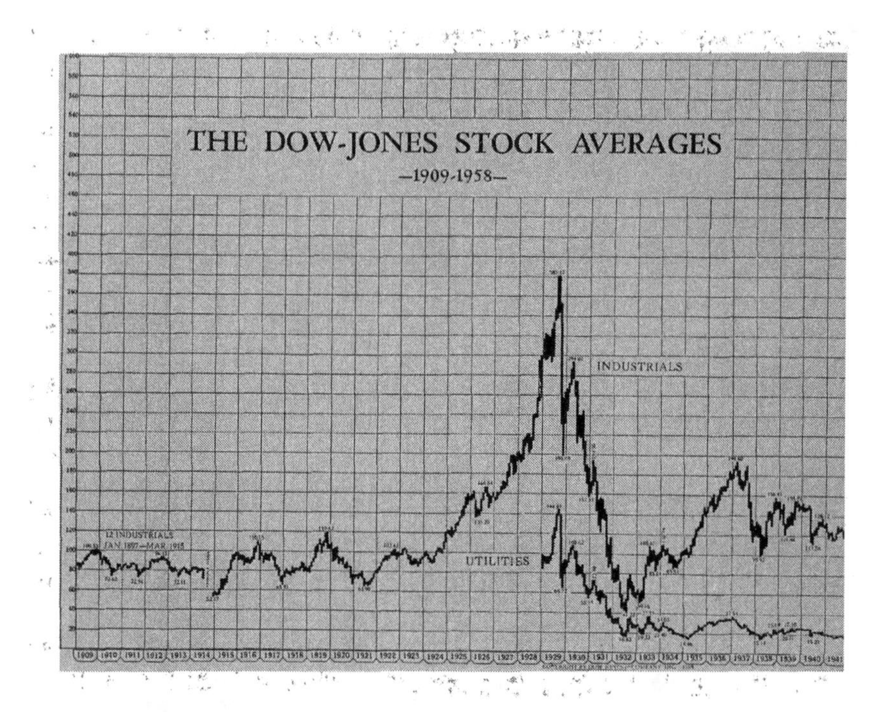

The "technical approach"

So, over the years many have found that the use of charts is extremely valuable, as a sort of guidepost that helps to measure these psychological changes in the market place. This is called the "technical approach." Charts are of real value as they enable one, to a certain extent, to avoid personal opinions and preconceived ideas, hopes, and perhaps wishful thinking. They tend to keep one on the winning team and indicate when to switch to the other side. This is the key to stock market profits. In essence, they often arouse the investors' suspicions that the most obvious interpretations of current events, both economic and business, may not always be the right ones.

We are all prone to believe that a decline in business profits will cause a decline in stock prices and vice versa. Yet, it might be well to recall 1946, when the trend of earnings was pointing higher but stock prices collapsed. Or we might remember the early part of 1949, when earnings began to go down and the market started up. Even late in 1957 and 1958, when a deep recession was widely advertised and predicted and business actually did decline, stock prices advanced over 200 points on the Dow-Jones industrial average. It is unnecessary to theorize on this contention (the importance of public psychology) when price changes in the security market over the years have so clearly proven this truth. Selection in making a security purchase is equally as important as timing. Amid the greatest inflationary prosperity this nation has ever known there have been many stocks (in categories

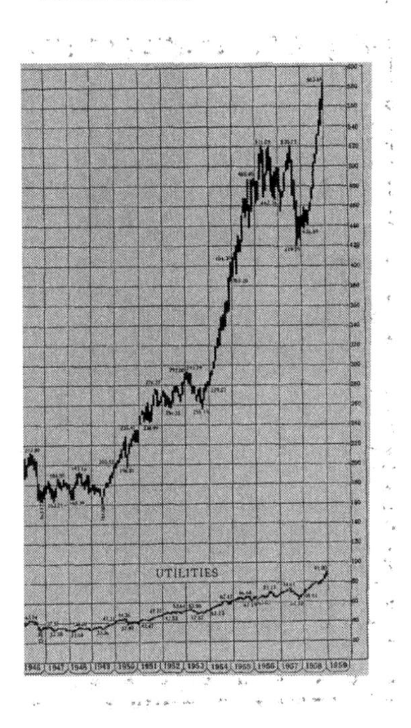

such as textiles, sugars, liquors, coal, lead, and zinc, to name a few) that have declined substantially as a result of narrowing profit margins and other adverse factors.

In using charts to interpret public psychology several things are important. First, one should not read into a chart something that isn't there. Swim with the tide. Do not fight a trend. Second, one should not try to uphold or justify a previously expressed opinion if it turns out wrong—change to the winning side. No one is infallible. You are bound to make mistakes. Thirdly, and above all, do not join the crowd which constantly advertises how right they have been. People know when you've been right without your advertising it, and they also know that you wouldn't express an opinion, or write an article, or make a speech, or go to the office any more if you were always right. Charts should be used only in conjunction with the constant study of the basic statistical and economic background of the market. It's the combination of these two factors that pays off. Obviously, no one can have complete knowledge of all the up-to-date information on the many companies in existence today. That is why we in our firm have many security analysts—experts in their various fields—to help us in our work.

After studying about 47 different chart methods, I have come to the conclusion that too many different types of charts or chart methods are bad, for one will many times contradict the other. You can never reduce to a mathematical formula anything so variable as the buying and selling of securities by human beings motivated by different opinions and purposes. The student of charts not only examines the psychological state of mind of the investor and the relative buying and selling pressures, which are reflected daily on the ticker tape, but he also studies economic and company reports. Coupled with a little horse sense and a little luck he thus becomes a correlator of all the factors that go into making a definite forecast on the price movement of a specific stock or group of stocks.

To be a qualified, time-tested technical student of markets he must have had many of his forecasts go wrong, just as a good quarterback sometimes finds that his judgment has been wrong. He must have miscalled some plays, and he should tell his clients frankly when and if he makes a mistake. Unfortunately, he doesn't often do this. You cannot learn this more scientific approach to the market in a hurry. You must first analyze the economic trends going on around you. You must be a constant reader and try to keep abreast, not only of the current business news, but also of all the phases of international affairs as they may affect the market.

What are some of the other factors that provide a background for arriving at any conclusion on the market or on any specific stock?

♦ One must have a clear understanding of the role that *taxes* play in the present economy. Especially formidable to high income investors, taxes often preclude extensive profit taking in the market and are mainly respon-

Events of world-wide significance are always a pervading market influence. Wars begin and end (here, Pearl Harbor and Hiroshima), international incidents threaten—all affect the course of security prices.

sible for many investors' reluctance to sell a long-term position, even when it would otherwise be to their advantage to switch from one issue to another.

♦ So long as earnings and dividends are well maintained, *fear* will be at a minimum. This is one reason for the firm action of a general market, despite such bearish factors as we had in 1959—the steel strike, rising costs of labor, and tighter credit conditions.

♦ The *government* plays an active role in creating more confidence in industry and the securities market. By boosting initiative and morale, it has stepped up new money expenditures, thereby creating large sums, a portion of which has been going into purchases of securities.

♦ It is most important to keep in mind the tremendous amount of funds being placed in the stock market today, by *pension funds and institutional investors*. It is estimated that pension funds have assets of $30 billion and are acquiring sound stocks at an annual rate of $3 billion or more. It follows that large amounts of top quality stocks have been taken out of the market and are in strong hands. The result is a shrinking supply of such stocks.

♦ The *role of management* in a competitive economy is also most important. It is common knowledge that the plush years of the "seller's market" are over, that competition in all phases of business is increasingly keen, and that companies with shortsighted or lethargic management are in a least favored position. Able and aggressive management, on the other hand, must recognize the existence of a "buyer's market," and streamline its operations.

♦ The investor has to remain constantly alert to *the international situation*, so as to gauge whatever effect the increasing or decreasing tension abroad might have on corporate sales, earnings, and dividends. Sudden and unexpected international incidents, such as the fall of France, Pearl Harbor, the start of the Korean War, or the trouble in Berlin, always pose a constant threat to the over-all stock market picture and produce sudden and sometimes drastic changes in the prices of securities.

♦ Developing *new products* as a result of research leads good management into vigorous campaigns to capture a larger share of the market from competitors. Results of the $40 billion which industry has spent on research over the past several years are just now coming to light and will eventually reach flood proportions.

Visualize for a moment the vast upheavals that will occur when atomic power is used commercially. Consider, too, the numerous time and labor saving devices which will stem from research in the fields of electronics and automation. For example, Radio Corporation's research laboratories at Princeton, N. J., employ over 1,000 persons—scientists and engineers—on fundamental research.

♦ Although not so important as the foregoing, *"broker's loans"* (the total of funds borrowed to support securities purchased on credit) and the *"short interest"* (the total amount of the outstanding shares which have been sold "short" in anticipation of lower prices) are also fundamental elements contributing to the ebb and flow of stock prices. Both of these factors were major contributors to the stock market collapse of 1929. However, broker's loans are comparatively small today; the majority of stock is bought for cash.

As you know, one can sell stocks he doesn't own in expectation that he can buy back at a lower price. Respecting the current short interest, although it has been at its highest level in twenty years, much of this stock has been sold short "against the box" in order to protect a long-term profit in the same shares, which are actually owned by the short seller. It is, therefore, not considered to be quite the same as a short sale by one who does not own his stock outright, and who thus must cover sometime, or "buy in" the stock which he previously sold short.

Multiple judgments move prices

In conclusion, it is the composite of thousands of independent judgments based on some or all the factors listed above, that determines the price of a stock. As indicated, this projection of judgment causes violent swings in stock prices, sometimes out of all proportion to the values which are finally published. Essentially, it is the problem of the analyst and forecaster to attempt to correlate all these various factors together. With the recent development of new and better products, I, for one, believe the opportunities for gain are even greater than they ever were, although it may take a little shopping around and patience to uncover some of them. Thus, with teamwork, along with lots of careful research, some of the fundamental forces reviewed above and which underlie stock price movements may be converted into important stock market profits.

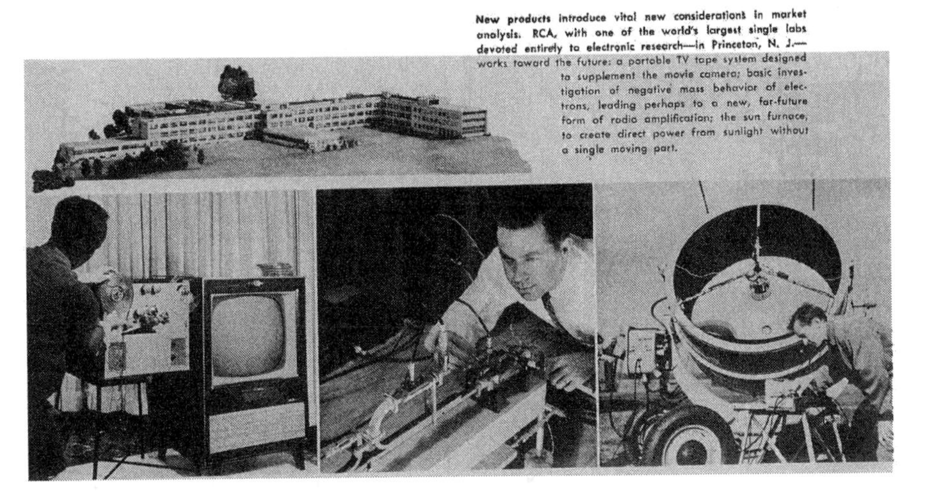

New products introduce vital new considerations in market analysis. RCA, with one of the world's largest single labs devoted entirely to electronic research—in Princeton, N. J.— works toward the future: a portable TV tape system designed to supplement the movie camera; basic investigation of negative mass behavior of electrons, leading perhaps to a new, far-future form of radio amplification; the sun furnace, to create direct power from sunlight without a single moving part.

The Organization and Functions of a Research Department

THE INCUBATOR OF IDEAS

Henry A. Loeb

IN DISCUSSING the functions and describing a well-integrated research department, it is necessary to look back over the past twenty years to get a proper perspective. As a recognized profession, statistical analysis is relatively new. Prior to 1933, and particularly in the Gay Twenties, people bought securities on the basis of hunches, inside information, and tips; and the public by and large had no real information concerning the securities they were buying. With the depression an analysis of the stock market as a public service was made. A new conception was developed, providing for full disclosure of all pertinent corporate facts, as evidenced by the passage of the Securities Act of 1933 and the Securities Exchange Act of 1934.

With this development the security analyst came into his own. To obtain at least a fair understanding of a given listed company's affairs it was no longer necessary to be an "insider." This development is more or less unique in this country, for in most nations companies do not provide sufficient information to permit an intelligent evaluation of their securities. In effect, this restricts the possible sources of risk capital which are so important in a dynamic economy; for the public participation in capital formation can be based only on confidence, which is dependent on reliable and sufficient information.

HENRY A. LOEB became a partner of Carl M. Loeb, Rhoades & Co., in 1939 and has been in charge of their investment department since 1946. He is also a member of both the New York and California bars.

The history of the 20's brought to light the necessity of investment bankers and brokers developing fully integrated research departments; and with emphasis on full disclosure, these research departments have become a valuable and necessary part of an organization. People looking for investments want the facts and not tips. In the United States a great deal of money has been made (and lost) by following rumors and hunches, but actually nobody can expect good luck to last forever, and now with the wealth of information available to the investing public there is no excuse for substituting intuition for research.

Specialization is the key to thorough understanding

A well-integrated research department is set up to cover all phases of investment and investment banking. The organization usually provides for a group of younger analysts, whose primary duty it is to become acquainted with certain industries and to follow the companies in these industries. This function involves a thorough knowledge of all sources of investment information, such as investment manuals and services, annual and other reports, and management interviews. During this period specialization is important, as a thorough understanding of one industry is necessary training for future analysis of the entire economy. It also gives an individual the opportunity to contact and discuss industry problems with executives in the particular industry. These contacts can become increasingly valuable.

The selective and critical portion of security analysis also requires a thorough knowledge of the industry involved and of the real position of the industry in the national economy. These latter functions are performed by senior statisticians who, through their long experience, have acquired broader knowledge and better judgment. On the basis of all information available, an attempt is made to judge the potential of individual industries and companies. By this screening process the research department attempts to develop ideas which can be used in recommending investments to customers.

The great appeal of security analysis for the young businessman lies in the fact that the national and—more and more—the international economy is his chosen field and he can apply himself not as a dilettante but as a professional. The young graduate entering a specific industry will acquire familiarity with it; but with greater specialization his versatility is limited and his professional fate may depend upon the future of this one industry. In security analysis some specialization is useful, but here the basic demands are better satisfied by shifting one's main interests. With the flux of general business and technological developments, the good security analyst must be a master in many fields—a great challenge but one that may bring many rewards.

Security analysis requires more than book-learning alone—the analyst will come in contact with many types of people. His technique will never become an end in itself but will always be a means to grasp the meaning of the facts. In this direction it may be worth considering a divergence of opinion concerning the desirability of having the security analyst be at the same time analyst, investment counselor and investor. Some firms hold that the security analyst is most useful if his judgment is not biased by having to worry about the investment decisions of clients or even a per-

This large research department—at Loeb, Rhoades & Co.—has 64 members, 33 of them senior analysts, and uses closed circuit TV to show *instantaneously tape reports* on current trading. Better than 2,100 different stocks and bonds are listed. The library (right) is an important part of the department.

sonal stake in the correctness of his judgment. I have always felt that security analyses should not be carried on in an ivory tower, and that participation in buying and selling securities for customers and one's self is the final step in bringing to life all the facts and figures that the security analyst has spent so much time and effort in compiling.

Financial reports are a basic analytical tool—shown here are recent prize-winners chosen by Financial World magazine.

The glamor of "new business"?

Recently young men applying for positions have all indicated that they wanted to go into "the new business department" and that security analysis, as such, was not their objective. This is the wrong approach both from the point of view of interest and rewards. The success of most firms in the securities business is dependent upon its day-to-day business and this in turn succeeds or fails in ratio to the quality of the advice and recommendations of the firm. Therefore, the individual with the ability to develop successful ideas both affirmative and negative will be rewarded. His success will also lead to developing clients of his own.

After all, analyzing the national and world economy and the implementation of ideas into action is the backbone of the securities business. It would be silly to waste the talents of a good securities analyst when a new business situation arises in a field in which such analyst has specialized. Therefore, there is no hard and fast line between the "new business department" and the security analysis department. When a situation arises in a field in which an analyst is a specialist, he is called in to work with the new business department for advice as to its merits. Only after these are determined do the functions of the two departments separate.

The separate function of the new business department is in the field of negotiation, and time alone determines whether an individual has a flare in this direction. He may be a brilliant analyst and yet not have the ability to negotiate a "deal." Therefore, he may be successful if he sticks to analysis and fail if he insists on limiting his objective to the new business department. I emphasize this problem as too many young applicants for positions have been influenced by the glamor of "new business" which requires certain very rare talents and is more restricted because of the limited number of personnel required.

Rewards for the novice

As in every other profession, it is difficult to tell the novice where he is going to end up. Many a security analyst will never get beyond technical competence and is likely to end up in one of the large research organizations where methodical research is used to lay the groundwork for more significant accomplishments. On the other hand, there is a considerable need for individuals who combine a thorough knowledge of the techniques of security analysis, familiarity with industry and individual companies, and judgment. With the pressure of investment funds rising steadily, the role of the analyst in an investment trust, a bank, a brokerage house, and insurance and pension funds, is demanding but rewarding.

Knowledge of securities is basic in almost every phase of investment banking and brokerage, and those with this knowledge and judgment have unlimited opportunities. The number of officers and partners in large institutions who are graduates of the research department is increasing steadily.

The Research Department at Work

UNCOMMON VALUES IN COMMON STOCKS

Walter Maynard

THE FIRM OF Shearson, Hammill & Co. in each year since 1949 has published at approximately mid-year a portfolio of stocks entitled "Uncommon Values in Common Stocks." These portfolios have been widely advertised, for the purpose of emphasizing the importance which the firm attaches to research. With the exception of two years, these lists have consistently outperformed the averages by a substantial margin, and for the ten years ended June 30th, 1959, showed an appreciation of approximately 666% compared with a gain over the same period of 296% in the Standard & Poor's 500-Stock Index. The following chart indicates this performance in graphic terms:

The publication (and subsequent successful performance) of such portfolios is, of course, a rigorous and definitive test of the quality of the work of a research department. Therefore, the process of creating them, which is essentially the art of arriving at a successful evaluation of securities, is probably worthy of a little closer examination.

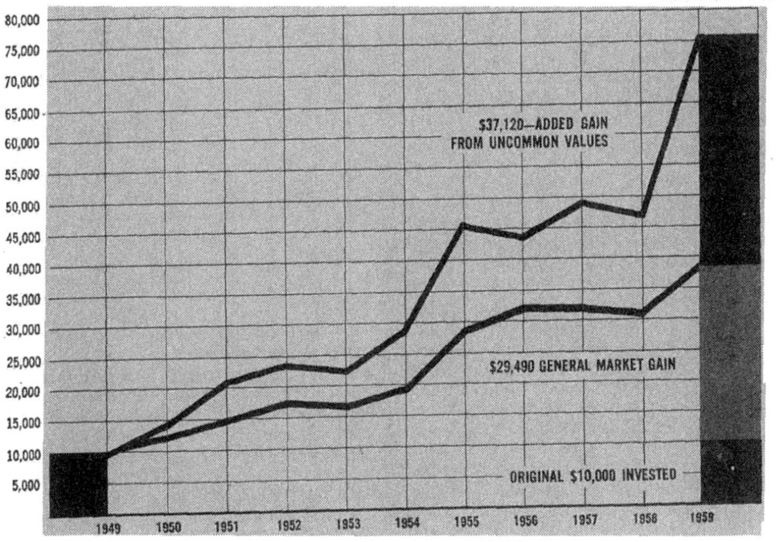

Not including $14,310 Accumulated Dividends

WALTER MAYNARD has been in the securities business since his graduation from Harvard in 1928. He is now a partner in Shearson, Hammill & Co., in charge of the firm's research and investment advisory department.

Experience has shown that the process of evaluating securities in a complex economy such as ours is an exacting business. Certain of the larger financial firms in New York have highly developed research departments devoted to this end. These departments characteristically contain a number of specialists—so-called senior analysts—who concentrate in specific industries. They, their assistants, their stenographers, their file clerks, and librarians comprise large organizations in themselves. The senior analysts are college-trained men, and when they have attained some stature in their profession command salaries which many financial men in other communities would look at with envy. The way in which such a department works to create a successful portfolio of "Uncommon Values" is described in succeeding paragraphs.

Three standards of selection

To begin with, it is necessary to set up certain standards for selection: to be a candidate for inclusion in a list of uncommon values a stock must enjoy a broad market—the buying generated by the publication of these lists is very substantial. Secondly, since it is assumed that the portfolio of uncommon values will be held for a full year, the companies whose stocks are chosen must be those of well entrenched businesses which have earned the regard of investors by a solid and consistent performance profit-wise. Third—and this is where the "uncommon" comes in—*there must be in the outlook for each one of these companies some favorable plus factors not as yet clearly discerned* in the market place. It is the detection and correct evaluation of these plus factors that distinguishes good quality research in the security field from the routine statistical compilation that passes for research in some quarters.

The actual process of selecting uncommon values involves many elements, including visits to plants, discussions with company officials, interviews with competitors, customers and suppliers, compilation of economic background through conversations with trade association officials and economists, an evaluation of relative market positions as determined by comparative studies, and a judgment as to future demand for the security in question.

Raytheon—an uncommon value

A specific example of the practical working of the process might be of interest. During the early 1950's the business of the Raytheon Corporation had been in a process of change and evolution. Between 1950 and the end of 1954 the price of the stock moved in a range between 9 and 15. As part of his job of keeping track of the electronics industry, the analyst responsible for following the progress of Raytheon began to feel, toward the end of this period, that the company's affairs were taking a turn for the better.

Over the next two years he made no less than seven separate visits to talk with the company's management. During this period the improvement that was taking place in the company's operations resulted in a price range for the stock between 15 and 25. Early in 1957 he recommended that Raytheon, then selling in the low 20's, be seriously considered as a candidate for Uncommon Values. An intensive period of study then ensued, in which the full information-gathering resources of the firm were utilized.

The standing of Raytheon with the Defense Department was checked, the capability of recently recruited top executives was investigated, the banking resources available to the company in the event that it should need to finance a greatly increased volume of business were ascertained, and opinions as to its standing as a maker of electronics components for missiles were sought from other missile manufacturers. Finally, the conclusion was reached that a very substantial jump in earnings was in the making, and that missile activity itself was due for a tremendous rise. In July of

1957, at a price of 22, Raytheon became one of the ten "Uncommon Values in Common Stocks" for the following year.

A severe setback in the stock market subsequently took place in the autumn of 1957 which carried the price down to a low of 17½. A careful re-evaluation suggested that this setback was purely temporary, and this subsequently proved to be the case. Beginning in October of 1957 the stock rose almost without interruption until in April of 1959 a price of 74 was reached.

At this time the analyst who followed the affairs of the company became aware that a large company with a heavy stake in the electronics field was seeking the services of a Raytheon executive who had played an important part in bringing about the surge in manufacturing efficiency and earnings that had provided much of the motive power for the advance in the stock. Since a price of over 70 seemed to take account of much of the further earnings improvement that lay ahead (although in only three years earnings had jumped from the $.23½ per share of 1956 to $3.08 per share in 1958), it was determined that the prudent path lay in a recommendation that profits be accepted.

Subsequently, the price of the stock, in common with most other electronics and missile issues, dropped severely to a level in the mid-40's. This thumbnail case history provides a clear example of the creative aspects of the work of the security analyst.

Compile, evaluate, judge

This process of compiling information, evaluating it and finally forming a correct judgment concerning it, which in due course (it is hoped) will be confirmed by "the bloodless verdict of the market place" is an intellectual exercise of a fascinating sort. Moreover, it is a process of this kind, possibly without the formality of an organized research effort, that lies (or should lie) at the base of all purchases of securities for investment. It can readily be appreciated, therefore, that the best possible research should form the basis for all security transactions, and that the work of research in the securities field can be challenging enough, and certainly rewarding enough in a material sense, to attract the best brains that our universities have to offer.

Raytheon's "box-car" radar antenna, 50 tons and 104 feet long, is part of the U.S.A.F. SAGE air-defense net.

Leadership in electronic development, which helped make Raytheon such an "uncommon value," is maintained in labs like this one, where microwave tubes are designed.

Prime contractor for the Navy's operational Sparrow III air-to-air weapon was Raytheon. Success with such "first-generation" missiles helped Raytheon win further Defense work.

Research for the military helped develop this battery/transistorized depth-finder for the civilian market—and for the fisherman who "has everything," except electric current in his boat.

Speculation or Investment?

A CHALLENGE FOR THE AMBITIOUS

Gerald M. Loeb

IF YOU EVER want to accumulate some capital of your own—speculate, don't invest.

"Investing" means trying to put your savings in a safe place and getting some income from them. In the case of high-grade corporate bonds, this income was a shade under 4¼% in 1959. Money invested at compound interest of 4¼%, even if tax-free, doubles itself in approximately 16 years. Dow-Jones industrial stocks had a yield of about 3¼% in 1959.

Yields from common stocks usually are higher than yields from corporate bonds. The situation in 1959 was a result of inflationary fears and tight money. The after-tax income yield of stocks was therefore considerably lower than was the case in high-grade corporate bonds. The difference isn't important because neither the corporates nor the stocks if bought primarily for safety and income are really safe.

Investors earn "minus income"

Since the bonds are top grade and should be paid off at maturity, their lack of safety lies in the almost certain fact that the dollars which are received at maturity will not buy the same values as the dollars which were originally invested. Occasionally they will buy more, but most of the time they will buy less. In recent years, the cost of living has been advancing faster than the after-tax take-home income paid by securities. In effect, investors have been getting "minus income." Borrowers have had the use of money for better-than-free.

In the case of stocks bought for safety and income the real determinant of whether they meet investment objectives has been the change upward or downward in the price of the stock rather than in the dividends received. The dividend rate has had an indirect value of great importance but only in affecting the price of the stock.

"Investing," therefore, is more theoretical than real. Investors are speculators without fully realizing their status.

The speculator seeks capital growth

"Speculating" means trying to put your savings where they will increase in value. Any income received is incidental. One cannot say how long it will take to double your money when speculating. That depends on the ability of the speculator and the economic conditions prevailing over the period of the speculation. The speculator has many advantages over the investor. The greatest advantage is that he strives for gain and seeks at the same time to minimize risk. He is, in effect, watching the road and watching the traffic signals. The investor tends to be lulled into a false sense of security and often neither points his car in the right direction nor watches its progress until it is too late. The investor pays varying rates of income tax on his interest and dividends that run as high as 91%. The speculator in pure economic theory does not owe any tax at all and in many countries does not pay any tax at all.

The United States, because of the need for revenue and the realities of the political situation, taxes the profits of the speculator at varying rates up to a current maximum of 25% on so-called "Long-Term Capital Gains." This is really more a form of capital confiscation than a tax. It persists because it is collected from the minority of voters. The majority is not well enough versed in Adam Smith to understand how it works indirectly against them as well.

Despite this discrimination against it, speculation offers more potential take-home profits than investing. In the chapter entitled "Strategy for Profits" in my book on how to make stock profits, *The Battle for Investment Survival,* I point out that the "annual price spread between the high and low of prominent stocks is many times the annual dividends paid." It is amazing, too, how even our very best equities can move over a wide range. It is not necessary to buy some highly risky low-priced "cat or dog" shares to realize high percentage gains from speculation. For example, in almost every period of market improvement one can find one of the best blue chips that will double in price in a year or two. Standard Oil of New Jersey doubled from its low of 1950 to its high of 1951. Ford Motor doubled from 1958 to 1959.

GERALD M. LOEB is a partner of E. F. Hutton & Co. He is a well known analyst and the author of "The Battle for Investment Survival."

The successful speculator advances by leaps and bounds: $10,000 becomes $20,000; $20,000 becomes $40,000; $40,000 becomes $80,000; $80,000 becomes $160,000. The rate of gain for the winner far exceeds anything even remotely possible in the way of compound interest.

Every young man a speculator

Youth deserves to speculate. They owe it to themselves. Certainly those who are just starting out in business should be ambitious enough to test their own abilities while they are young and exploring the business world. Obviously, not all are going to succeed. It is time enough to admit natural limitations after having given natural qualifications a chance to function. Security and pensions are for the aged and the unsuccessful. They should have no place in the thinking of young people until they have made a try at reaching the moon and have some real practical measure of the length of their reach.

Unfortunately, the term "speculate" has incorrectly been associated with gambling and recklessness. Gambling means betting on an outcome over which the gambler has no control or foreknowledge. Speculation means taking a calculated risk on an intelligent estimate of future possibilities. Practically every great success in this world of a national as well as corporate and personal nature has come from intelligent and successful speculation.

Taking a calculated risk: here, an American consortium explores for new sources of crude in Southern Arabia, in the Sultanate of Muscat and Oman. This is a seismic exploration crew on location.

The Analytical Approach to Tax Exempts

ASSESSING THE RISK

Robert C. Riehle

The Port of New York Authority has joined with federal, state, city, and private money to develop Idlewild's 655 acres. The great airport, when completed, will represent $150,000,000. Below, the Verrazano-Narrows Bridge: cost, $320,000,000 financed by the Authority's revenue bonds; approaches, built by the U. S. and the state will total $124,000,000—"without which the bridge itself could not have been financed."

To begin with a basic rule: bonds are priced commensurate with *quality* (relative freedom from risk) and *marketability* (how widely and favorably the issuer is known). They are, of course, payable in the future. Hence, an issue's investment worth is gauged by the anticipated ability of its issuer to meet all debt service commitments on schedule, particularly during periods of depressed economic circumstances. The quest for assurances of future ability to repay is broad, detailed and intriguing for it covers the spectrum of economic, political and social relationships.

A municipal borrower may finance through two basic media: (1) general obligation and (2) revenue bonds. By definition, debt incurred through general obligation bonds is secured by the full faith, credit and taxing power of the issuer—it is an unqualified promise to pay. Revenue obligations, on the other hand, are secured by a lien on the earnings of a facility owned and operated as a municipal enterprise. The latter, of necessity, has come into extensive usage of late. Though admittedly a more expensive means of financing, revenue bonds leave a community's general obligation borrowing capacity unencumbered to secure loans for school and other non-revenue producing enterprises.

Basic elements of bond quality

Of the two broad categories of tax exempts, revenue bonds analytically are the most fascinating. They have been employed to finance some of the nation's most glamorous projects, ranging from toll roads and major jet-age airports to port facilities and vast hydro-electric installations. Due to the limited liability characteristic of a revenue-secured obligation and the problems indigenous to the various undertakings, an analyst has to be a jack-of-all-trades. While he is by no means an authority, he must have a working knowledge of the general costs and techniques involved in operating water, sewer, electric, gas, port (air or sea), transit system, toll road or bridge facilities. Fortunately, the analytical approach is common to all revenue projects for all are vulnerable to similar contingencies.

New projects, of course, offer greater investment risk than going concerns. At the time of financing precedent to construction, the earnings potential of a new project is unproven; the investor has to rely upon feasibility studies. As a result, investors have come to rely on the findings of engineers whose feasibility reports have proven reliable. Naturally, lenders expect to be recompensed interest-wise for assuming an investment risk in an unproven project vs. lending money to expand an existing and proven one.

The New York State Thruway was financed by revenue bonds.

A "construction loan" typically capitalizes interest during the estimated construction period; i.e., bond proceeds cover not only site, right-of-way, construction, legal, architectural and financial cost but also bond interest accruing during the estimated time of construction. Principal is seldom scheduled for repayment until the time engineers estimate that the project will attain a sound earnings footing. Capitalizing interest usually is a satisfactory safeguard but there are occasional embarrassments; construction costs can be underestimated or the construction period so prolonged that the interest payments provided from bond proceeds are exhausted long before the project goes into operation. E.g., the construction costs of the West Virginia and Illinois Turnpikes were grossly underestimated; supplemental bond issues had to be sold to complete both projects, raising debt service requirements beyond earnings capabilities realized immediately after the projects went into operation. Cost escalation always dilutes debt service coverage. This hazard can be minimized by selecting (1) those issues financing construction which duplicate an existing facility where the original material, labor and time requirements are known; or (2) those where major cost items are covered by contractors' firm construction bids.

National emergency has also worked to the investor's detriment in construction projects: For example, World War II stopped construction of one of Dade County's (Fla.) causeway projects for the duration of hostilities. Capitalized interest was soon expended, being sufficient to weather only reasonable construction delays. Earnings have been so marginal since completion that the toll facility has never been able to make up its defaulted interest.

As a general rule of thumb, successful toll facilities connect major population centers, offer significant time and distance savings and are not competitive with existing free routes. Parkersburg Bridge, West Virginia, was constructed as a toll facility in 1952 in direct competition with a free crossing a few city blocks away. The success of the new crossing depended upon the state highway department constructing a business by-pass approach. Lacking adequate funds, the department has not been able thus far to fulfill its moral obligation. Needless to say, the bridge is in default.

Another general admonition — beware of projects wherein feasibility is contingent upon capital expenditures by some other government than the borrower. This pitfall is best illustrated by the case of the "bridge without a river," easily the most ludicrous situation in the annals of municipal finance.

In 1950, revenue bonds financed construction of the Decatur Bridge over the Missouri River between Decatur, Nebraska and Onawa, Iowa —with the approval of U. S. Army Engineers. It was built over a dry stream bed at a saving of 10%—the river then cutting a new path a few thousand feet to the east. Army engineers proposed to put the river back in its original channel by the time the bridge was ready for use. However, federal funds for river stabilization were not appropriated until 1955.

While the facility is still in default, it now spans a river and has regained some lost dignity.

Regardless of the mode of finance (general obligation or revenue bonds), a one-industry community requires thorough investigation both from the standpoint of the company's competitive position in its field of endeavor and the age and efficiency of its physical plant. Communities frequently view a substantial local industry as Santa Claus—and vote lavish capital improvements, the resulting tax burden to be carried principally by industry. On the other hand, a local industry can place increased demands on municipal plant.

When a community finances utility additions to meet industrial demands, a long term service contract extending for the life of the bond issue is desirable. Several years ago, Gulf Oil Company closed down its Sweetwater (Texas) refinery. The city's water plant lost its major consumer, but its revenue bonds remain secure, for Gulf continues to honor a long term purchase contract.

Municipal bonds closely related to nationally prominent industries are a comparatively recent innovation and are growing in popularity today. Analytically, of course, issues of this type stray into the realm of corporate finance.

Covenants for the prudent investor

Because a revenue bond is payable solely from utility earnings, the investor is necessarily concerned with the long range health of the revenue-producing facilities. Consequently, he expects management to bind itself legally (a) to maintain the utility in good operating condition and (b) to run it in an economic manner so that earning power will not be impaired during the life of the bond issue.

This is accomplished through certain basic enforceable covenants and provisions of the bond indenture. Their inclusion is so commonplace that the absence of any one, depending upon how essential, rightly or wrongly makes management's motives suspect; the investor will buy the bonds only when compensated by a higher than average rate of interest for the additional risk involved.

Conventional covenants include a ban on free service, a physical segregation of utility funds from general municipal funds, a pledge to charge adequate rates, segregation of debt service funds from operating funds, a prohibition against issuing prior lien bonds, a covenant to operate and maintain the plant for the life of the debt, a prohibition against the placing of encumbrances on the plant as well as a prohibition against the sale or disposal of the plant except as the bonds are retired from the proceeds of the sale, a covenant binding the obligor to provide periodic outside technical assistance, full insurance coverage (including use and occupancy insurance—bridges, for example, have been especially disaster-prone through structural defect, acts of God and even fire), periodic reports of operations, and independent audits. Provision should be made for the appointment of a trustee to represent the bondholder and protect his interest in the event of default. These covenants are requisite to a good quality revenue bond.

Of primary importance also is an assurance that future borrowing payable from the same earnings base will be held within reason. This is accomplished through an "earnings test" in which the issuer reserves the right to issue additional bonds of equal dignity and lien on earnings, subject to assurance that available earnings will cover future debt service requirements with something to spare.

One last observation before leaving revenue bonds—as a general policy, diverting utility earnings to general municipal purposes may be politically efficacious (minimizing the tax burden is always good politics). But when abused it makes for neither a healthy utility nor secure high quality bonds.

The protective covenants written into revenue bond contracts are not customarily employed in general obligation loans. However, investors in general obligations have the same basic considerations in mind. The assurances they seek are developed in somewhat different ways.

First, assurance is sought that there will be no worrisome increases in debt in the future. This assurance is found in the happy combination of modest debt plus governmental facilities which are adequate for present and prospective needs. If debt is high, credit is apt to be poor. Even if debt is low, credit is not apt to be high where a community possesses a grossly inadequate plant or badly deteriorated facilities; either of these holds a strong suggestion that much debt will be incurred as time goes on. As a case in point, Cumberland, R. I., nearly a decade ago had a moderate debt, modest tax rate, and a century-old frame high school. Although the building had been condemned years ago, proposals to issue bonds to construct a new one were repeatedly defeated by the taxpayers, in the interest of economy.

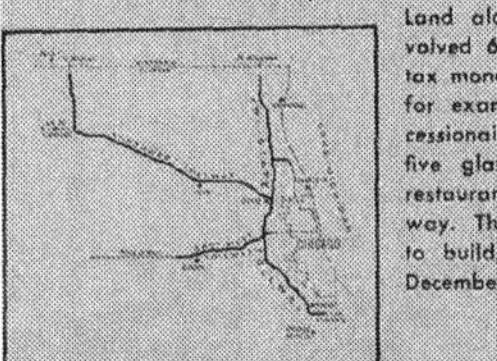

Financing of Illinois' Tollway was originally planned for $377,000,000. *During construction* on the 187-mile project outside Chicago, costs rose so rapidly that additional bonds totalling $64 million were needed. Interest ran at $38,000 per day while contractors struggled with record rains in the summer of 1957, icy winters, and tortuous property acquisition. Land alone cost $56 million, involved 6500 separate parcels. No tax money was used on the road; for example, it cost private concessionaires $13 million to build five glass-enclosed "over-the-top" restaurants along the right of way. The tollway took 27 months to build, was opened in full in December 1959.

ROBERT C. RIEHLE has been associated with Moody's Investors Service for six years and ranks today as a Senior Security Analyst. He is a graduate of Rutgers Univ.

Eventually, the building burned down and Cumberland residents had no choice but to triple their debt to build a replacement. Due to inflated building costs, procrastination proved expensive. Informed investors, however, had long anticipated the debt increase and resulting diminution in quality of Cumberland's bonds.

Secondly, the investor seeks assurance of ability-to-pay. In this regard, he is not concerned with the present ability alone; there must be something left in reserve to take care of a rainy day. In many states taxes for the payment of bonds and interest may be levied without legal limit as to rate. Hence, superficially, it may seem that bond security is never in question. But bond quality depends upon more than legal security. While the debt service portion of the budget may be amply secured under the letter of the law, the whole structure of a governmental budget must be healthy. Recurrent budget crises do not lead to a high credit standing.

The influence of economic geography

From the investor's point of view, quality bonds not only promise a lastingly conservative debt structure, but also offer assurance that ability to meet maturing principal and interest will not be impaired under depressed economic conditions. To a very large extent, the investor's concept of ability-to-pay is essentially a matter of economic geography. Among agricultural districts, best credits typically are found in areas where the soil is deep, fertile and well watered; sub-marginal farmland typically produces poorer risks. A diversity of crops is usually considered desirable. Preference is shown for areas where farm income is received in each month of the year, over the single-crop farm economy dependent upon a single annual harvesting and marketing.

The prosperity of communities dependent upon extractive activities is tied to the quality, longevity and productivity of their mines, quarries, or oil and gas wells. In industrial communities investors are concerned with the size, type and general standing of the industries represented. The relative and prospective profitability of the manufacturers would be important to some. Others will be equally concerned with the potential stability of employment and payrolls which affect community income. In commercial, banking and service centers investors are concerned with the scope and relative stability of the trade area. Communities which are extensively dependent upon seasonal business and tourism are not especially favored. Unquestionably the keyword in evaluating ability to pay is *stability;* conservative investment abhors change in a satisfactorily secure situation.

Municipal credit is more than cold economics and legal covenants: it has a human side —the management factor—judged by the overall caliber of personnel and the relative degree of administrative efficiency and sophistication over a span of several decades. An exercise of bad faith is an expensive luxury, for the borrower is long penalized by a limited market and punitive interest costs. Investors still recall a school district which achieved brief notoriety during the '30's by withholding debt service monies from its paying agent; then announcing that it could not meet debt service payments on schedule. As the borrower anticipated, the market for its bonds was immediately demoralized and the school district was able to retire its obligations through open market purchases at substantial savings. Today, emphasis has swung from distinctions between misfeasance and malfeasance to a study of the statutory mandates and restrictions which states have or have not provided to safeguard local management practice.

Unfortunately, municipal credit is too vast a field to explore in one short article. Its investigative procedures and financing media are limited only by the ingenuity of the analyst in an industry which is continuously searching for new methods of financing the capital needs of this fast-moving Twentieth Century.

Evaluating Foreign Securities

THE WORLD AS AN INVESTMENT

Carl Marks

TODAY THERE IS a greater and broader interest in foreign securities than ever before; no corner of the globe has been bypassed in the search for the overlooked investment opportunity. The American public has indeed become "stock-minded" on an international scale.

It is true that foreign corporations have different accounting methods and that restrictions, regulations and numerous other deterrents have discouraged many. However, there are available prime investments of an international character that are well-known and that offer the buyer the advantages he is seeking. This might be higher income, speculation, diversification, etc. In the better quality category we have such shares as Royal Dutch, Philips Lamp, Unilever, International Nickel, British American Tobacco, Imperial Chemical, the South African companies such as DeBeers, and others too numerous to mention. With reasonable study and experience one can find the kind of bond or share desired for the purpose for which it is acquired.

A particularly liquid international investment: local bottlers, guided from New York, have been established in 77 countries—from the Congo to the Philippines.

Another well-known type of foreign investment was also at the height of its activity during the past year. I am referring to the new companies or new subsidiaries being formed in foreign countries. Everyone is aware of the extensive propaganda by government agencies, national organizations, important political figures and others in recommending the creation of a foreign enterprise in a foreign country with the financial support and know-how of the investor. We have the International Bank, the Export-Import Bank, numerous financial organizations specifically set up for the purpose, conventions, suggestions for tax benefits, proposals for international development associations, international financial investment firms and even tax incentives, all intended to encourage Americans to invest their funds in a business abroad.

CARL MARKS has long been associated with the foreign securities field, as president and chairman of Carl Marks & Co., which he founded in 1925. He is also a member of many international organizations, among them the Pan American Society, the Philippine-American Chamber of Commerce, and the American-Brazilian Association.

"Venture capital" does not adequately describe the dangers involved in this kind of project. Looking over the past history of such investments, it is difficult to find a foreign operation abroad which would have exceeded the success of an equivalent investment right here at home. And present conditions are no more encouraging now than they have been in the past.

The primary risk in any foreign investment is undoubtedly the power of a foreign sovereign over the private investor in another country. Any enterprise created in a foreign country is subject to so many unforeseen governmental actions, regulations or restrictions that I often wonder how a favorable decision to build an enterprise in a foreign country was reached in the first place. Nationalistic tendencies, political changes, exchange regulations, restrictions and expropriations are probably the most obvious deterrents. In many cases the difference in ethical standards has led to partial or complete loss of the original investment. A foreign corporation financed by American residents does not necessarily have the protection of the American governmental agencies or the International Bank. It is obvious that our Congress cannot pass laws protecting capital investments abroad unless they wish to insure such risks with o. national resources. Nor can we in these cases prevent the consequences of such economic changes as have occurred in Cuba, Venezuela, Argentina or Egypt.

Favors high liquidity

I guess I have made it clear that I am definitely set against recommending a foreign investment in the form of a new enterprise or subsidiary. I am certainly in favor of helping these foreign countries, but not at the public level. I have no objection to "venture capital" being loaned by our government or any other government to another government for projects intended for the general public welfare or the raising of living standards. At least, loans at the national level appear to me to have a chance of permanent claim and no sovereign action can be used to obliterate the assets of a foreign investor. I am definitely opposed to the type of foreign investment which cannot be negotiated quickly.

However, the "liquid type" of foreign investment described above is desirable from every point of view and should find a reasonable place in everyone's portfolio.

The unprecedented demand has found the American banks and brokers well prepared for this type of business. Close bid and asked quotations are being maintained in New York and many of the other principal cities of the U. S. in all active issues, and transactions in many instances run into many thousands of shares without affecting the market.

part 

THE MONEY MANAGERS

The Function of the Investment Advisory Service

THE GENTLE ART OF CONSERVING CAPITAL

Edward C. Delafield

THE PRIMARY responsibility of the investment advisor is to provide continuous supervision of the security portfolios and other investments of his clients (individual as well as institutional). However, investment supervision requires far more than a mere knowledge of security values, and successful portfolio management involves not only expert judgment but the coordination of many special skills and professional talents. Moreover, various clients differ widely in their desires and aims, and no two portfolio management problems are identical. Typical is the problem of the trustee who is under pressure to provide a high return to the life beneficiary (interested solely in current income) but who is obligated at the same time to consider the safety and enhancement of principal which is the prime interest of the remaindermen under a trust. It is not enough, therefore, to say that any given security is a "sound investment." It must as well be suitable for a given individual or institution and fit its long-term policy objectives.

EDWARD C. DELAFIELD was educated at Princeton, held various banking positions before becoming senior partner of Delafield & Delafield in 1937. He is a director of many business and charitable organizations.

The operations of an investment advisory business tend to fall into four principal categories: (1) investment research, (2) policy determination, (3) portfolio management, (4) tax and estate requirements.

An investment research department must be staffed and equipped to acquire and maintain current the knowledge of a wide range of data in the fields of economics, industry, business and finance, and it must be competent to interpret the available facts with sound judgment. These facts, it should be noted, cannot be obtained solely from published sources (statistical manuals, government releases, etc.); the competent researcher or security analyst develops his own sources of information through his enterprise and knowledge in establishing worthwhile contacts in a wide range of companies and industries.

Policy determination is, of course, the core of an investment advisory organization. The finance committee or other group responsible for major policy decisions consists necessarily of men not only experienced in all phases of the business but also with a wide range of outside business contacts—men who have proved the soundness of their judgment as to economic trends and basic security values. To this committee must flow all the data, reports, findings and opinions of the research staff, to be discussed and weighed against facts obtained by each member of the committee from his own varied outside contacts and associations. The responsibilities of this committee include, first, the formulation of a basic policy through an interpretation of the judgment of the research staff and, second, a decision as to the economic or business outlook, including which industries will be favorably affected and which unfavorably.

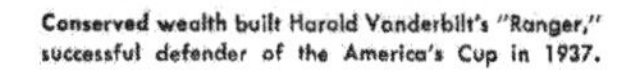

Conserved wealth built Harold Vanderbilt's "Ranger," successful defender of the America's Cup in 1937.

Created wealth, the boom of the 50's, has developed a new leisure class—here skiing in California's High Sierras.

A central function: supervision

With this general policy as a base, this committee must determine, subject to the varying aims and needs of different clients, the most suitable portfolio balance (fixed-income securities vs. common stock) in relation to the economic and political situation. It must also provide similar guidance as to industry diversification among common stocks, and approve or disapprove individual securities for current investment. An essential function of this committee is to exercise constant supervision of securities held in accounts and to maintain continuously a list of securities considered favorable for investment—for holding or for buying.

Portfolio management involves the responsibility of translating the decisions of the finance or policy committee into specific recommended action for the investment portfolios of individual clients. It might perhaps be more accurate to say that the function of the portfolio manager or account executive is to meet, as far as possible, the needs and aims of each particular client within the broad framework of the firm's general investment policy. The competent account manager must be not only thoroughly grounded in economics and experienced in analyzing security values, but also a keen and sympathetic student of psychology in understanding and attempting to adjust his clients' problems. These problems frequently involve far more than the mere selection of securities to buy or sell, and the portfolio manager must have access to expert judgment on many subjects outside the direct realm of security values.

The investment advisor's responsibilities cover not only the protection of his client's property during the owner's lifetime but the provision for the future of his family as well. Legal and tax experts must be retained to render opinions on many vital questions such as wills, trusts, the gifting of properties, the purchase of life insurance and a variety of matters which, if not correctly handled, can result in serious financial loss to the client and/or his beneficiaries. With the high taxes of these times, it is of paramount importance to make certain that estate taxes, both current and prospective, are minimized by all the means provided by law. Maximum conservation of family wealth can be achieved by the coupling of carefully thought out testamentary plans and/or gifts during life, with continuous professional investment advice.

In short, it seems clear that a competent investment advisory firm must be composed of individuals with a wide variety of talents and interests. It must function as a well drilled team in order that any client, whether individual or institutional, may receive the full benefit of a sound investment policy based on competent knowledge and interpretation of conditions that exist at any time. To the prospective trainee, the profession offers an exceptionally broad range of experience and opportunity.

The Professionally-Managed Mutual Fund—I

"THE WORLD'S FASTEST-GROWING PHENOMENON"*

Arthur Wiesenberger

If you are like most other Americans, you own some life insurance and have some money in a savings bank. You know, therefore, what these basic financial organizations can do for you.

Open-end investment companies—more popularly known as "mutual funds"—provide another basic financial service and are valuable for people who desire, and are ready, to invest in stocks and bonds. The sole business of a mutual fund is to invest the money entrusted to it in selected securities, for the benefit of its shareholders. A mutual fund can be a complete investment in itself.

The number of shares of most mutual funds changes constantly. New purchasers receive new shares, created by the fund to supply the demand. And when the owner of mutual fund shares wants to sell them, the company itself will repurchase and retire them. In this respect the mutual fund differs from the closed-end investment company—a feature that is an important characteristic of this method of investment.

Basically, a mutual fund is simply a large investment account—owned not by just one person but by many separate shareholders. They share the net income and profits or losses from the securities their company owns, in proportion to the number of shares they hold. The company is operated by professional managers, supervised by a Board of Directors or Trustees. Costs of operation are divided among all the shareholders and deducted from the earnings on the securities owned.

Few people have the experience, time or facilities to set up an investment program properly—much less to supervise it constantly. The investment company enables them to place their money in the hands of professional managers, who invest it for them and are continuously responsible for it. Thus an investment company is a means of applying organization to the investment problems of people in all walks of life.

In this way, a farmer in Iowa, a doctor in Chicago or an oil driller in Texas can, collectively, have as diversified an investment program as the wealthiest man in Wall Street. In other words, the smallest mutual fund investor enjoys precisely the same diversification, the same continuous supervision, as the largest.

Investors offered wide choice

Desirable as it may seem, there is no single investment company or mutual fund that can meet the desires of all investors. The existence of such a fund is an obvious impossibility, for the simple reason that the objectives of investors vary so widely.

Some investors seek or wish as much immediate income as is obtainable; others can afford to sacrifice income now in the hope of achieving an increase in capital which could provide a higher income later on. Some can afford to take a greater amount of risk in investing for either of these objectives; others must try to reduce their risks by setting more conservative objectives. Probably the majority of investors must work out a compromise among the various possible objectives, weighing each factor in the light of their individual circumstances.

Neither a single investment company nor one program made up of different investment companies, therefore, can provide a standard "prescription" for all investors. For this rea-

* TIME, June 1, 1959.

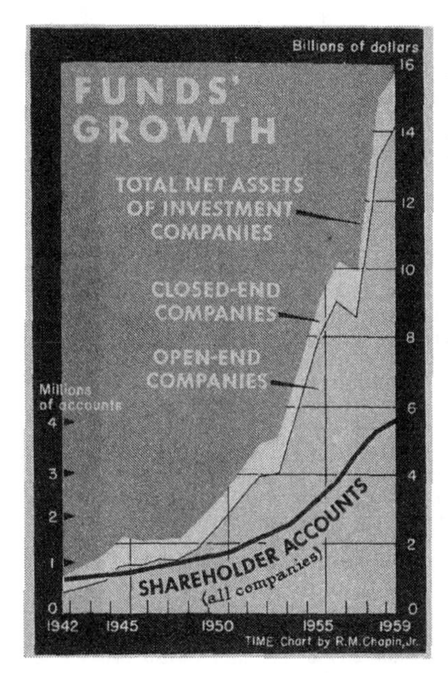

son there exist many different types of services which are available conveniently through mutual fund shares. In fact, the array may seem at first somewhat bewildering. Most funds, however, can readily be so classified as to make it fairly simple for the investor who has determined his investment objective to make an intelligent selection, or to have his financial adviser or investment dealer do so for him.

The first step: deciding why

Setting the goal must come first. Far too many people make direct purchases of securities because they think the prospects for a particular stock or bond are good, or because it appears to provide a high yield, without stopping to think whether or not it is the type of security which can reasonably be expected to provide what they really want. The same error can be made in selecting investment company shares. The investor should first clarify in his own mind just why he is taking the risk which is inherent in any investment —whether it is long-term growth of capital he seeks, income now or in the future, a chance to hedge against the effects of inflation, or some other specific purpose.

Just as many investors have more than a single objective, so do some investment companies try to provide the answer to more than one investor requirement. A particular fund, for example, may follow a "middle-of-the-road" investment policy with the combined objectives of long-term growth of capital, reasonable current income, and greater stability of both principal and income than common stocks alone provide. This means that the investment company itself has decided how much relative emphasis should be placed on the various objectives. If this decision meets the investor's own needs, a simple answer may be provided and a single mutual fund may constitute a suitable investment program.

Another investor, however, may find that no single fund is just what he wants, or he may prefer to make up his individual program from a number of different types of funds. Both investors have a wide choice. With their decisions made as to their own investment objectives, they are ready to consider the types of investment companies available and narrow the choice down to the specific funds with the same objectives.

Major types

While extreme variations of investment policy may exist even within single classifications, the following broad designations will cover all types of mutual funds: diversified common stock funds; specialized common stock funds; balanced funds; income funds; bond and preferred stock funds; funds investing in securities of foreign corporations. At the 1958 year end, diversified common stock funds accounted for 53 per cent of the total net assets of open-end investment companies, followed by the balanced funds with 27 per cent.

Diversified common stock funds

Oldest and largest group in the open-end field are those companies that invest all, or almost all, the money under their control in

PRINCIPAL CLASSIFICATIONS OF OPEN-END COMPANIES

Type of Fund	Total Net Assets 12/31/58	% of Total
Diversified Common Stock	$7,369,744,000	53
Industry Specialized	810,880,000	6
Balanced	3,685,814,000	27
Income	925,511,000	7
Bonds and Preferred Stock	193,796,000	1
Canadian (Sold in U. S.)	443,644,000	3
Canadian (Sold in Canada)	437,450,000	3

common stocks or in other securities with common stock characteristics. They are by no means all alike or intended to serve the same purposes; on the contrary, investment objectives, policies, methods and results differ widely from fund to fund and management to management—as does management experience, competence, and degree of risk and success.

Some invest primarily in the better known stocks of large corporations—the standard type of investment-quality shares often described as "blue chips." Others may specialize in "growth company" shares. Some concentrate in shares of less well-known firms where greater opportunities for profits or income are believed to exist. Many, of course, combine various types of common stocks or shift their portfolio emphasis from time to time.

Some funds lay greatest stress on current income, while others emphasize capital appreciation. There are funds that remain almost fully invested at all times. Others try to reduce fluctuations by switching a part of their assets into cash or high-grade bonds when market conditions for equities appear unfavorable to them.

As a general rule, diversified common stock funds are intended for that part of an investor's program that he believes should be concentrated in common stocks, in the hope of achieving either capital growth or better income, and in which he can afford to take the risks inherent in owning equities. However, because some funds follow a policy of full investment at all times, while others at times shift partly into cash or defensive-type securities, the most suitable uses for specific funds may vary.

Funds that follow a policy of almost full investment at all times appear suitable primarily for investors who want to keep a definite portion of their capital invested in common stocks. They are also suitable for trustees, who may select one or more investment company issues to represent the common stock portion of an account.

The more completely managed type of common stock fund may, in addition, provide close to an entire investment program for the investor who does not need the element of defense a continuous holding of high-grade bonds and preferred stocks can give. Whether a common stock fund intends to remain fully invested at all times or to vary its holdings in accordance with the management's judgments on the economic and financial outlook is frequently stated in the prospectus. Records of past results and portfolio composition are also helpful in identifying investment policies.

For investors who want to place special emphasis in their accounts on a particular industry or geographical area, there are many common stock funds for a variety of distinct purposes. A few of these have existed for many years; most have been formed more recently.

Specialized industry funds provide a means of purchasing a diversified group of stocks in a single industry or group of related industries such as various forms of energy, transportation, chemicals, etc. Most of these are intended primarily as supplements to diversified stock programs, providing broad diversification plus professional selection and supervision within a limited field which may be of special interest to the investor. Some, however, invest in fields so broad as to encompass most of the industrial scene.

Balanced funds

Investment companies that at all times invest some portion of their assets in bonds or preferred stocks, or both, in addition to a portion that is invested in common stocks, are generally called balanced funds. The term "balanced" is used in a broad rather than a narrow sense. As one large fund has stated, "in our use of the word 'balanced' we have in mind not an equal balance, as between fixed-income securities and common stocks, but rather a flexible program in which bonds, preferred stocks and common stocks are utilized in such varying proportions as seem prudent in light of investment considerations as they exist at any given time."

The objective of a balanced fund usually is to provide a complete investment program. Hence balanced funds follow more conservative investment policies than does the typical common stock fund. Balanced funds seldom show as large gains during a period of rising markets as most common stock funds. By the same token, they can be expected to decline less in bear markets. Unless income is their primary objective, balanced funds may yield less at times than many common stock funds; their income is likely, however, to show less fluctuation from year to year.

Of course, the mere fact that an investment company keeps part of its assets in bonds and preferred stocks at all times does not in itself indicate that a conservative policy is being followed. Bonds range in quality from virtually no risk to a degree of risk comparable to or greater than that of a speculative common stock; the range in quality of preferred stocks is as great.

In practice, it is sometimes difficult to draw a precise line between balanced funds and common stock funds. Many mutual funds are clearly one type or the other, but there are also companies that fit neither classification in all respects. In any event, rather than relying upon labels, investors should refer to the statements of the managements in the companies' prospectuses and reports.

ARTHUR WIESENBERGER, senior partner in Arthur Wiesenberger & Co., is the author of "Investment Companies," an annual reference work published since 1941. He has lectured and written extensively on finance and business.

Past performance is not an assurance of future results. But long-term management performance records are the best available guide to the quality of management in individual cases, provided that the results are considered in the light of the company's objectives, the characteristics of the company's investments, and the period selected.

Income funds

A separate classification is made for a group of mutual funds whose primary objective is to provide a relatively high rate of current return. Some invest in bonds and preferred stocks, as well as common stocks, while others invest chiefly in common stocks. Their distinguishing feature is the emphasis upon high immediate income return and the willingness of management to take normal risks of loss to obtain it. Most bond and preferred stock funds might also be considered income funds, but are not included in this classification.

Income funds seek to provide a higher-than-average rate of return by concentrating their holdings among certain securities that, in turn, currently yield more than the average high-grade stock or bond. Such high-yielding issues are found in situations where the risk, either to capital or income, or both, is above average, or the prospects for future growth are below average. In some cases the securities are little known and may in fact be undervalued.

Income funds are chiefly of interest to investors who need immediate income and who are willing both to de-emphasize potential growth of capital and to assume the risks described above. If the investor's objective is clearly defined and he understands the compromise he is making in regard to risk and growth possibilities, income funds may provide a suitable answer to a specific problem.

Bond and preferred stock funds

Diversification and supervision are just as important and valuable to the investor in senior securities as to the buyer of common stocks. Direct diversification of bonds, however, is likely to be quite difficult for the investor of modest means. Almost any type or grade of bond can be duplicated by the purchase of mutual fund shares, with the added advantages of diversification and continuous professional supervision. A few funds that hold preferred stocks alone, or a combination of bonds and preferred stocks, are also available.

These funds can be used as component parts of individualized investment programs or for specialized purposes. For example, an investor who wished to divide his capital equally between good-grade bonds and "growth stocks" might decide to place half in one or more bond funds meeting his specifications and half in one or more diversified common stock funds that specialize in issues believed to have good growth prospects, rather than to use a balanced fund. Other combinations are possible for various individual purposes.

In different circumstances, bond and preferred stock funds may be used to supplement holdings in other types of funds. An investor, for example, who felt that there were good appreciation possibilities in low-grade bonds might use the shares of such a specialized fund to take advantage of an expected general improvement in prices. Or if he feared a general market decline, the investor might convert part of his more volatile holdings into shares of a high-grade bond fund. Before switching from any company into another the investor should, of course, realize that in most instances a sales charge will be incurred and should measure this added cost against the possible advantages.

Just as in the cases of common stock funds and balanced funds, the prospective user of bond and preferred stock funds should examine the policy as stated by the management and indicated by past results before making any commitment. Long-term performance is unfortunately more difficult to appraise in these cases, because of the lack of suitable standards of comparison. The relationship of the prices of holdings to their par or face values and call prices may be a helpful indication of policy.

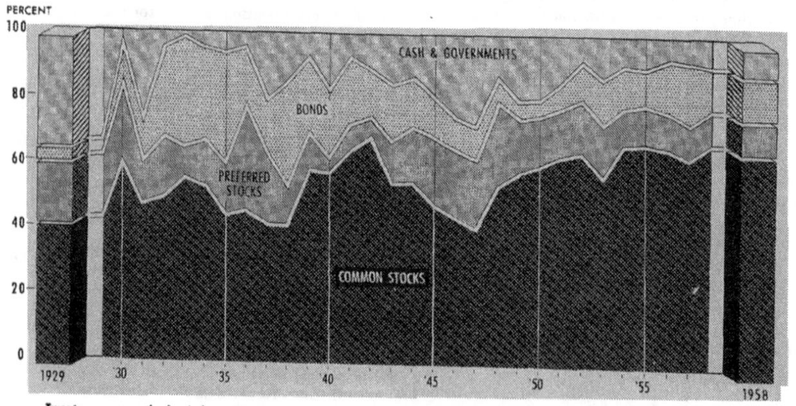

Twenty-year growth of a balanced fund shows continuing wide fluctuations in types of holdings, to meet market conditions.

Sources of information: investors interested in particular open-end funds should review the individual companies' annual reports and prospectuses for information on the sales charge included in the offering price of the shares of most mutual funds, the fees, expenses, etc., before making any decision to buy or sell these shares. Reports are available from all companies and may be obtained without cost or obligation directly from the companies or from most investment dealers.

The Professionally-Managed Mutual Fund—II

PEOPLE, ECONOMICS—AND INVESTMENT COMPANIES

Edward B. Burr

AT THE END of June, 1959 investors held a total of 4,294,000 accounts in 179 United States investment companies—an increase of over 3.5 million accounts since the end of 1940. The value of these accounts on June 30 was about $16.7 billion, almost 16 times the $1.06 billion value of shareholder accounts 18½ years earlier. Today's shareholders, who live in all parts of the United States and in many foreign countries, include men and women of all economic and income levels, and include also institutional investors of all kinds—labor unions, corporations, colleges and universities, fiduciaries, etc. And while the average investment company account had increased during this 18½-year period from $1,400 to $3,900, many accounts on June 30, 1959 involved as little as $100, many had a value well in excess of $100,000.

This growth pattern during the past 19 years has made the investment company business one of the fastest growing financial institutions in America. Why have so many more people and institutions assigned a steadily increasing amount of their investment funds to the purchase of investment company shares?

Consider first the investment needs and desires of modern men:

Today a man with money to invest has, in most cases, a full-time job. He works for a living. He works even if he is president of a large corporation. He's short of time; he doesn't have enough time to follow market and general economic trends to the extent necessary if he were to handle his own investment accounts.

A man with money to invest today is cautious. He's usually thinking of his long-term financial needs. He knows it's not easy for an amateur to choose stocks or bonds wisely or without undue risk.

Finally, the amount of money that a man has to invest today is often moderate. As a rule, he doesn't have enough capital to buy ten or twelve stocks and thereby spread his investment risk.

Investment company shares meet each of these needs.

The assets of an investment company consist of carefully selected securities—the securities of 50, 100 or even more business and industrial corporations—generally stocks, oc-

EDWARD B. BURR is a graduate of *Bowdoin College in 1946 and the* Wharton School of Finance and Commerce. In April of 1958 he assumed his present position as *Executive Vice President of The One* William Street Fund, Inc.; his prior affiliations included the Institute of Life Insurance and the National Association of Investment Companies, where he was executive director.

casionally bonds, sometimes both. When a man buys shares in an investment company, in effect, he buys part ownership in all those securities. The investment company collects the income and passes his share along to him in the form of regular dividends, usually four times a year.

Investment companies are designed to provide the investor with three major advantages and services:

- professional management of investments;
- diversification among many different securities—reduction of the risk of loss by spreading shareholder investments among many different securities;
- convenience—an entire investment program in one package, together with a ready market for his shares if an investor wishes to sell.

There are two basic classifications of investment companies—the closed-end companies and the mutual funds open-end companies. Their chief differences are related to their capital structures and to the manner in which their shares are distributed.

Until the middle 1920's all investment companies were of the closed-end type. A typical closed-end company has a fixed number of shares outstanding, all in the hands of investors. To buy closed-end shares, an investor must buy at the prevailing market price, through a securities dealer or broker, from another investor who owns the shares and is willing to sell. Thus, investors buy and sell shares of closed-end investment companies in precisely the same manner as they buy and sell shares of any corporate stock listed and traded on major stock exchanges.

The second classification of investment companies, the open-end, is often called the "mutual fund." It is "open-end" because the typical mutual fund has no limit to the number of shares it may issue, and is issuing new shares daily and stands ready itself, at any time, to buy back its own shares from investors who wish to sell.

Funds are revalued daily

The price an investor pays in buying mutual fund shares—and the price he receives when he sells—is established by the actual pro rata value of his shares related to the total value of the assets the investment company owns. This value, the "per share asset value," is determined daily and is the quotient of the total assets of the company divided by the total number of its own shares outstanding.

An investor who purchases or sells shares of a closed-end company pays, of course, the brokerage charges involved in all securities transactions on the particular stock exchange where the purchase or sale takes place. Mutual fund shares are unlisted securities; they are purchased from securities dealers, in some instances from direct representatives of the investment company and, in some cases, from the company itself.

Thus the costs of distributing shares of open-end investment companies are ordinarily included as a sales charge added to the per share asset value. The sales charge varies between companies and often varies with the size of the purchase, and usually covers two transactions—for in most companies the investor pays no further charge if he wishes to sell his shares back to the company.

Internally, particularly with respect to portfolio management (though not necessarily portfolio policy), the two types of companies are quite similar, and their personnel requirements in this area are quite alike. For in both types of companies the securities are bought by professional investment managers, men and women who have the training, the experience, and the time that sound investment management requires.

To decide which securities should be bought, which held and which sold—to decide *when* to buy and when to sell—every investment company depends upon research. Some investment companies maintain their own research departments; others employ investment counselling firms which service one or a few closely allied investment companies.

Mr. Inside: the industry specialist

The key figure in investment research is the industry specialist. He concentrates on the stocks and bonds in a single or a few industries. He keeps abreast of all developments which may affect prices, dividends, and earnings of the securities in his special field, and his recommendations to buy or sell are vitally important in determining whether the investment company buys, continues to hold, or sells any of the securities in his industry.

To be successful, the industry specialist must have imagination and develop judgment. He must feel the concrete signficance behind the abstract figures of an earnings statement. He must think independently and yet be able to take advantage of the comments and evaluations of others. He must not only be able to absorb an enormous amount of information, but he must have the ability to assess its reliability and know how and where to get more.

He gets his facts by reading corporation reports and statements, newspapers and trade magazines, by attending meetings of associations concerned with his industry specialty, by interviewing and getting to know corporation presidents, treasurers, and other top management people.

Statisticians and junior security analysts assist him by sifting and correlating the mass of information that is available. They compile the figures he needs, prepare graphs and charts, etc. But it is he, out of his experience and ability, who sums up the outlook for the industry; he who recommends which securities the investment company should buy in his industry, which securities the investment company should sell—or whether the investment company should take any action in his industry at all.

The industry specialist makes recommendations—but his is seldom the final responsibility. For his recommendations must be balanced against those of other industry specialists. This balancing is accomplished, in part, at regular meetings of the entire staff in which each industry specialist airs his views.

Many participate in decisions

The final decision to act or not to act according to an industry specialist's recommendations rests with a portfolio manager in some companies, with a portfolio committee in others. The manager or the committee weighs the relative recommendations of each industry specialist and decides how the investment company's funds should be invested.

The portfolio manager (or committee) is usually aided in his decisions by a market analyst, by bond specialists, and by one or more economists.

A market analyst is concerned with the securities market as a whole. He decides when preferred stocks or bonds may be a better buy than common stocks or vice versa. He may also help the portfolio manager to compare the relative merits of each industry and may recommend the industry which he believes offers the best investment opportunities.

A market analyst may base his recommendations upon his views of general economic conditions or upon intricate computations of stock price movements, or upon both. By examining the technical behavior of the market he is often able to discern indications of future changes in security prices.

A striking example of the modern approach to mutual fund sales is the advertising campaign of the Dreyfus Fund. Their lion is familiar to millions of people.

A bond specialist is an expert on interest rates. He advises which bonds are the best buys or sales, whether it is better to buy or sell bonds which mature in a few months, or bonds which may mature in as much as several decades.

The economist, as in most business organizations, concerns himself with business as a whole. His research and studies are directed toward answering such questions as: "Is unemployment likely to increase or decrease? What's the outlook for general price levels?"

Each of these men—the industry specialist, the market analyst, the bond specialist, the economist—must have not only ability, but each must be *confident* of his ability. He must sum up in his own mind a great many facts, figures, and opinions, come to an independent conclusion, and then present his recommendations to the portfolio manager (or committee) for final decision—recommendations which will be tested by actual developments.

It's not difficult for the portfolio manager of an investment company to determine whether a member of his research staff is competent, for actual market experience will quickly show whether a specialist's or an analyst's recommendations have been sound.

Capable security analysts are in great demand and are well paid. They are well paid because a man who knows how to make money with money is an extremely valuable investment company staff member. They are well paid, too, because there's keen competition for competent security analysts, not only between investment companies but from brokerage firms, insurance companies, and from investment advisory services as well.

Sales and distribution: extensive and dynamic

The performance of investment companies has had much to do, certainly, with their growth in recent years, as has the fact that investment company share ownership meets a genuine investor need. Important, too, in the growth of the open-end companies has been the development of extensive sales organizations.

There is no single pattern of sales organization in the open-end investment company business. A great many mutual fund managements are affiliated with "sponsoring companies," wholesale distributors which, on order, sell shares of the fund to retail security dealer firms whose salesmen have received orders for its shares from investors. This follows closely the distribution pattern of many manufacturers—from producer, to wholesaler, to retailer, to consumer.

In other companies, the salesman is an employee of the sponsoring organization itself, selling only the shares of the mutual fund or funds managed by his employer's affiliated management company. In still other mutual funds, no sales organization is maintained, the shares being issued directly to the investor by the mutual fund itself.

More and more, the mutual fund salesman is becoming a family financial counselor, working with his client and with his client's other financial advisers to plan a coordinated estate. He works to ensure that his client's financial program is a balanced one—one which includes an adequate, readily available fund of cash to meet emergency needs, one which includes a program of life insurance sufficient to protect his client's family should he die, and one which, among other investments, includes properly selected mutual fund shares.

The mutual fund salesman has the responsibility to guide his client toward choosing an investment company whose investment policies best coincide with the needs, objectives, and financial circumstances of his client. For no two investment companies are exactly alike, and a program of investment in mutual fund shares should be tailor-made for each individual client if the program is to best serve the client's needs.

The career of mutual fund selling is a rewarding career—rewarding not only in financial return to the successful salesman, but also in the sense of performing a useful service to clients. For both the investment companies themselves and their salesmen are providing a unique and valuable service for modern investors: to the man or woman of limited resources they are bringing the same professional investment management and diversification which only the wealthy investor could once afford; and to the modest investor they are providing an opportunity to participate on a sound basis in the growth and profits of the American economy.

Investment companies, in the final analysis, have grown during the past two decades for precisely these reasons and because they do, indeed, offer a service which fits the investment needs and wishes of the American people.

ALLERTON C. HICKMOTT has been vice-president of the Connecticut General Life Insurance Company since 1949. His qualifications include a Phi Beta Kappa key and a background in the insurance field beginning when he joined Connecticut General as analyst in the investment department in 1917. His office today is in their award-winning new Hartford headquarters building.

The Keys to Successful Investment

SCROOGE AND THE BRIGHT YOUNG MAN

Allerton C. Hickmott

To THOSE over fifty, the term "money manager" may evoke the image of a super Scrooge counting his golden sovereigns with meticulous and avid care. To the graduate of our great business schools it may mean the handsome young man with vision in his eye and a slide rule jauntily tucked into his breast pocket. More than forty years in the business leaves me with the feeling it might unfortunately be either, but I hope it is somewhere in between.

The fluctuations of the security markets and the gyrations of individual components present a continuing challenge to those of us who are trying desperately to protect the dollars given over to our supervision by donors, policyholders and stockholders. Each group has a completely different desire—expressed or implied—but the one common hope is that they will not *lose* money. The future may require growth in spendable capital; maintenance forever of a comfortable income; or, indeed, the greater use to which donations may be put.

At the beginning of the century the prime investment was that made in mortgages, secured by the farm that produced the food, or the home in which a man lived. This was lending against the security of basic things; the necessary tools of the way of life that could be captured for the debt and resold because of primary importance. This was also the general era of the financing of the recently emerged railroad systems. Here, with some similarity, the best individual credits, the most desirable pieces of paper, were those loans secured by a lien on important segments of railroad physical property—terminals and main line facilities—not particularly related to the earning power of the railroad as a business entity.

"Things"-type thinking

As late as the Twenties, the emphasis was much the same. As the great electric and gas utilities expanded and needed money for additions to plant and equipment, investment officers were still adamant about "bricks and mortar" as security for their lending. One of the early laws relating to investment by Savings Banks was particularly clear as to the requirement for this kind of security. I wrote the law, and I can well remember the insistence of its sponsors on a utility's ability to generate its own electricity or to manufacture its own gas. But changes have occurred gradually in investment philosophy. It developed the hard way, really, sparked by the proof, through reorganization procedure and torment, that *things,* in and of themselves, were not as vital as the use to which they might be put. There was a gradual but steady growth in the conviction that business alertness, basic operating skill, and imaginative management, were firmer reeds on which to lean than specific tools—either generating units, or steam locomotives, or terminal facilities in great metropolitan areas. It became increasingly evident that the character of the borrower outshone his pledged security. I believe this to be the most significant change of this century in primary investment thinking.

The effect of direct placements

When direct placements (direct negotiation of loans between borrower and lender) came along, all sorts of new frills appeared in the individual contracts. Without a broker to police the loans or an intermediary to originate the business and follow it after completion, the operating experts in the investment departments of the great banks and insurance companies had a field day. Here was an area in which to put into practice the cherished theories developed in ivied walls—to a point, I am told, that one borrower spent so much time making sure he was in compliance with the restrictive covenants of his loan contract he

Investment favorites change, says author Hickmott. Sixty years ago prime money went into mortgages, secured by the land, the house—basic things easily captured and easily disposed of to satisfy the debt. "Bricks and mortar" security dominated American finance even as late as the boom years of the 1920's when the great utilities expanded and empires were built—sound financing called for loans firmly tied to real physical properties.

completely forgot to send in the interest payment. This, of course, is the exaggeration that always accompanies the entrance into new fields of investment. Changes in operating techniques and entrance into a new field always involve a period of gestation.

The life insurance industry has a particular investment goal. It must provide future dollars to satisfy contracts maturing with the death claims of its policyholders. This, of course, is over-simplification of a broad complex of heterogeneous commitments. However, it points up the desired and needed portfolio—a means of assuring the future in-flow of maturing investment dollars to provide for payment of claims whose incidence can only be theorized.

The importance of dollars is vital, because they constitute the medium of obligation payment. For this reason, securities bearing fixed interest and principal payments at stated

UARANTEE THE MILK-AND-HONEY FUTURE?

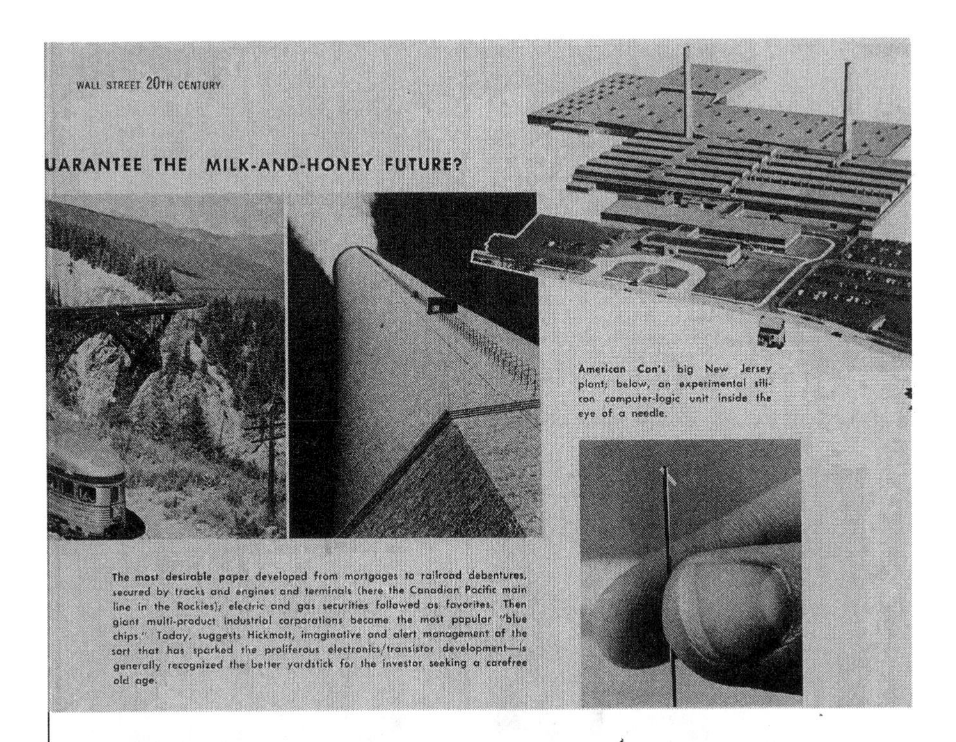

American Can's big New Jersey plant; below, an experimental silicon computer-logic unit inside the eye of a needle.

The most desirable paper developed from mortgages to railroad debentures, secured by tracks and engines and terminals (here the Canadian Pacific main line in the Rockies); electric and gas securities followed as favorites. Then giant multi-product industrial corporations became the most popular "blue chips." Today, suggests Hickmott, imaginative and alert management of the sort that has sparked the proliferous electronics/transistor development—is generally recognized the better yardstick for the investor seeking a carefree old age.

times have always made up the bulk of life insurance company investing. Thus the vital problem of the life insurance "money manager" is to select and develop an investing pattern that will provide the required future dollars plus the desired cushion of surplus for contingencies (and for his better sleep o'nights). In the case of the stock life company, there is also the ever-present interest of the stockholder who owns the company, risks his money, and for whom the "money manager" works—a multi-lashed whip indeed for a troubled brain; delicate cleavage between orthodoxy and bravery. Despite the thoughtful textbooks, despite the elaborate case studies of the past, there are no well-defined paths, no detailed rules to be mastered by intensive study. I have seen fantastically detailed forecasts, and the simplest of "stomach feelings" produce no panacea for the time when the blood is running in the streets.

So, what does the "money manager" do?

Memories, patience, and the orthodox

What do I do? Consult the supermen? I have never, really, met one. Interrogate the financial prophets? Their opinions are as legion as their numbers. If by some extravagant penance I could sit on the right hand of Wisdom herself, I might easily suspect that her pronouncement of today's correct course was in some way victualled by last night's indiscretion. But it is not a completely frustrating way of life. It becomes apparent, over the years, that yesterday's solution of a problem is a small stone in the long a-building lodging of experience. Memory comes back, hazily, to prevent the same mistake. Patience rewards those who stick it through. Orthodoxy is a grim business, but no life insurance portfolio can be suitably developed without some basis of it. The chance is always too great to warrant the high-wheeling swing into imagination unless, of course, one is blessed with a lion's share of luck; and *that* could be the stock-in-trade of a near-sighted blonde with a sharp pencil poised blindly but intently over the offering sheets.

Favorites change. The prime rails give way to the sprawling utilities. The utilities are shouldered aside by the great industrial corporations with their multiplicity of products. But even so, an orthodox selection of railroad bonds has in some instances suffered no greater deterioration in the recent years of advancing interest rates than has been experienced by other investment units of comparable original credit. Interest rates have done more than credit rating or popularity, for that matter.

And so we creep along, measuring past performance against future prospects. The main line of a major railroad becomes the central generating unit of an area utility. An important oil company believes it may be advantageous to make a package of its retail outlets, borrow money on them (no matter what fancy name they give to the deal) and thus free up working funds to their general use.

It is a new, unorthodox type of investment. We study and weigh it by our own standards of future money for future needs and the rate of return that may (from its newness, its unorthodox character) provide cushion earnings. Here enters, just as an aside, what our advantage may be over the pretty blonde. It is the imaginative(?) stone on the rock foundation, or a rapidly growing chain of stores, or a chemical giant who wants someone else to provide the transportation equipment to deliver its products. There are many pots of gold under the stone if you can stomach the search and get there early.

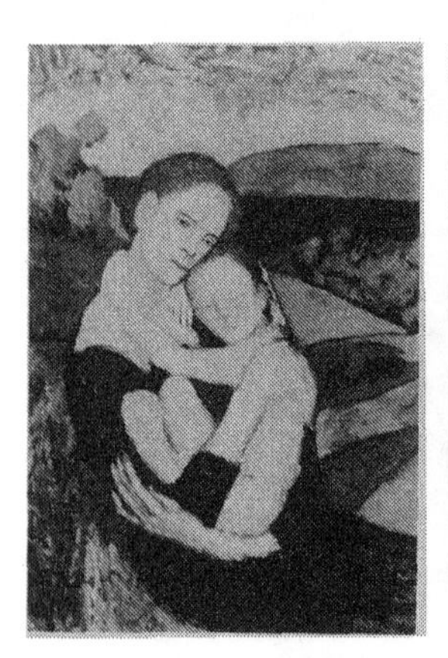

Is art the sure investment? Hickmott suggests caution, but today's prices and enthusiasm indicate that at least the very rich buy treasures for appreciation as well as beauty. Picasso's "Mother and Child" brought $152,000 at auction in 1958 in a constantly-rising market for the Impressionists and Post-Impressionists. A year earlier New York's famed Parke-Bernet Galleries auctioned the Lurcy Collection of 65 modern French paintings and objets d'art for an all-time record high of $2,221,000. Closed circuit TV and "invitation-only" were necessary to control the throngs of bidders.

What to do with tired money

As the financial economy stumbles along through its many phases, unpredictable gyrations produce periods of low interest rates and easy money. Everything sells at the same price and nothing yields much of anything. This is the time to throw away the battle flags. Let others be brave. Money becomes tired, and when squeezed too hard for that extra dribble of income it fights back with uncanny bitterness. That extra ¼ of 1%, that investment that is "probably just as good" can conceivably rise to haunt the "money manager" with all the horror of Banquo's ghost. One of the most astute of my contemporaries had sound advice for these periods—"Throw away the yield book."

I believe no more sound admonition could be given to those people torn between eagerness to improve performance and the conviction that in such times the credit risk is not worth the faulty candle. Calculated risks, yes. These we always take. But when the "money manager" neglects what might be termed investment integrity, there really should exist some power to politely send him fishing, and call back, temporarily at least, the blonde with the sharp pencil. You cannot fight basic economic forces, and you cannot perform with elaborate and finished skill in an area of artificiality. Finally, a feeling of omnipotence breeds quick disaster.

Periodically, there occurs a "flight from the dollar." This is used here to mean growing uncertainty as to the stability of accepted exchange media. It is evidenced by a desire to speculate in tulip bulbs—East Indian shares—even the purchase of a farm as a hedge against the day of Revolution. Twenty years ago, at a meeting of investment men, an eminent economist wisely pointed out that running a farm is back-breaking work, and in addition queried as to whether the revolutionaries would respect the rights of property.

I have collected books for forty-odd years, a hobby that has preserved for me a measure of relative sanity and a retreat from the exigencies of a muddled economy. This mania has been pursued thoughtfully, but despite careful attention to quality it is only recently that the collection could have been sold without loss. The profit is my enjoyment—and collections of books, engraved gems, objets d'art, should always be totted up with this foremost in mind. This rambling is to warn investors from what seems an easy road to affluence. The distinguished Rembrandt, the noble folio, the exquisite gem from the treasury of some famed courtesan is seldom the whole—only a part of a motley and varied gathering of amenities.

Can equities guarantee your milk-and-honey future?

But there must be some way to avoid erosion of future dollars! Inflation is the periodic ogre lurking in the dark at the top of the stairs. Is the stock market the answer? Can equities provide the comfortable years in a summer climate where the sun always shines and pretty girls in shorts are continually offering cool drinks of milk and honey? Can participation in the Space Age produce units of purchasing power that will outsmart the cost-of-living index? I don't know. It is today's glib answer to the threat of inflation. I have a friend who for years bought IBM and carefully locked it up to his supreme satisfaction. I also have a friend who has gradually dissipated his nest egg by quick and frequent excursions into a gallimaufry of "growth stocks." The employer who is buying retirement protection for his employees wants equities in his contract—but sometimes I suspect he hopes to provide lower cost to himself by the magic of the "assured" future growth of his equity coverage.

The one great imponderable in burgeoning industries is the explicit time when enjoyment of the presumed increment is achieved. It is a one-shot operation—the time the cake is cut to provide a finer house to live in, steak every day, even the Cadillac to spite the Joneses. No one should be brave enough to neglect current income or belittle the fact that 4% current and 2% growth *may* provide something more tangible than 2% current and 4% growth. I look back at 1921 and 1929, at 1933 and 1938—and today I wonder, too.

It seems to me that experience is the key, that elaborate correlations of "disposable income" and the production of babies could be misleading; that an individual stock only goes up when more people are buyers than sellers (irrespective of its theoretical prospects or price/earnings ratio); and that if you can be patient and reasonably brave you might evolve into the desirable combination of Old Scrooge and the boy with the magic slide rule.

An Investment Career In Commercial Banking

VERSATILE MEN AND MONEY

Brian P. Leeb

THERE IS AN OLD SAYING in Wall Street that investing is an art and not a science. Those individuals in Wall Street banks whose responsibility it is to manage the investments in a wide variety of individual funds may not be popularly thought of as artists; but in the sense that it is the artist's objective to achieve a sense of unity out of a mass of formless and conflicting details, there is a similarity in the challenge which comes with the assignment of portfolio management and the making of investment decisions. The successful investment man combines a broad knowledge of investments, familiarity with securities markets, sound judgment, attention to detail, an imaginative approach, and skill and patience in dealing with people to achieve worthwhile results. Wall Street offers an interesting and profitable career to young men who wish to accept such a challenge.

In a large commercial bank the career opportunities in investments are especially wide and varied. They range from investment research and the management of customers' portfolios in the trust department, to the management of the bank's own investment portfolio and the underwriting and/or selling or trading in United States Government and municipal securities by the bond department. Each of these activities requires special skills and knowledge; each is becoming increasingly complex and the province of highly trained specialists.

Trusts are growth area

One of the fastest growing segments of most large commercial banks is the trust operation. This has been particularly true in the postwar period, reflecting in large part the rapid growth of pension and profit-sharing trusts and investment advisory accounts and, to a lesser degree, estates and trust accounts. Fundamental to the management of these portfolios is a good investment research staff. In some instances, research and portfolio management are combined in a single staff, but because of the special talents and training required in these functions, the preferable practice is to keep them separate. Consequently, a good investment research operation will offer an attractive career opportunity to qualified young men.

The basic function of research is to select suitable securities for the varied needs of the trust department's customers. To fulfill this purpose, an experienced staff of analysts and statisticians is employed, backed by younger members in various stages of training. In order to obtain maximum benefit from accumulated experience, the individual analysts are assigned specific industries, with which they become thoroughly familiar. Every available source of information is used, including investment manuals, annual and interim company reports, trade papers, magazines and newspapers. Since much of this material would be difficult to understand and appraise without a knowledge of accounting and statistical principles, the analyst is expected to have a working familiarity with these subjects.

Economists broaden specific research

In addition to the gathering of factual information, research concerns itself with the formulation of investment judgments. Industries and companies must be viewed from a much broader angle than is possible from a study of the statistics alone. To assist in the comparisons of various industries and companies, other tools are used. Specialists from the economics department are consulted on questions in their sphere, as are members of the banking and foreign departments. Outside consultants are employed to advise on problems in their areas of special interest. These include experts in particular industries such as oil, electronics and nuclear energy, for example, as well as people versed in technical aspects of the securities markets. Detailed charts are maintained on a large number of stocks, since this way it is often possible to note an important trend—a trend which might be missed in a general statistical review.

Besides preparation of the regularly scheduled industry reviews, the analyst is called upon to perform many other jobs of an investment nature. Individual and corporate customers of the bank forward inquiries which must be answered; other departments of the bank seek his assistance in connection with their lending problems; and he must be as well versed in evaluating bonds as he is stocks. As the bank's representative, the impression he creates during interviews with important company officials can influence "new business" decisions.

Since the fortunes of the industries and companies he follows are subject to many outside forces, the analyst must keep well informed on a large number of general topics. Developments in Europe and elsewhere cannot be ignored, for example, nor can the political situation in our own country. Population trends, changes in the tax laws, money market conditions, labor problems and a host of similar subjects must be studied and made part of the day-to-day equipment of the bank's research specialists.

At regular intervals the analysts present their findings on an industry, or a special situation under review, before a group of their colleagues. Sufficient information is provided beforehand to familiarize the participants in the discussion with the important facts. The objective is to point up the strengths and weaknesses of the securities and to compare their future potentials with those of the many other securities which are available. This is the end result of the investigation and a judgment must be made. Finally, the investment recommendations must be communicated to those who make practical use of them, the portfolio managers.

Portfolio management demands ready judgments

Portfolio management in the trust department of a large Wall Street bank involves applying the judgments reached through investment research and a knowledge of the operations of the various securities markets to the problems of individual investment accounts. These are of three main types: estates and personal trusts, investment advisory accounts, and corporate pension and profit-sharing funds.

Settling decedents' estates and managing trust accounts for individuals are historically the oldest types of business carried on in personal trust departments. The management of funds of this type requires a broad knowledge of a wide variety of securities, familiarity with statutory law and court decisions regarding the duties, powers, and responsibilities of executors and trustees, knowledge of the income tax law, and the exercise of sound judgment in adopting the correct investment program for the needs of the individual beneficiaries of a particular trust account. A bank acting as executor steps into the shoes of the decedent. The investment officer must become familiar with all the investments owned by him, which may include some of doubtful or no value, as well as blocks of securities not owned by the general investing public, which

BRIAN P. LEEB has devoted over 40 years to the banking profession. For the past 25 years he has been head of the Personal Trust and Pension Trust Divisions of Bankers Trust Company, and since 1956 has been a Senior Vice President and Director responsible for all the fiduciary and agency activities of the bank.

are called "closely held" securities. He must decide which investments to liquidate in order to meet claims against the estate, including those of the tax collector. He may be called upon to liquidate a family business, or to arrange through investment bankers the public offering of a large block of stock.

In managing trust funds for individuals, the portfolio manager has to take into account both the needs of the persons entitled to the income of the fund as well as the rights of those who will receive the principal of the fund when it terminates according to its terms. The choice of investments is governed not only by the bank's investment policy but also by the terms of the instrument creating the trust and, in some cases, by the laws of the state under which the trust was established. Ordinarily, the portfolio of investments will consist of a rather wide variety of bonds, preferred and common stocks, and, in some cases, real estate and mortgages. The types of bonds in individual accounts will depend on the tax status of the beneficiary. The portfolio manager must be familiar with United States Government, state and municipal, and corporate obligations.

Counselling is new role

As compared with the settlement of estates and the management of trust funds for individuals, acting as investment advisor is a comparatively new type of business for a Wall Street bank. In such accounts, the bank undertakes to give individuals or corporations continuous investment supervision of their assets, but the individual or the corporation makes the final investment decisions. In many estate and trust accounts, the portfolio manager works with individuals who act as co-fiduciaries with the bank and share investment responsibility with it. In a large number of such accounts, however, the bank acts as sole executor or sole trustee and, therefore, has the sole responsibility.

In investment advisory accounts, the portfolio manager must be in frequent contact with the owner of the investments and must understand his problems and objectives. The choice of investments for investment advisory accounts is, naturally, somewhat wider than for trust accounts, since many individuals can appropriately include among their investments venture-type situations which would probably not be appropriate for trust funds. Corporations such as savings banks, insurance companies. and charitable and educational institutions frequently engage the services of banks as investment advisor. Such appointments often require the portfolio manager to attend formal meetings of boards of trustees and investment committees.

Trusteeships of pension and profit-sharing funds established by corporations for the benefit of their employees are the newest types of appointments undertaken by banks' trust departments. Nationwide, assets in these funds aggregate some $24 billion, and it is estimated that fully one-half are managed by Wall Street banks. A distinctive characteristic of these funds is their dynamic growth rate, now estimated at an aggregate of $3 billion a year. The portfolio manager thus has the responsibility not only for managing the assets in which the funds are currently invested, but also the task of selecting suitable investments for the sizable amount of new money contributed to the funds on a regular basis. Since these funds are exempt from taxation, tax-exempt state and municipal obligations are not generally appropriate holdings for the portfolio; but with this exception, a wide range of investments is often found in these funds, including common stocks in liberal proportions, preferred stocks, United States Government and corporate bonds, federally insured and guaranteed mortgages, conventional mortgages, and real estate acquired on a sale-and-leaseback basis.

In the aggregate, these funds have taken their place along with life insurance companies, mutual savings banks, fire and casualty companies, mutual funds, and public pension funds in the forefront of the nation's institutional investors, and are an important factor in the market for corporate securities, and play a vital role in supplying capital for American industry.

In the vast majority of cases, corporations give their bank trustees the sole responsibility for making investment decisions. In view of the importance of these funds to the corporations establishing them, a most important part of the portfolio manager's responsibility is discussing and reviewing investment policies and programs with corporate managements.

Also included in the operations of most trust departments are a corporate trust division, which provides fiduciary services for government and business in connection with debt financing requirements, and a corporate agency division, which is responsible for the issuance and transfer of the stock of companies and for the servicing of other equity securities' requirements. These activities also offer important career opportunities in themselves, but since they are not primarily in the investment area, they are mentioned here only in passing.

A mighty challenge: the bank's own funds

Commercial banks also offer careers in the investment banking field. In the management of its own investment portfolio, policy is established and transactions are effected to balance the changes that occur as loans and deposits rise or fall. Trends are analyzed and possible future demands are anticipated in order to offset any drastic changes in basic relationships. All the aspects of changing market conditions, rate of economic activity and interest patterns help determine the actions necessary to maintain a satisfactory portfolio under all circumstances.

In smaller country banks the portfolio is generally handled by the president, together with determination of loan policy and administration of the bank. The larger city banks normally have portfolio decisions made by top management and administered by a senior officer who is a specialist in this field. This investment officer is responsible for a portfolio that is an important percentage of the bank's total assets. For some of the largest banks this may mean administering an investment of over one billion dollars.

In addition to the sizable investments of the bond portfolio, many of the large banks are also dealers in these various securities. Banks are limited to dealing as principal only in obligations of the United States, governmental agency issues and general obligation state and municipal bonds. Their operation is similar to that of an investment banking firm.

Several of the large banks are major factors in the vastly important government bond market. As any other dealer they maintain firm markets in all outstanding issues of bills, notes, certificates and bonds of the government and also the various obligations of the many federal agencies. Volume in this field is measured in terms of hundreds of millions each day. The outstanding marketable government debt is now about $185 billion and recent studies show that the market for these securities is continually broadening.

Bankers serve the municipal market

Closely allied to the government bond trading is the municipal operation, the underwriting and trading of city and state obligations. This is a much broader field, consisting of many firms, in which "dealer" banks serve an important part of the market. In fact, during one recent year four of the first five principal managing underwriters were banks. In the past ten years the tax-exempt field has experienced a tremendous growth. In a decade outstanding municipal debt rose from less than $21 billion to over $58 billion. In the same period the annual volume of new financing increased from $3 billion to approximately $8 billion. Some experts in the field forecast an annual rate of $13 billion in new financing by 1965.

With the recent growth in both Government and local debt, banks offer a wide variety of investment banking opportunities. In order to serve the customer it is necessary to have fully qualified men. The rapid increase of business has created added pressure on the already limited supply of trained portfolio managers, salesmen, analysts, traders and underwriting specialists.

To most people, a large commercial bank is merely a place where we deposit or borrow money. However, behind the orderly rows of banking desks lie the same stimulating opportunities that have recently attracted so many young men to the investment business. The scope of investment activities of a large Wall Street bank offers a young man a wide choice of careers to suit his particular interests and talents. The entire field is growing and, contrary to many out-dated opinions, it is interesting and dynamic. To insure a continuing flow of competent men who will accept the challenge and the responsibilities, bank salaries and benefits are fully competitive with other positions in the financial field. For a young man interested in investments, a large commercial bank offers careers that are unique in their opportunities.

Brokers of yesterday . . . through the years commuting trains have perhaps changed less than their riders.

The Role of the Customer's Man

'SELF-EMPLOYED' ON WALL STREET

William J. Ruane

THE ROLE OF a customer's man is one of the most interesting in the investment field and it should be regarded as a challenge for any young man considering the securities field as a career. Success in the job will go to the hard working individual who can combine the critical attitude of an analyst, the persuasive manner of a salesman, and the bedside manner of a country doctor.

The basic function of a customer's man is to aid his clients by giving them sound counsel on their investment problems. He must be able to diagnose the needs of the clients and develop a suitable portfolio to meet those requirements. The job is not completed by merely purchasing a list of stocks. The securities must be supervised and changed as economic trends in general and company developments in particular would seem to dictate.

The account man's day is divided into three parts: a study of the current news, a study of particular companies which may have merit for investment, and consultation with present and prospective clients.

A study of developments in the political, economic, and scientific fields is as important as being abreast of strictly financial news. There are few developments in any of the foregoing fields which will not affect the fortunes of one or more companies in American business. Security analysis, in part, requires the interpretation of ordinary news and its application to individual companies.

The day is gone when the "well-connected" young man could enter Wall Street with no knowledge of a balance sheet or an income

Today's customer's man works in attractive, efficient surroundings. Here a conveyer belt system links 31 desks for speedy sending of orders and messages, and the office is tied to various exchanges by phone and teletype.

WILLIAM J. RUANE graduated from the University of Minnesota in 1945 and from the Harvard Business School in 1949. He is with Kidder, Peabody & Co., a leading investment banking firm.

statement and immediately proceed to make a substantial income on his connections. Today a period of training in the use of the analytical tools of research is necessary to prepare the future account man to service his customers with intelligence. He must learn how to appraise the relative and absolute values behind the security of a particular company selling at a particular price. A graduate entering the investment business is well advised to spend a period of time in the research department of a firm, developing experience in the approach to appraising the worth of a security, be it bonds, preferred or common stocks.

After completion of such a training program the process of education does not end. In fact it is merely beginning. A certain part of each day will be devoted to the appraisal of a wide range of companies with a view to selecting the most attractive and appropriate investments for his clients' money in the light of the existing economic conditions.

Attractive stocks are the tools of the account man and he develops investment ideas in many ways. The most common way is to receive the idea from the research department of the firm for which he works. The end result of the work of the security analyst in the research department is the application of an interesting stock idea to the accounts of the customer's man. It is the responsibility of the account man, however, to make himself thoroughly conversant with the investment idea, so that he may buy it for his clients with the conviction that comes only with knowledge. Further, it is not uncommon for the account man with experience to develop interesting ideas of his own.

A great deal of satisfaction is found by the customer's man in translating the analytical opinions formed by economic and security analysis into a sound and profitable investment program for his clients. Each customer will have a different investment problem. A young married businessman with a good income needs different advice from an elderly widow who lives on her income from securities. This job is accomplished by a proper analysis of the customer's needs, supplemented by a certain amount of salesmanship to persuade the customer to take the action which is indicated by intelligent interpretation of the facts. Careful research and analysis will only produce income for the customer's man or his firm if he is able to convince his clients or prospective clients of the merit of the advice.

Where customers come from

One of the principal problems a young man faces when entering the securities field in the position of account man is that of building a clientele. Initially it is done by developing leads which his firm will give him. Once a nucleus of customers has been obtained, the clientele of a customer's man of sound judgment is to a large degree built up by radiation —that is, through the recommendations of his satisfied clients. As the customer's man develops experience he may be assigned by his firm to service banks, insurance companies, mutual funds, and pension funds.

A young man should enter the securities field with thoughts of becoming a customer's man only if he feels he has a sincere interest in financial analysis combined with sales work. There is no concrete product to sell or produce; one is always dealing in intangibles. The early few years are often not too rewarding financially and the task of building a clientele is difficult.

Despite the initial difficulties of starting a career, in the long run the opportunities in the securities field can exceed those found in the average industrial concern. One advantage which is inherent in the job is the opportunity, through the development of investment acumen, to build up one's own capital. Further, there is no limit to the earning power of the individual. Since a customer's man is essentially in his own business his income should be proportionate to the time and energy he himself applies to the job. The more successful customer's man is also taken in as a partner in his firm. In addition, it is not unusual for an alert and imaginative account man to be the key individual in the formation, financing, or merger of companies while performing his regular duties.

Finally, there is a real need and opportunity for young men in the investment field because of the high average age levels of the men now in the business. These many advantages and possibilities serve to make the job of a customer's man one of real attraction for anyone interested in the investment field.

The Role of the Institutional Salesman

SELLING TO THE SOPHISTICATED INVESTOR

J. William Middendorf, II

Universities and foundations seek yield. Yale's two new colleges, shown here, will represent donations of $17,500,000 when completed in 1962. Of this, $7,500,000 is money to support the buildings, part of permanent endowment and available for investment.

PERHAPS THE most significant phenomenon affecting Wall Street in the post-World War II period has been the rapid institutionalization of capital resources. The assets of life insurance companies, mutual funds, and banks have grown at unprecedented rates, until today these institutions are the predominant factors in the purchase of the merchandise of Wall Street. A study published by the S.E.C. in 1956 pointed this up: in 1954 net purchases of newly issued securities by institutions exceeded those of individuals by 9 times, representing an increase from 7½ times in 1951.

Life insurance companies have until recently been the leading net purchasers. Corporate pension funds, receiving their original major impetus during World War II under the influence of war-time frozen wages and high profits taxes, have increased tenfold in size since 1944 and are now among the most assiduously cultivated investing institutions. Assets of open-end mutual funds have increased a similar amount in this period.

More than one billion dollars are invested by General Electric's Pension Trust. Joseph Pomeroy, (left) is the 20,000th current GE pensioner; through the years investment income has paid $200 million to more than 60,000 GE employees.

The growth rate of assets of other institutionalized pools of capital (such as the fire and casualty companies, state trust funds, banks and their trust departments, charitable foundations and union pension funds) while all seeking varied avenues of investment, shows no signs of slowing down. The energetic institutional salesman in a reasonable-sized firm, supported by good underwriting and research departments, should find this one of the most profitable avenues to success today in Wall Street.

Years ago it was the generally accepted custom for investors to take securities from the banking fraternity on faith, but that faith became badly shaken in the 1930's. Invest-

Insurance companies swing immense weight: some of Prudential's assets are represented by gleaming regional headquarters (left, their Chicago home); but vastly more is invested in securities. Fire and casualty companies stress liquidity—to meet crises like famed San Francisco quake-and-fire.

Big city banks, like New York's Manufacturers Trust, generally buy a mixture of short-term governments and long-term tax-exempts.

J. WILLIAM MIDDENDORF, II deals with institutional investors regularly as a partner of Wood, Struthers & Co., in charge of insurance stock research and trading. He graduated from Harvard in 1947, received his Master's in Business Administration from N.Y.U. in 1952.

ment departments in such institutions as life and fire companies (which had been generally one-man affairs more or less run by default as a relatively unimportant end of the business) in the middle 30's began to develop their own research to implement their buying.

No longer could the "customer's man" from the investment banking house, whose "advice" was dominated too often by what he happened to have in his satchel, expect to succeed in the old way of doing business. A whole new professional investor class has since developed in our American financial institutions, which today usually have research departments equal to those of the best investment firms.

Further, it became apparent that the institutional salesman also had to become more knowledgeable. Since rarely can one man be a specialist in the many facets of investment, this in turn led to specialized departments within the leading investment firms. Now, the successful salesman calling on institutions must be alert to all the complex desires of as sophisticated a group of investors as can be found anywhere in finance.

The reasoning of these sophisticates

What has brought this about? The growth of investable funds under the control of institutions, for one. The changing investment needs of the institutions, for another.

- Life companies seek to balance dollar liabilities with dollar-pay assets, but lately have bought equities, sometimes to their legal limit, to provide a slight hedge against further debasement of the currency.
- Fire and casualty companies generally seek to balance their loss reserves and other immediate liabilities with liquid assets in the form of cash or government bonds, other reserves with medium term tax-exempts, and surplus funds with tax-exempts and equities.
- Mutual funds often are 85% or more invested in equities and generally seek capital appreciation with some current yield.
- State funds, formerly limited to government bonds, have recently been permitted to buy corporate bonds in a majority of states. Yield and safety is their goal.
- Savings banks, most of which are in New England and the Middle Atlantic states, seek primarily yield with safety and buy mortgages, with government bonds and cash as liquid reserves.
- Savings and loan associations, which need not be so liquid, buy mostly high-yielding mortgages.

- Union pension funds seek yield, the majority buying governments and mortgages.
- Corporate pension funds seek yield, but due to recent policy changes, have been heavy buyers of equities.
- Charitable foundations and universities seek yield and generally invest in a balanced list of corporate bonds and equities.
- Big city banks buy short governments and for their time deposits, long-term high yielding tax-exempts. Smaller banks buy first mortgages on local real estate and government and municipal bonds.

Tax laws play a large part in investment decisions. Pension funds, universities and charities pay no taxes and rarely buy tax-exempt bonds unless the yield is extraordinary and quality still excellent. Life companies are taxed in three steps and the Federal tax on earned interest plays an important part in investment decisions. Due to this some high yielding tax-exempts are now being bought. Fire and casualty companies pay only a 7.8% tax on income from commons and most preferreds but 52% on government and corporate bonds. Many now have tax loss carry-forwards so are buying corporates instead of the more usual tax-exempts. Insurance companies own local state obligations to meet state requirements for business done in the state.

All details of this sort should be well known to an institutional salesman before he calls on the buyer. Furthermore, the idea he presents in his call should be timely and appropriate—frequently patience is required before such an atmosphere manifests itself. The average buyer is besieged with calls and research material, and to make enough of an impression to receive orders the successful salesman must make his visit count. Institutional buyers generally shy away from what is called a "salesman's swap"; perhaps the best guide is the self-directed question: "Would I undertake the trade if in his position?"

How to meet the customer

How does one meet the buyer for the first time when he has been assigned to a new account? The ideal would be to be taken over by the salesman previously covering the account if he has gotten along well with the people involved.

Failing that, an introduction by a mutual friend is an excellent idea. Generally, however, it is not a particularly good idea to be brought down to the buyer on the arm of the director, who announces something to the effect that, "Charley here should be fixed up with some business." The salesman may be put subconsciously at a real disadvantage and his job will be that much more difficult.

A good meeting ground is at functions such as an Analysts' Society meeting, a bankers' dinner or the like. It is better for the new salesman to meet the buyer in a professional atmosphere than at a social affair. Generally, institutional buyers are a pretty serious lot; they are not overpaid for the really hard work load and responsibility they carry; and they often have little time for frivolities designed solely to induce an atmosphere *simpático*.

Today's successful institutional salesman must be up-to-date on all phases of the money market, and should possess a broad general knowledge of equity values. Accuracy and attention to detail, particularly when preparing a report or handling an order, are obviously essential qualities. Persistance usually pays off, even when the first several calls seem to lead nowhere. If the customer comes to depend on the salesman and seeks his advice, he has done his job well. As important as it is to gain his respect, one must also get the buyer to like him and if sincere, this will come automatically.

Institutional buyers rarely pioneer. In equities, they stick mainly to "blue chips," usually choosing the leading companies in a growing field. This has been a successful formula over decades. A salesman may get discouraged at the seemingly laborious committee procedure that his well-thought-out idea must go through. The facts of life are that this is generally the standard procedure. Even if his idea is a good one, it may not be accepted because the committee may have available to it information that precludes the idea fitting into its portfolio.

Finally, even though it is important to have a good general knowledge of securities and to be alert to rapidly changing conditions, it is also wise to know one field well. It should make the job of understanding other fields a good deal easier, and should give one the confidence essential to becoming a successful salesman.

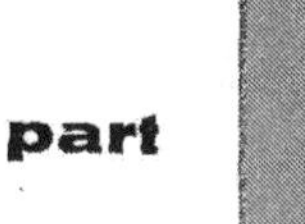

part VI

HOW THE MARKETPLACE WORKS

REPORT FROM THE FLOOR

Kenneth R. Williams

DURING THE LAST few years it has been the policy of the New York Stock Exchange to offer an indoctrination course on the various operations of the Exchange to allied members, registered representatives, institutional investors, portfolio managers, and others using the Exchange in their day-to-day business. Included in this course is an unprecedented visit to the "floor" during trading hours. Before these special visits were inaugurated, the floor was restricted during trading hours to members and floor personnel of the Exchange. Since a new precedent has been established, let's take advantage of it by going on one of these special visits.

We start at a member firm's booth, occupying a small space at the outer edge of the trading floor. It is manned by a telephone clerk who monitors the direct wire to the firm's office and a partner of the member firm. The partner has a "seat" on the Exchange and acts as a floor broker for his firm.

The action begins as an order to buy 100 shares of General Foods is received by the telephone clerk. He writes down the particulars and hands the order to the broker to execute. Using all his experience and knowledge, our broker sets out to buy the stock at the best possible price. He hurries to "post" 8, and enters the General Foods "crowd." Post 8 is the only place on the floor where GF (ticker symbol) is handled, and the crowd that he enters consists of members interested in buying or selling this particular stock. In a loud, clear voice, our broker shouts, "How's General Foods?"

Our broker's cry is an abbreviated way of saying, "What is the bid (highest price) and what is the offer (lowest price) at which GF stock will be traded, and what is the size of the market?" Any broker in the crowd may bid or offer. One or more brokers may be bidding or offering at the same price. When all the bids and offers are consolidated, the market quotation is given to our broker. Thus far he has given no indication as to whether he is a buyer or seller or merely seeking a quotation.

However, with this quick information, our broker now knows the market, the number of shares for sale, and the price of the last sale which is indicated on the post. A prompt decision, based on his judgment, must be made. The crux of the situation is as follows: (1) he has one hundred shares of General Foods to buy for his customer, who has not limited the price but has indicated that he will pay a fair price in the current market; (2) the market as a whole is steady; (3) the offering price is one quarter of a dollar above the last indicated sale; (4) price fluctuations in General Foods are generally about three-eighths to one-half dollar between sales at the current price level; and (5) there is only 100 shares offered. If he does not take the offering at once, someone else may or it may be withdrawn. So he quickly decides and shouts, "Take it!" The contract is closed.

After the contract is closed

Since all transactions on the Exchange are made verbally between members with no receipts or exchange of papers given or taken, he has bought the General Foods stock for his customer at the offered price. It only remains for our broker to tell the seller the name of the brokerage firm to which he should deliver the stock. The seller in turn gives him the name of the firm that should receive payment. The seller also gives a stock exchange reporter stationed in the crowd the number of shares, the name of the stock, and the price at which he sold them. The reporter notes the data on a slip and hands it to a carrier who dispatches the information to the ticker department over a pneumatic tube system. Under normal operating conditions a sale takes place only from one to two minutes before notice of the sale appears on ticker tape all over the country and becomes a matter of public record.

Our broker, having made his purchase at the best possible price, must now send a report back to the customer. He or a page carries the report slip giving the particulars, including the name of the brokerage firm that sold the stock, back to his booth. The telephone clerk at the booth calls the report back to their firm's office, which in turn notifies the customer of his purchase. The next day a written confirmation is sent to the customer. All that remains is the payment and disposition of the stock certificate to finish the transaction.

At the completion of this General Foods sale (when our broker shouted, "Take it!"), a completely new auction market in General Foods begins. Members in the crowd holding orders in the stock renew their bids and offers. This is one of the basic rules of the Exchange. There are other rules, too, all designed to insure an orderly auction. For example, if two

This battery of operators at the New York Stock Exchange furnishes instant quotes to brokers on all "Big Board" issues.

brokers offered the same amount of stock at the same time at identical prices in the auction market, and our broker bought one hundred shares, which one would sell him the stock? Since both are on equal standing, they would match each other with coins to determine who makes the sale.

Our broker who has just made the fairly simple transaction of purchasing 100 shares of General Foods is a "commission house broker." He is a member of the Exchange and a partner of a member firm that does business with the public. The order that he just executed originated after a customer contacted his firm's office or branch office. This order was transmitted to our broker via the telephone clerk at his booth on the floor.

Floor partner handles average 40% of firm's business

His job, then, is to direct the floor operation of his firm and to handle as many of their orders as possible. Each time clients of his firm buy or sell securities, they are charged a gross commission in accordance with the stock price. Part of this commission is allocated to the member who executes the order on the floor. Obviously, our commission house broker tries to execute as many of his firm's orders as possible, averaging about 40%. There are occasions when he cannot be on the floor to handle his firm's orders. At such times, a specially designated group of brokers will act for his firm. Stock Exchange members acting in this capacity are called "two-dollar brokers," a term which goes back to the days when the floor broker's average commission amounted to two dollars. Today the scale for executing floor orders runs from $1.25 to $4.35 per hundred shares.

Many of the orders given to our commission broker by his firm's clients are limited in price and away from the current market. Since he cannot possibly watch out for or handle these orders, he delegates the responsibility for them to a special category of members called "specialists." They act as his agent. A brief look at history will help explain how and why the specialist came into being.

In the "call system" of trading used when the Exchange was founded in 1792, the entire

TO BUY ONE HUNDRED SHARE

Any single transaction in any one of the approximately 1,100 issues listed on the New York Stock Exchange begins when a member's name appears on the wall-mounted annunciator board. The member goes to his firm's phone clerk, receives the order (top left)—his job: execute it at the best possible price. Then . . .

list of stocks was called one at a time for trading. Sometimes it took all morning to go through the list. By the year 1867, American industrial enterprise had grown to such an extent that investors became impatient with this outmoded and time-consuming system of trading. Eager buyers and sellers found more ready markets out on the streets. The Exchange then abandoned the call system and introduced continuous trading for all listed stocks. This was accomplished by erecting "posts" on the floor of the Exchange (today there are 18), and assigning each stock to a location at a designated post. The governors ordered that thenceforth all dealings in any stock would take place only in the immediate vicinity of its location. This was indeed a revolution! Up to this time brokers had been able to remain in their "seats" during the call and had control over all their orders. Suddenly, with the new order, there were simultaneous markets all over the room. It was obvious that a new brokerage technique had to be evolved. Certain members solicited member firms and offered their services to handle their orders in a special group of stocks located at a single post. They agreed to stay at the assigned post and assume full responsibility for executing the member firm's orders entrusted to them. For their services, they charged the usual commission allocated a floor member for executing an order. Thus, the specialist system was born. With refinements, it remains essentially the same today.

The functions of the specialist

Today, a specialist has two major functions, as an agent for member firms and as a dealer in his stock specialties. As an agent, he executes the orders for his member firm customers at the best possible market prices, reporting the transactions to them. He also supplies

OF "BIG BOARD" STOCK

The broker enters the "crowd" to execute his order. "What's the market?" "An eighth bid, offered at a half!" "Sold a hundred at a half!" The contract is closed—and brokers walk 12 miles daily to make such trades.

Record of the transaction goes by pneumatic tube to the ticker room five floors above. In under two minutes the sale will be teletyped to tickers, like that below, all over the country.

Actual certificates of ownership are ultimately sent to customers by transfer clerks using high-speed filing equipment.

The floor is a busy place, 10 to 3 30, five days a week, filled with a market crowd that on a normal day includes 800-900 active trading members, 1,200 other employees. 1,106 bond issues are traded at the post at left, about 75 stocks at each of 18 main floor posts—total daily volume: better than 2,200,000 shares (average) and a ton of paper remains to be swept up every night.

them with quotations, sizes of markets, sales prices, and other information relevant to their orders. His function as an agent requires a factual knowledge of the rules governing trading, as well as a deft handling and placing of orders in the swiftly changing auction market.

The specialist's function as a dealer is actually a "risk-bearing function." He is required, under the rules of the Exchange, to maintain a fair and orderly market in the stocks in which he specializes. He cannot always depend upon his customer orders to establish the auction market (at times even so-called "blue-chip" stocks have few or no orders near the current market prices). In such instances, the specialist is obliged to act as a dealer—buying or selling at his own risk to maintain price continuity. This furnishes the cushion and liquidity so essential to the operation of the Exchange because investors inevitably direct their dealings to the most stable or liquid market. However, no specialist is expected to maintain a market that runs counter to the normal sources of supply and demand.

Ike's heart attack tripled specialists' risk

The Stock Exchange requires that each specialist be adequately capitalized in order to perform his dealer functions. It has been arbitrarily established that a specialist must have available capital to purchase at least 400 shares of each stock in which he specializes. Needless to say, this capital requirement is minimum. Generally speaking, considerable more capital is utilized. For example, on September 26, 1955, the Monday after President Eisenhower's heart attack, when a selling wave hit the market, the stock inventory of the 350 specialists in 115 separate groupings increased $23.5 million to a total of $73.4 million.

In order to ascertain the percentage of dealings that specialists maintain in relation to the daily volume, the Exchange has gathered voluminous statistics over the last quarter-century. Their purpose is to formulate an index or yardstick for the guidance of specialists in their dealings. These specialist dealings are audited four times a year. On the basis of the audit a specialist and his group are given their percentage of dealer participation in their stocks. They are also given the current index of all specialists, in all stocks. At the present, the ratio of specialist dealings is about 15% of twice the reported volume. Applying this index, it is apparent that the specialist is on the average either the buyer or the seller in one out of every three transactions.

As a whole, specialists purchase 80% of

their dealer transactions on declining prices in order to cushion the market. The same ratio holds true for their dealer sales at rising prices in order to furnish liquidity to the market. If a specialist falls below the current norm in the percentage of dealer or stabilizing transactions, he is notified by the Exchange. For continued sub-normal dealer functioning, he may lose his registration as a specialist.

Up to this point in our visit to the floor, we have witnessed a transaction and been introduced to various types of brokers. Our picture will be more complete if we take a brief look at some of the underlying principles and rules of the auction market.

Action only when the price is right

We start with an important common denominator: each share of a corporation's stock in a particular category represents identical privileges of ownership as do all shares of the same class. Thus, when buyers or sellers enter the auction market of a specified security they know they are bargaining for identical items. Competition to buy or sell is price-wise. The pricing unit of the Exchange is by eighths* of a dollar and one hundred shares has been adopted as the round-lot unit of trading. These essential factors make for the unique two-way auction market operating on the Exchange. Buyers bid up in competition with each other for stock, and the highest price that will be paid is the bid price in the market. Sellers, similarly, offer their stock in the open market and the lowest price at which the stock will be sold is the offered price. When the bid price is raised to the offered price, or the offered price is reduced to the bid price, a transaction takes place. The buyer and the seller have had a meeting of their minds and the contract is consummated. In fact, no one has ever bought or sold stock on the Exchange unless he has agreed through the medium of his broker that the price is acceptable. Each listed security has a bid and an offer at all times, for the reason that the specialist must maintain a fair and orderly market.

Does the quotation and size of the market indicate the ability of the market to trade? By no means, for a broker or specialist will divulge only as much of his order as he thinks is in the best interest of his customer. Do auction markets remain fairly stable? No—the market is swiftly changing and ever moving. New orders to buy or sell change the quotations of the market. The simple fact that a customer may cancel any order up to the moment of its execution also makes for many changes in the market. Likewise, world and financial news, along with changing price patterns of other stocks, are dynamic factors.

Does it pay to quote a stock and its size before giving an order? Active stocks generally have close markets. To get a quotation takes as much time as making an execution. This may mean wasted time and missing your markets. In thin markets, however, it is good policy to get a quotation. One of the most troublesome problems to brokers and customers is the general lack of understanding of how swiftly the auction market changes, and that at the conclusion of each sale a new auction begins in which former privileges may be changed.

A thin market makes for a big spread

What is a thin market stock? Many securities at times have very few orders in the hands of brokers or specialists. This unusual lack of supply or demand may create a wider

* This derives from the earliest days when our new nation adopted the term "dollar" from the Spanish pillar dollar, the coinage most widely used in the Western Hemisphere during revolutionary times. It was the "piece of eight" that we first read about in *Treasure Island*. This pillar dollar was divisible into eight parts or "bits." Two bits was a quarter of a dollar, four bits a half dollar. In 1792 the new board of brokers adopted this pricing system, which has remained the same ever since.

KENNETH R. WILLIAMS, a graduate of Columbia in 1928, has been a specialist on the New York Stock Exchange for more than 25 years.

spread than usual between the bid and offered prices. Any sizable order generally requires negotiation. A fairly large order may have to be resolved by selling to the orders on the specialist's "book" and to the specialist, as a dealer, at agreed prices. The order may have to be merchandised to interested clients, generally known by the specialist; or the order may have to be executed over a period of time with the help of the specialist. With the approval of the Exchange, the specialist may make a block bid for his own account, outside the auction market.

How does one become a specialist? Any member may notify the Exchange that he wishes to become a specialist in certain stocks. His registration as a specialist will be approved upon demonstration of an ability to operate a "book," knowledge of the rules, and experience with specialist duties. He must have sufficient capital, be associated with other specialists, and must prove that the new function will be a service to the Exchange.

May a specialist compete for his own account with orders on his book? It is mandatory that he shall subordinate his interest to those of his customers. Furthermore, no professional trader or specialist may compete with any public orders to buy stock unless he is the first bidder at a stabilizing (minus) price. A specialist must not divulge orders entrusted to him, except to represent them in the market.

What advantages does a specialist have? Not being able to compete with customer orders, he has more freedom of dealer action at the opening of the market, for the simple reason that customers generally hold back their orders to see how the market opens. The specialist has the advantage of noting the preponderance of orders on his books. At times this may indicate the direction in which a stock will move. To the uninitiated, many buy orders might be interpreted as indicating that a purchase is in order. The specialist learns that the reverse is generally more likely. Many orders on the buy side of his book make a so-called "down" book; many sell orders constitute an "up" book. Let us assume that the book has a scattering of buy orders and a very heavy number of sell orders. Eliminating all outside factors and influences, can he make a forecast as to the direction the stock will take?

Nature abhors a vacuum as does the auction market. We find that the lightly ordered down-side presents not only a thin market but a lack of bids for a seller to hit. Conversely, the thick up-side presents many opportunities for potential buyers. Should the abundance of orders on the sell side of the specialist's book start to appear on the ticker tape, it stimulates other buyers to make further purchases of what appears to be a liquidating bargain. The classic illustration of this thesis is demonstrated by almost every new company that has been extraordinarily successful. Tens of thousands of shares change hands at very low prices, thousands at moderate prices, and hundreds at high figures; but practically none at astronomical heights when, ironically, selling is indicated. The psychology of mass selling is well recognized. The housewife will pass up a single item on the supermarket shelf, but hundreds of the same item mixed up in a bin suggests the appearance of an irresistible bargain.

"The first loss is the least costly"

A knowledgeable specialist learns by experience that his first inclination to buy or sell is generally the best. Likewise, he learns that the first loss is the least costly. He sees this demonstrated every day when a customer places a sell order on his book at a price slightly higher than the market. Then, as the market falls away, the customer reduces the price of his order—however, still behind the market. This process of reducing his order continues until finally, in a desperate burst, the customer sells out at or near the low price of the day, and the chances are that the stock of the frustrated seller is purchased by a patient dealer.

Membership on the Exchange presents excellent opportunities for the ambitious young man. It requires an aptitude for matching names and numbers, for thinking fast and reacting quickly. Basic judgment and native shrewdness come high on the list of qualifications, with the foreknowledge that mistakes mean monetary losses. Ability to work efficiently under pressure is vital. It is the performance of a service with intangible goods, yet it gives great satisfaction, pride of professional accomplishment, and an excellent livelihood.

OUTDOORS TO INDOORS

THE AMERICAN STOCK EXCHANGE

The American Stock Exchange is better than 100 years old and began informally, about the time of the California Gold Rush, under the open skies at Wall and Hanover Streets. Handling issues not listed by the New York Stock Exchange, the "Curb Market" grew till a wonderland of excitement filled Broad Street (south of Wall) in fair weather or foul. On June 6, 1919, the members voted to come indoors. The move was made in 1921 to a building at the present location, 86 Trinity Place.

The vast air-conditioned Trading Room, 152 feet long, houses one bond and 21 stock trading posts. About 340 members appear on the floor, assisted by phone clerks ranged along the east and west walls in tiered seats.

Today's telephone clerks operate from positions where they can easily see every member. The hand signals are unchanged from the days outdoors.

Dressed for any weather, Curb brokers traded in violent heat, extreme cold, rain, snow, sleet. The broker signalling at left to a telephone clerk in a building window wears a bull's-eye cap for easy spotting from above. Even earlier, the same signals provided the same amazing split-second accurate communication.

The Management of a Brokerage House

PEOPLE AND

Watching the tape

MONEY AND PROBLEMS

Lloyd W. Mason

THE MANAGING PARTNER is a relatively new member of the brokerage and investment fraternity. At least, it is a relatively new idea for a brokerage firm to designate someone to assume the responsibilities of a managing partner. But in the last generation many brokerage firms have grown to such size that a formal and conscious definition of management's function has become essential.

Until the time of the first World War, most of the major brokerage and underwriting firms were relatively small partnerships. If the partnership interest was divided up more or less evenly, management decisions were usually reached around the partnership table and then one of the members of the partnership was assigned the job of implementing the decision. Often things were done with a great deal of informality.

If the firm was dominated by a single man, the senior partner usually operated as the autocratic, old-fashioned boss. The business was usually small enough for him to keep a finger in every pie and know in considerable detail everything that was going on in the firm. In most firms the membership on the New York Stock Exchange was registered in his name and he spent much of his time on the floor of the Exchange. The housekeeping chores were generally assigned to an office manager who acted as a foreman to supervise the help, get out the payroll, see to it that the windows were washed and the wastebaskets emptied.

The need for a professional approach to management problems became apparent as many units in the industry grew to substantial size and the business became increasingly complex. Today, it is not uncommon for a member firm to have a thousand or more employees, and to have gross income of $25 million or more, to maintain offices in a dozen different states and to handle a vast variety of different types of business—listed and unlisted stocks and bonds, underwritings, private placements, mergers and research and advisory services.

As brokerage and underwriting firms grew in scope, there was a parallel refinement and growth in the science of management. When the college professors go to work on the "management function," they frequently break it down into four main stages: planning, organizing, integrating and appraising. Certainly all of these functions must be consciously undertaken by the modern investment firm's management. But, of course, these functions are common to the managements of any type of business enterprise. These theoretical bones can take on meaning for us only if clothed with specific facts from the investment business.

With what, in fact, does the management of a big investment firm deal? Well, there are at least six main categories:

1. People.
2. Money.
3. Accounts and records.
4. Locations and communications.
5. Laws and regulations.
6. Public relations and business development.

Let's look at several of these areas in terms of our four functions.

People

For example, people. Because we are a service industry, the real assets of a modern investment firm are its people. Because the personnel in our industry must be highly trained in a whole battery of specialized skills, the management must plan the recruiting, training and supervision far in advance of actual needs.

The investment firm has three categories of employees—the clerical and service staff; the professional staff, made up of accountants, statisticians, analysts, etc.; and, finally, the key to the success of the firm, its sales force.

It is the obligation of management to visualize the need in each of these categories far enough ahead of time to permit them to be recruited and trained. It is necessary not only to anticipate the growth of the individual firm, but to keep a sharp eye on the age level and the rate of erosion of the current staff, so that both additions and replacements are on hand as needed.

The organizing function must be brought into play so that jobs are defined, ladders of advancement clearly delineated, and the interrelation of various groups within the firm clearly established. The organization chart

Nerve center of the big brokerage house is the wire and order room. Moving belts carry incoming and outgoing orders along the tracks, between offices and departments, practically "untouched by human hand".

LLOYD W. MASON joined Paine, Webber, Jackson & Curtis following World War I, in which he served with distinction as member of the British Royal Flying Corps, winning the Distinguished Flying Cross. He became a partner in 1929, and managing partner in 1947. He has also served as a vice president of the Association of Stock Exchange Firms.

and the manual of procedures, things utterly unheard of in this industry a generation ago, are now constantly on management's desk for revision and refinement.

When the people have been hired, trained and put into their respective slots, the firm management then faces its most difficult task of all. The professors call it "integration," but we generally describe it in more homely terms as simply getting everybody to work together harmoniously and efficiently so that we get the job done. The whole chain of command in a modern investment firm is designed to further this purpose. Whether the firm is organized as a partnership or a corporation, the authority always flows from ownership, which sets broad policy, to functioning management, which is then normally arranged in a hierarchy from the managing partner downward.

Two types of organizational set-ups are generally blended in the typical large investment firm. There is, first, the breakdown of functions—underwriting, sales, accounting, communications, business development, research, etc. For the large national firm there is also the geographical organization, with senior members of the firm acting under the managing partner as regional supervisors. Under the regional supervisors one finds managers, co-managers, assistant managers, etc., as individual circumstances require.

We are just beginning to develop effective procedures to measure and evaluate personnel policies. Various tests that are applied in the industry include:

(1) the rate of personnel turnover,
(2) average labor costs for the performance of different functions,
(3) average length of service,
(4) ease of attracting new employees, and
(5) direct interrogation of personnel to discover attitudes toward the firm and its management.

We won't attempt to analyze each of the four functions (planning, organizing, integrating and appraising) in all six areas, but rather go down the list to find some of the things that are unique about the brokerage

Customers visit a brokerage office.

and investment industry that must be handled by management.

Money

Money is certainly one of the most prominent areas to consider, as its management in the investment firm is quite different from that in the industrial corporation.

An investment firm has three main sources of funds: the capital of its partners or stockholders, the free credit balances of its customers that are left with the firm, and, finally, collateral loans from commercial banks. It is the job of the policy determining group in the firm to decide how much capital shall be kept clear to finance the brokerage operations of the firm, how much shall be available to commit in underwriting operations, and, finally,

TICKER TAPE
. . . A Million Rolls a Year

Seen everywhere in the financial world is the quotation ticker, which flashes the buying and selling prices of stocks and bonds, nationwide, from the country's principal exchanges. Quotations are sent to more than 500 cities over nearly 4700 tickers—machines which eat up about 1,000,000 rolls of tape each year. That's almost 190,000 miles, enough to circle the world nearly eight times.

The first tape printing ticker was the invention of Edward A. Calahan, who developed his device shortly after the Civil War, when markets were nervous and the price of gold was fluctuating rapidly. At that time the only rapid reporting instrument was a Gold Indicator, a crude visual gadget made of three overlapping discs. Calahan, a telegraph operator on the floor of the N. Y. Stock Exchange, developed a machine that would print letters and figures on a paper ribbon—and was granted his patent on April 21, 1868. The ticker got its name because early models ticked like a clock (the ticker's escapement unit, in fact, closely resembled a clock mechanism).

Thomas A. Edison made the next major improvement in the ticker in 1870. His two-wire Universal Ticker proved much more efficient than the three-wire Calahan ticker, and General Lefferts of Western Union bought the rights from Edison for $40,000. Edison later related that just before the $40,000 offer, he was trying to work up enough courage to ask $2,500 for his invention. Edison's original design was so sound that it has come down through the years practically unchanged. (More than 1000 Universal Tickers still operate with complete satisfaction in Western Union's baseball service.)

"What do you think the invention's worth?" young Edison blurted out. "$40,000, replied Lefferts calmly.

Today, the country's principal stock and other exchanges are

Watching the trades on the N. Y. Stock Exchange tape.

Mr. Bache inspects a new private wire system for Bache & Co. offices.

The control center in Los Angeles for the nationwide automatic private wire system used by E. F. Hutton & Company.

of course, how much shall be kept on hand for operating expenses.

Once these policy determinations are made, the job of controlling and managing the various capital accounts is the duty of the managing partner, though he may delegate this responsibility. In larger firms a sum may be allocated to the municipal department, another sum to the trading department, a third to the underwriting department. The executive in charge of these divisions then manages the money entrusted to him, under the supervision of the managing partner.

Likewise, the management of bank loans may be delegated, but whoever performs the function is assuming responsibility of great served by Western Union's high-speed ticker, printing 500 characters a minute. This ticker was first placed in service in 1930—the extra speed became necessary when a record volume of 16,410,030 shares were traded during the market crash on October 29, 1929. Tickers then in use ran nearly three hours behind the market—that day, never equalled since, used about 15,000 *miles* of tape.

City parades in New York are most always the occasion for an avalanche of floating ticker tape from brokers' offices along lower Broadway. It is estimated that about 30,000 rolls, each with about 1,000 feet of tape, are tossed during an average "hero's welcome." But it's generally not good, new tape because office boys save used tape for just such occasions. The record parades were those for Lindbergh and MacArthur, where 50,000 rolls apiece were cascaded into the street. . . . Mr. Calahan really started something.

NYSE order slips go here for tape transmission.

Tape moves continuously across this special Merrill Lynch, Pierce, Fenner, & Smith device, used by their research department.

Operators check tape for accuracy, against actual buy and sell slips.

moment to the success of the firm. The amount of money borrowed and the cost of money are vital factors in the over-all net results of the operation. Nor can loan and money management be performed in a vacuum. Banks are, themselves, valuable clients of brokerage and underwriting firms. It would be foolish to ignore the potentialities of reciprocal business. Likewise, local prides and prejudices must be borne in mind as well as dollars and cents.

Accounting

A wag once said that a financial firm was simply in the business of manufacturing numbers on paper. In the superficial sense this is true. But there is nothing superficial about the fact that accounting and record-keeping represent the biggest items of expense after the cost of sales.

Actually, little management thought was given to this phase of the business until the '30's when the financial industry began to look to the modern business machine as a partial solution to the hard times then prevailing. Today mechanical data processing is almost universal in the financial industry and new, more efficient means of handling accounts and records are a constant concern of management.

A new data processing laboratory is now in the process of construction in Wall Street. New methods are adopted as rapidly as they become available. All of the leading firms are planning years ahead in this regard, and studies are being launched today that may completely revolutionize this phase of the business over the next decade.

Data processing is vital today in handling's Wall Street's growing volume. Here computers, which deliver final customer statements from magnetic tapes, are shown going into Bache & Co.; at work for Merrill Lynch and for Reynolds & Co.

Locations and communications

Next to newspapers, the financial industry has the most extensive private communications network in the country, with literally hundreds of thousands of miles of leased lines spreading out from the big financial centers, like Boston, New York, Chicago and San Francisco, into every city of any size in the country. It is not at all uncommon for a major nationwide firm to have a communications bill of over $1,000,000 per year. Needless to say, this creates a unique set of problems for brokerage management.

Our leasing and general housekeeping problems, of course, are similar to those of any

An automatic stuffing machine (left) puts statements into envelopes at a rate of better than 20,000 a day, yet needs almost no supervision.

Stock certificates proceed sedately (right) to vault safe-keeping at the end of the day. Paper valued in billions is contained in these safes.

multi-unit service organization, though there are a few architectural considerations that only the broker with a board room has to consider.

Laws and regulations

The sheaf of rules and regulations, laws and taboos that surround the modern financial institution would have long since strangled a less hardy animal. A modern brokerage firm must operate under the regulations of the Federal Government exemplified in the Securities and Exchange Commission; under the National Association of Securities Dealers, a quasi-Federal body; under the individual laws of each state in which it has an office; and under a book full of regulations applicable to each Exchange of which it is a member. The whole complex is so vast, so difficult, that it is no secret to the regulators themselves that with the best intentions in the world, little violations are constantly occurring. But it is still one of management's major responsibilities to educate its staff—to explain, interpret and to enforce within the firm this body of edicts.

The New York Stock Exchange and the National Association of Securities Dealers both require registered representatives to pass extensive examinations designed to assure that they are familiar with the regulations governing our industry. The fact that all sales personnel receive schooling in this area is a great help to management, but it is still necessary to constantly refresh people's memories, to interpret regulations, and to spot and stop any violations that occur. Managements of most firms even go beyond this and set up a code of ethics of their own. These policies, enforced within the firm, set the tone of a fiancial house and afford an opportunity to build a unique character for the firm.

The determination of firm policy, of course, always flows from the partnership as a whole, or the board of directors if the firm is organized as a corporation. It becomes a function of the management team to follow through and assure that the policies are, in fact, carried out on down the line.

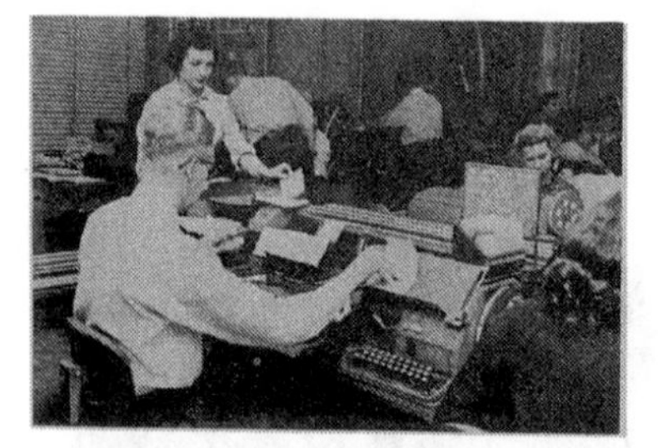

The nation's largest brokerage house, Merrill Lynch, Pierce, Fenner & Smith, Incorporated, is also the phone company's biggest civilian customer. Here, a teletype operator at work.

Heart of the wire and order department at Merrill Lynch, Pierce, Fenner & Smith, Incorporated: 130 offices in 114 cities are connected to ten floors at 70 Pine, all through this room.

Account executives meet with M L, P, F & S Vice President Rubezanin. Below, a clerk in the dividend department records dividend checks received in the day's mail.

It is only in recent years that public relations and business development programs have been considered apart from ordinary sales effort. Since the end of World War II, however, management has been forced to view these functions as separate activities and plan and budget accordingly.

Though each major firm in Wall Street approaches the problem somewhat differently, the research department is always the keystone to the arch. Modern securities research began many years ago, usually with a single man writing a daily market letter. Today, all of the larger firms have a score or more men in securities research. The publications of a firm's research department and the reputation of its analysts are two aspects of a firm that are constantly visible to the public. The quality and form of work turned out in the research department is a constant concern of management, because it is so much in the public eye.

In recent years advertising that is designed both to produce retail customers and to create an institutional image in the public mind has become almost universal. As both advertising and security research expenditures represent a major slice of the budget, and as their long-term influence can be tremendously powerful in determining public reaction toward the house, firm managements have found it necessary to allot an increasing proportion of their time to policy determination and administration in this area.

And tomorrow . . . .

After management has finished the extensive tasks outlined above, it still has one more big job to do and that is provide for its own succession. Only today's management can train the management of tomorrow, and the final job of management is to provide for orderly succession. It is a task that the industry has just begun to approach in a conscious and scientific manner, but management is alive to the need. Today's manager is constantly searching among junior staff personnel for men with the qualities of mind and heart needed to carry on the big firms of the Street. And it is here that the greatest opportunity rests for young men entering the financial industry today.

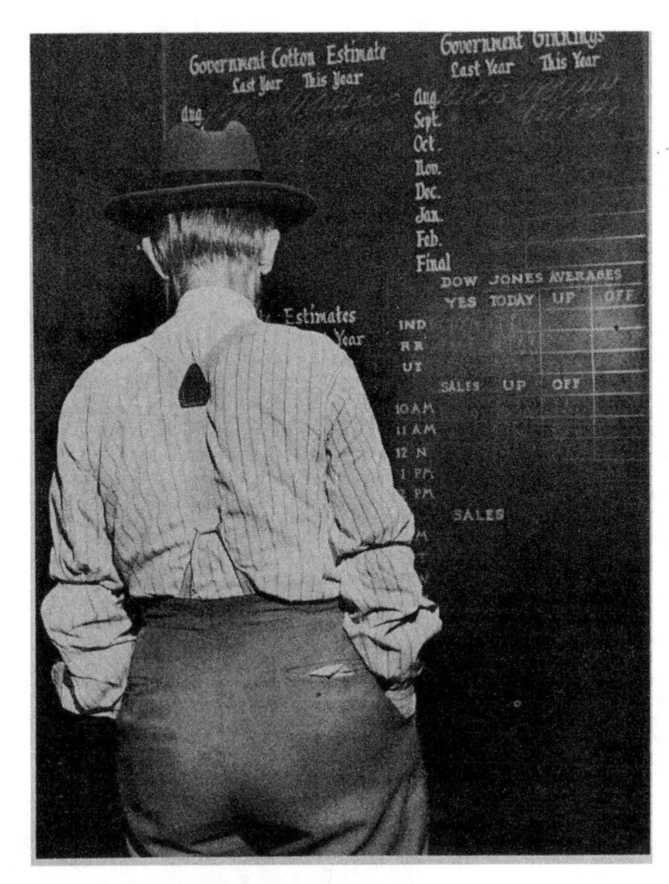

The Mississippi Delta: a cotton planter checks the government cotton estimate for September in the brokerage office of J. G. Lusk, Greenville, Mississippi.

Commodity Markets—Today and Tomorrow

THE PRICE IS ALWAYS RIGHT

Jerome Lewine

THE POSITION and function of the organized futures market or commodity exchange in the economic life of this country has been much misrepresented and little understood. When the price of an import commodity advances sharply, an investigation by a committee of Congress or by a government agency usually follows. The futures market is customarily attacked as the cause of the trouble. Few attribute the changes in prices to the operation of economic forces.

Yet, these markets have survived over 100 years of active service to commerce and industry. Why is it that they can be so indiscriminately condemned and yet maintain an important place in our economy?

Why our economy needs organized futures markets

The answer lies in the fact that as long as we have a capitalistic economy in which the free marketing of goods is preserved, these markets serve a true and necessary economic function. They provide an essential instrument of free enterprise, which is a place to sell goods at any time and at any price one sees fit. These are the modern market places where buyers and sellers congregate either in person or through brokers to buy and sell our basic commodities at open and competitive auction. These are the places where the law of supply and demand finds its freest expression in a constantly shifting price level which is broadcast to the entire world. These are the modern substitutes for the old market place to which producers would bring their goods for sale to such dealers and consumers as might gather on the spot. Today, these market places are linked by radio and wire to the entire world so that a jute merchant in Calcutta can know instantly the price at which burlap is currently selling on the Commodity Exchange in New York, and the cotton merchant in Lubbock, Texas can find out by telephoning his local broker the price at which cotton is selling on the New York Cotton Exchange.

The oldest organized futures market in the United States is the Chicago Board of Trade, which was founded in 1848. This is the great grain futures market of the world. It affords a central place for trading in wheat, corn, oats, barley, rye, soybeans, and a number of other agricultural commodities.

The New York Cotton Exchange was founded in 1870. This is the world's center for the marketing of raw cotton of American growth. The Cotton Exchange also provides facilities for trading in raw wool futures and wool top futures.

Without enumerating them, all sorts of other basic commodities are traded in exchanges in many sections of the country.

Only those commodities fit into the pattern of futures trading which are susceptible of uniform grading, which can be stored readily, and which are not subject to sudden or extensive deterioration in storage. The reason for this is that anyone who sells a commodity on a futures market commits himself to do one of two things:

(1) to make delivery of the quantity called for by the futures contract at some time during the month in which the contract matures, or

(2) to offset this commitment before maturity by the purchase of a futures contract maturing in the same month as his contract of sale.

A seller who wishes to liquidate his futures contract by making delivery must have the commodity available at a delivery point specified in the Regulations of the Exchange; and the lot must meet all the terms and conditions of such Regulations as to grade, quantity, quality and the like.

It is obvious from the existence of futures markets in the variety of commodities mentioned above, that such markets provide an important service in their respective fields. Giving consideration to the two World Wars of the past forty years, and the deep economic depression of the 1930's, the persistence of our futures markets demonstrates the genuine need

The Cotton Exchange

which they fill. A brief survey of the functions performed by these futures markets may assist the reader in appreciating their value.

The economic functions of commodity exchanges

The first and most important of these economic functions is the opportunity which they afford to a producer, dealer or consumer of the commodity to reduce his price risk by what is known as "hedging." This function of the futures markets corresponds to the shifting of such risks as fire, theft, etc., which are commonly covered by insurance.

Other benefits which are provided by futures markets were summarized by *Fortune* Magazine:

"By offering a continuous market, the commodities in question become liquid—they can at any time be converted into cash at prevailing market prices without the difficulty of searching out a customer who happens to want the actual goods at once.

"By providing a daily list of published quotations, they make it comparatively easy for either purchaser or seller of the actual article to be sure that he is not paying more or receiving less than a fair price—something that is especially of value to such people as farmers.

"By bringing together data on general supply and demand as well as prices in other markets (information which the Exchanges gather for the benefit of traders) they tend to minimize price fluctuations due to local conditions—to make a larger, fairer, and more accurate market."

It may also be added that the Exchanges perform two other important functions:

(1) They establish standards of grading, and standards of trading in a commodity, which lends stability and certainty to trading in the physical commodity as well as to trading in the futures contract, and

(2) they provide a guarantee of credit to both seller and buyer so that it is not necessary for either party to inquire as to the credit standing of the other.

The seller of a futures contract who commits himself to make a delivery usually has the option to deliver the contract grade (which is frequently spoken of as the "basis" grade) or any one of a number of other specified grades of the commodity, at premiums on or discounts from the basis grade, as fixed in the bylaws. In some cases, as in cotton, deliveries may be made at any one of a number of cities.

How futures contracts are cleared

One of the outstanding characteristics of futures markets in the U. S. is the system of clearance of contracts which has been generally adopted. An understanding of this system is essential to a complete comprehension of the use of futures markets by trade interests.

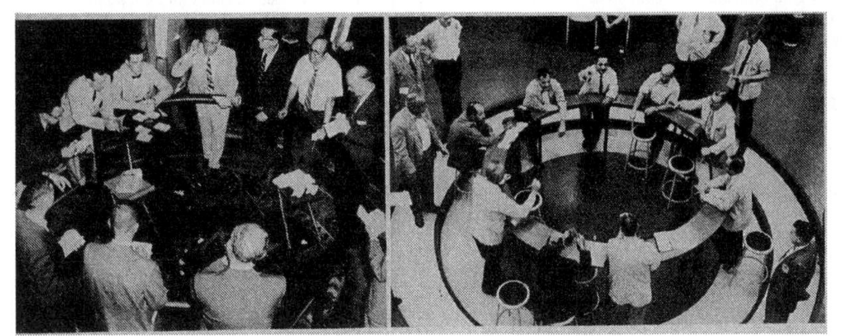

The Commodity Exchange

The Sugar Exchange

Every contract executed on the floor of the Exchange must be cleared through a clearing house operated in conjunction with, not as an integral part of, the Exchange. The clearing house is run by a separate stock corporation whose stockholders must be members of the Exchange. However, the members of the clearing house are limited to those members of the Exchange who can meet very stringent financial requirements, since the members of the clearing house "carry" all contracts and guarantee their performance in full without qualification or limitation. Thus, a contract which is done on the Exchange by a member, either for his own account or for the account of a non-member, must be "given up" to a clearing member if the member executing it is not himself a member of the clearing house. The clearing member is required to maintain margin with the clearing house for all contracts carried by him and he, in turn, receives margin from the member or non-member for whose account a contract is carried.

Thus, a buyer of December cotton has a contractual commitment to receive cotton for December delivery through the clearing house; and the clearing house in turn has a contractual commitment with some other clearing member to deliver that cotton. The clearing house is therefore always in balance as between open purchases and open sales in any delivery month. These open commitments, however, fluctuate from day to day, as the clearing members add to or close out their open positions with the clearing house.

It is this offsetting of contracts (because of their identity in any given delivery month) that enables a person who buys or sells a futures contract to take advantage of the second alternative mentioned above, i.e., to close out his position without taking or making delivery, merely by the execution of an equal and offsetting contract.

This is what gives the futures markets the flexibility and liquidity which cannot be had in party contracts outside of the Exchanges. It also provides financial security to Exchange contracts. It is a matter of record that no party to an Exchange contract has ever sustained a loss since the system of clearance was adopted. Finally, it is the feature which enables a buyer or seller on the Exchange to use its facilities for hedging purposes. It thus

JEROME LEWINE, senior partner of H. Hentz & Co., entered the firm in 1900 and became a partner in 1915. Mr. Lewine has been chairman, president, and director of many commodity exchanges, and was the first president of the Commodity Exchange, Inc. He was on the board of managers of the Cotton Exchange, and served three times as president of the Raw Silk Exchange.

provides one of the principal economic advantages of these markets.

In an article entitled "The Insurance Service of Commodity Exchanges," Dr. S. S. Huebner of the Wharton School of the University of Pennsylvania describes hedging as follows:

"Hedging refers to the practice of making two contracts of an opposite though corresponding nature at about the same time, one in the *trade market*, where the actual physical commodity is handled, and the other in the *speculative market* furnished by commodity exchanges. Thus, a purchase of cotton in the trade market is promptly offset by a short sale for an equal amount on some exchange for delivery at some convenient future month. From that time on, assuming a close relationship between prices in the futures and cash markets and between the 'basis grade' and the grade actually held, the holder of the cotton is substantially freed from the gamble of a severe decline in price. Any loss in the cotton held is offset by a corresponding gain on the short sale. No matter how severe the decline, the dealer is always even as regards the wholesale price, and to this he may add the customary trade profit which he is seeking to earn through the physical handling of the cotton for clients.

"But when disposing of his actual cotton to some client in the trade market, a hedger must at the same time close out his short sale with a purchase on the exchange. In other words, both contracts are entered into at the same time, and in order to avoid speculation, both must also be terminated at the same time. Similarly, a short seller in the trade market, who has promised to deliver actual cotton to some client at some future delivery date, may insure his trade profit by hedging with a purchase of a future on the exchange.

"Being reasonably assured of their regular trade profit, middlemen are in position to operate on the basis of a smaller margin of profit per unit of commodity than would be possible in the absence of insurance against speculative loss, with the result that the differences between the price received by the producer and that paid by the consumer is materially reduced."

It is apparent from Professor Huebner's explanation of hedging that it is the special nature of the futures contract and the system of clearance that makes hedge operations possible. If such contracts could not be closed out by the making of opposite and equal contracts, the value of such a market for hedging would be greatly reduced.

The place of the speculator

The effective functioning of an Exchange is possible only if a reasonably broad and orderly market exists. Speculation serves the purpose of providing such a market. The word "speculation" has acquired an unpleasant connotation. However, it should be remembered that speculation is inherent in the very nature of merchandising operations. Every dealer who carries an inventory is speculating. Every farmer who raises a cash crop is a speculator. To the extent to which the farmer or dealer or consumer can shift the risk of adverse price fluctuations to someone who voluntarily assumes them, he minimizes his speculation. The party who voluntarily assumes such risk becomes the speculator in his place. Professor Huebner, in the article mentioned above, has the following to say about the function of the speculator in our commodity markets:

"Because of the presence of a large group of speculators, many of them always ready to buy or sell at any particular time, our leading commodity exchanges furnish a continuous market to producers, distributors, creditors and ultimate buyers. Such a market may be defined as one which enables buyers or sellers to obtain or to dispose of the commodity, even in large quantities, at any time during business hours, and at a price varying but slightly from the last previous quotation. Under normal conditions (and panic conditions are comparatively rare), the daily price range on commodity exchanges is surprisingly small, and all interests in the market may count upon either obtaining or disposing of the commodity at a very small sacrifice as compared with the last recorded quotation."

It must be admitted that despite the economic service performed by the speculator, it is his activity in the futures markets that has made them the football of politics. There have been notorious instances of attempts to "corner" a market which have had great publicity. Such episodes have hurt the standing of these markets in the minds of the public. Such activities, however, now belong to the remote past. Today, most of our domestic commodities are traded on Exchanges which are under the jurisdiction of a Federal agency known as the Commodity Exchange Authority. The regulations of the Authority limit the amount of the commodity which may be carried for the account of any one person, and provide other safeguards against manipulative activity.

Government regulations

The Exchanges themselves, recognizing the position which they occupy in our economic system, have, without exception, adopted rules

"Unrealistic and extravagant government price support programs are threatening the very existence of some of our exchanges . . . upset the entire economy of our nation."

and regulations for self-policing. Today, it is most unusual to find instances of improper manipulative activity on any organized Exchange. The Commodity Exchange Authority from time to time files a complaint against persons accused of such activity, but these are relatively few, and are of minor importance.

The fact is that when the price of a commodity rises or falls rapidly, the movement today is based upon some unusual happening such as the frost damage to the coffee crop in Brazil during the winter of 1953 which led to the sharp rise in the price of coffee. The futures markets actually serve to cushion the rate of change in the prices of such commodities, through the interplay of buying and selling forces meeting in a single market place. That this is true is clear from a comparison of the price movements of such commodities with those of commodities which are not the subject of futures trading. The impact of catastrophe or other unusual economic conditions has frequently led to extreme price movements in the latter group of commodities.

Our futures markets have proved themselves effective instruments in the operation of our free economy. Despite all of the investigations which have been directed at them for political reasons, Congress has recognized their value and has refrained from destructive legislation. If their functions and methods of operation were more generally understood by the public, their usefulness to the economy would be more fully appreciated.

When one considers how vital it is for the processor of a commodity to gauge with a conservative degree of accuracy the price movements of the raw materials that go into his product, it is apparent that it is of the utmost importance that he should have a complete knowledge of the commodity dealt in.

It is regrettable that currently unrealistic and extravagant government price support programs are threatening the very existence of some of our exchanges, especially those dealing in domestically produced commodities. Let us hope that it will soon be recognized by the taxpayers generally that a continuation of such costly schemes, which interfere with the inexorable law of supply and demand, can do much harm and upset the entire economy of our nation.

Over-the-Counter Operations

THE INVISIBLE

THE OVER-THE-COUNTER MARKET, sometimes referred to as the unlisted market, is the largest securities market in the United States. The only other market is the listed market, i.e., the market that is available on the national securities exchanges—the New York Stock Exchange, the American Stock Exchange, the Midwest Stock Exchange, the Pacific Coast Stock Exchange, the Philadelphia-Baltimore Stock Exchange, the Boston Stock Exchange, etc. On these Stock Exchanges, business is conducted under the auction system. To buy and sell in that market, an agent, more commonly known as a broker, must be employed to execute an order. This agent or broker charges a standard fee or commission.

In contrast to this auction system used on the Stock Exchanges, dealings in the over-the-counter market are conducted on a negotiated basis. Fair prices and close markets can be obtained by taking the highest bid and lowest offering from among the various bids and offerings shown for that particular security. This is termed "the inside market."

Where is the over-the-counter market, what is it, and how does it operate? It is the market without a market place. It is the market where all securities not listed on an exchange are traded. It is the market that does not function by any set mechanism. It is, rather, a combination of all of the financial communities in the country—those in the smaller towns and cities, as well as the Wall Streets, La Salle Streets, State Streets and Montgomery Streets.

These financial communities are composed of corporations and partnerships dealing in, and specializing in, the purchase and sale of

MARKETPLACE

H. Neill Brady

H. NEILL BRADY is vice president of Blyth & Co., Inc., and manages their National Trading Department, supervising trading activities in nine major cities, coast to coast. He is responsible for the company's long/short positions in 400-500 stocks and bonds.

securities of various types, and include the largest commercial banks and investment banking houses down to the smallest brokers and dealers. The departments of these firms—trading, sales, statistical, buying and municipal—along with officers, partners, salesmen, and staff personnel, all contribute directly or indirectly to the functioning of this market.

Such firms and banking institutions provide the working capital and operational facilities. However, more than that is necessary. A continuing flow of bids and offerings and purchases and sales is needed for the maintenance of an orderly and liquid market. Providing this fundamental need are the buying and selling orders originating from individuals, banks, insurance companies, charitable organizations, investment trusts, pension funds and trust funds.

Unlisted exceeds listed volume

It has been estimated that out of the approximately 55,000 to 60,000 different securities traded in the United States, around 53,000 are unlisted and traded over-the-counter.

These include virtually all bank shares and insurance company shares, all open-end trust shares, all railroad equipment trust certificates, all municipal bonds, most real estate securities, many Canadian and foreign securities, and many public utility, industrial and railroad securities.

Other securities, while listed, trade preponderantly over-the-counter. These include blocks of corporate equities handled as single transactions or through wide secondary distribution, along with the billions of dollars of corporate bonds and securities of the U. S. Government, its territories and instrumentalities. Also included are nearly all new issues of origination, along with securities emanating from reorganizations, divestment programs and "spin-offs." While some of these will eventually be listed on a national securities exchange, it is deemed of primary importance by underwriters and issuing corporations that the initial distribution and seasoning be accomplished in the over-the-counter market. Although exact figures are not available, another estimate places the daily aggregate dollar value of securities traded over-the-counter as exceeding that traded during a like period on all of the stock exchanges combined.

Therefore, we are considering a tremendously important market that performs a vital function in our financial structure.

Liquidity of a market depends greatly on the wide and speedy dissemination of accurate current quotations. Over-the-counter quotations are well publicized—ever increasingly so. The stock exchanges, through the use of ticker systems, render this service with efficiency. Such ticker systems are not available to the over-the-counter market, so other methods are utilized.

Newspapers throughout the country publish daily quotations of hundreds of the more active securities, with the *Wall Street Journal* alone listing over 1,000 daily and an additional 400 to 500 one day a week. The National Quotation Bureau publishes nationally each day the latest dealer quotations for almost 8,000 stock and bond issues, and in the course of a year lists quotations for over 25,000 different issues. Practically every dealer, broker and bank subscribes to this service and uses it extensively. Quotations are further publicized by the offering sheets and market lists continuously sent to extensive mailing lists by dealers and brokers.

The tremendous advancements in communications has played no small part in the prompt transmission to all parts of the country of market-influencing news and market changes of over-the-counter securities. This is accomplished through the liberal use of private leased wire systems, TWX, Telemeter, Western Union and the long distance telephone.

Thus, the over-the-counter market is a vast network of communication wires from coast to coast, linking securities dealers in every part of the country with other dealers, and enabling them—in a matter of minutes—to buy and sell unlisted stocks and bonds, either for themselves or for their customers. The effect of this wide publicity of quotations and speed of contact between buyers and sellers has been to increase trading volume and narrow market spreads. Today there is—over-the-counter—a broad, active liquid market functioning with facility.

Operating actively in the over-the-counter market are the trading departments of many broker and dealer firms. The dealer buys and sells as a principal for his own account, whereas the broker acts in an agency capacity, executing orders for the account of others. There are times when one assumes the role of the other, but the basic capacity under which each type conducts its business is rather sharply defined.

Professional leadership is required in the development and maintenance of a market. While the major component of the over-the-counter market is represented by non-professional interests, the bids and offers flowing from these sources must be brought together, and frequently supplemented by intermediate trading, in order to make a market. This is the task of the professional broker-dealer firms organized to devote their entire efforts to this work. These firms represent the keystone in the over-the-counter market structure.

An integral part of these firms are their trading departments which are organized to accomplish, in general, one of three things: to conduct a strictly professional trading operation, to maintain a service department for their sales organization, or to maintain a department which is charged with both responsibilities.

Some of these departments are purely local in their activities while others are national in scope. Staffed with up to twenty to thirty traders, a large department operating on a national scale may maintain hundreds of primary markets, with accompanying long or short positions having a value or liability of millions of dollars.

Trading as a career

As a vocation, trading in general, and position trading in particular, is a highly specialized line of endeavor. A trader's responsibilities are great and his duties are heavy. He is charged with representing his firm in the professional market and is given the responsibility of making primary markets and entering into commitments for his firm's account. He must exercise sound judgment at all times.

Perhaps the most important element in the

Trading rooms, like this at Blyth & Co., Inc., maintain liquidity in the OTC market through efficient handling of immense volumes of business. Brokers and dealers cross-country are tied in by the nation's most complex non-military communications net (see inset).

structure of the trading department is the personal knowledge and skill of the individual trader. These men bring to their work a knowledge of clientele, of securities and of security values acquired through long experience. Certain native qualities are also essential, including integrity in fulfilling obligations, capacity to absorb and retain news and figures, a flexible mind and the ability to make instantaneous decisions. All that is necessary to become a trader is training and experience, certain mental attributes, plus the application of basic common sense.

There are a multitude of technical factors directly pertaining to trading that a trader must know of. He must be continuously on the alert for changes in interest rates. He must watch for changes in dividend rates, not only in the securities which he trades but in other securities which could have a direct bearing on his own position. He must know what the federal and state taxes are on each security he trades and he must have a thorough knowledge of call prices, conversion features, types of delivery contracts, etc.

He should be familiar with all of the ramifications of arbitrage operations and secondary distributions. These operations and distributions are in the main effected in the over-the-counter market, and may have a direct or indirect bearing on the market in general, and on specific securities in particular.

He should know intimately the mechanics of stock exchange procedure. Over-the-counter trading relates so closely at times to trading on the exchanges that it is of paramount importance for a trader to have a comprehensive knowledge of this complex mechanism. A general knowledge of the investment banking and brokerage business is of inestimable value.

In addition, he must be familiar with the rules and regulations pertaining to his activities, as laid down by the Securities and Exchange Commission and the National Association of Securities Dealers.

Trading technique and procedures

Maintaining trading markets, from either long or short positions, necessitates the application of certain techniques and procedures requiring close and constant attention. Markets are established to develop profits from in-and-out transactions within the market spread, and to assist in the acquiring and maintenance of base positions.

Large volume, rapid turn-over of inventory, and short-term profits are the objectives of many successful professional trading departments. There are basic principles of operation which should be followed if these objectives are to be attained.

Continual liquidity of positions is of paramount importance. Needless to say, the business of making a market is not easy; nor can it be equally well done for every security. For active issues, traders can afford the risk of fairly large positions, knowing that these can be moved if necessary by small price concessions; but for small, inactive issues, the risks of positioning mount rapidly. Those who make markets are, of course, helped in a general way by the presence of many other traders with whom they can bargain. There is a continual shifting of positions among traders in response to changing customer bids and offers and to changing opinion regarding the market; and these shifts have the general effect of spreading the load of dealer positions. This is not an accommodation or friendship affair, however, and at any time a trader may discover that his market has melted away, leaving him with the slow and often costly task of working out of his position as best he can.

Losses should be taken quickly and profitable positions should be allowed to run. For the type of operation under discussion, scale-down buying in the acquisition of a position should seldom be used, whereas buying on a scale-up is sound procedure. In one instance, the position shows a loss from its inception, while in the other, the reverse is true.

Close competitive markets of size should be quoted. This will assure the maximum number of inquiries and transactions. Markets are determined by the law of supply and demand, and these inquiries and transactions present the immediate trend picture which is so essential to position work.

Statistical studies and pertinent items of information are helpful when used judiciously. However, in the final analysis, the market itself tells the immediate story and the successful trading operation is geared to flow with it, rather than attempt to challenge its trend.

"WHAT IS MARGIN?" is a question often asked of brokers. Actually, there is little difference between buying an automobile on the installment plan, and buying stocks on margin, except that the car buyer must pay his debt in regular payments, whereas the investor can sit tight for months or even years, making no further payments after the initial deposit, unless the value of the stock declines considerably.

The Federal Reserve Board tells both the buyer of the car, and the investor, how large their down payment must be. On securities, the current minimum margin requirement is 90%, which can be changed at any time by the Federal Reserve Board. This simply means that when you purchase a stock on margin, you must put up 90% of the value.

WALTER A. SCHOLL is New York Stock Exchange floor broker for Merrill Lynch, Pierce, Fenner & Smith, Incorporated.

What is Margin?

BORROWING BY THE BRAVE

Walter A. Scholl

A purchase of $10,000 would require a deposit of $9,000, and the balance of $1,000 would be owed the broker. How much interest the broker charges the customer depends on how much he, in turn, must pay his own bank, as the New York Stock Exchange regulations require the broker to charge a *minimum* rate of ½ of 1% more than the current brokers' call rate.

After the investor has made his initial 90% deposit, the Federal Reserve Board steps out of the picture, and the account is then subject to the New York Stock Exchange *minimum* maintenance requirements of 25%, although many brokers may require more than 25%. Under the present regulations requiring an initial 90% deposit, the chances are slim of getting a "maintenance call" for additional funds, as the stock must drop considerably. For instance, a purchase of 100 shares priced at $100 per share, requiring a deposit of $9,000, would leave an equity of $9,000. (Equity is the market value less the amount owed the broker.) The equity must at all times be at least equal to 25% of the market value of the stock.

If this was the only stock in the account, it would require a drop in price to about $13 per share before additional funds would be required.

MARKET VALUE	LOAN OUTSTANDING	EQUITY
$10,000	$1,000	$9,000
4,000	1,000	3,000
1,300*	1,000	300

**At this value you are subject to a small margin call, as equity is now less than 25% of value.*

At the present time, maintenance margin is more likely to be required of someone who may have purchased stock when lower "down payment" rates prevailed.

The Federal Reserve Board gets back into the picture if the margin buyer wants to withdraw funds or securities from his account, or wants to buy more stock on margin. He can collect any cash dividends paid on his stock even though his account has dropped below the 90% Federal Reserve Board minimum.

Margin range: 40% to 100%

Prior to the Security and Exchange Act of 1934, margin trading was quite common, and during the 1929 boom brokers frequently let their customers buy stocks on as little as 10% margin. Since 1934, when the Federal Reserve Board began to exercise its authority, the minimum rate has varied from 40%, which it was from 1937 to 1945, to a high of 100% in 1946—and when the 100% rate prevailed that meant, of course, that there was no margin trading at all. In recent years, figures of 50% or 75% have been most common. Although margin activity has declined sharply from what it was in the days before the Reserve Board entered the picture, experienced traders continue to put margin to use. Usually, they buy on margin because they can procure a larger percentage of profit. Of course, they stand to lose, percentage-wise, a larger share of their capital if the stock declines.

Margin can also be used by an investor who wants to buy his General Motors stock just like he buys a General Motors' Buick. He buys the stock on margin and gradually pays off his debit balance or loan. Other investors buy on margin so that they can get more dividends. Dividends are paid on all the stock a man owns, even though he may actually have paid for only part of it.

You have often heard of people who pride themselves on the fact that they pay cash for everything. Investors who buy stock outright and not on margin may properly consider this the more prudent course; but they are deceiving themselves if they believe this course is safe, or if they believe they can consequently put the stock away and not have to worry about it. All investors should be solicitous about their stock, whether they pay cash or buy on margin. Actually, because of the penalties he may have to pay, the margin buyer is apt to watch more closely developments that affect the value of his securities than is the cash buyer.

A wire clerk re-routes orders in a major brokerage house; above, the call board above the floor of the Exchange.

The Odd-Lot Dealer System on the New York Stock Exchange

FROM 1 TO 99

Harold W. Carhart, Jr.

HAROLD W. CARHART, JR., Yale '37, joined Carlisle & Jacquelin, a leading odd-lot house, on graduation. He became a general partner in 1950 and was elected a member of their Board in 1958. He is also a Stock Exchange member.

IN ORDER TO explain the principles involved in Odd-Lot transactions on the New York Stock Exchange, it is necessary to present the basic features which apply to buying and selling listed securities.

The unit of trading on the New York Stock Exchange is one hundred shares, or multiples thereof, and all sales, therefore, are based upon this unit. Obviously, many investors wish to trade in less than one hundred shares, and the Odd-Lot Dealer System has developed over many years to handle this particular phase of the securities industry.

An Odd-Lot is any number of shares from one through ninety-nine in any security listed on the New York Stock Exchange.

Since the unit of trading is one hundred shares, the Odd-Lot Dealer System has been evolved to afford the small investor the same opportunity to buy and sell securities as the larger participant in the market.

The biggest brokerage houses process millions of pieces of paper each year. The paperwork flow is speeded by banks of pneumatic tubes, conveyer belts, etc.—yet no one has replaced a careful eye for checking mechanical error (left, inspection of monthly statements before mailing).

The Odd-Lot dealer is a New York Stock Exchange member firm dealing exclusively in Odd-Lots, and as such, is a principal in every transaction, never becoming an agent. The Odd-Lot dealer will trade with any New York Stock Exchange member in any listed stock, in any amount from one through ninety-nine shares at a price based upon the next effective round-lot sale occurring after receipt by him of the order upon the floor of the New York Stock Exchange. The only fee the Odd-Lot dealer receives for his services is known as the Odd-Lot Differential. This differential is based upon the price of the stock involved: 12½¢ per share on stocks selling below $40, 25¢ per share on stocks above $40.

In order to perform these services with adequate speed and accuracy, the Odd-Lot dealer firms are represented by members of the New York Stock Exchange at every trading post on the trading floor. These brokers confine their activities exclusively to executing Odd-Lot orders in the stocks assigned to them at their particular posts. Since the Odd-Lot dealer is a principal in every transaction, these brokers are also responsible for the inventory assumed by the Odd-Lot dealer and consequently they must buy and sell round-lots in the open market to offset the cumulative effect of the Odd-Lot orders they have executed. These brokers at the various trading posts have no direct financial interest in the inventory of the dealer firms; they are representatives of the dealer firms and operate on a commission basis only.

Other Odd-Lot services

In addition to their primary function, the Odd-Lot firms perform various other services for the member firms of the New York Stock Exchange, among which one of the most important is the maintenance of order-servicing departments to assist their customers in checking prices and to ensure that orders have been executed at the correct price and time. They maintain the only record of the exact minute every round-lot transaction is reported on the New York Stock Exchange, and therefore customers may check prices at any time against their reports of executed trades as they have appeared on the New York Stock Exchange ticker tape.

Small shareholders on a plant tour: such trips are part of a continuing effort by American industry on behalf of the small investor.

In recent years, the New York Stock Exchange has placed more and more emphasis upon broadening the base of the ownership of securities in the United States. The Exchange has felt that if the ownership of business was placed in more and more hands, the system of free enterprise would be greatly strengthened by a wider understanding of, and participation in, the profits of our economy. Therefore the Monthly Investment Plan for the purchase of securities was originated. This Plan, in brief, provides a medium for the monthly or quarterly purchase of listed securities for as little as forty dollars per payment. The Odd-Lot firms, in conjunction with member firms dealing with the public, have developed a procedure to facilitate the handling of these accounts.

In conclusion, the essential purpose of the Odd-Lot firms is to provide a liquid market for the small investor who is becoming a more and more important factor in our economy. Odd-Lot transactions constitute roughly 20% of the total volume of the New York Stock Exchange, and if the Exchange is to maintain its position as the leading securities market of the world, the customer who trades from one through ninety-nine shares must be afforded the same facilities as the customer who buys and sells in larger amounts.

The Monthly Investment Plan

AGE OF THE "LITTLE FINANCIER"

Adolph Woolner

ON A DAY late in January, 1954 there appeared in the financial pages of a number of newspapers a news item to the effect that Mr. and Mrs. Norman Hoffman, of Mount Vernon, N. Y., a quiet suburb of New York City, had purchased $40 worth of a stock listed on the New York Stock Exchange—to be specific, 1.1794 shares of common stock of Anaconda Copper Mining Company. On the day (January 25) this modest purchase was made, a total of 1,866,220 shares with a market value in the millions of dollars was traded on the Exchange. Why then was a transaction involving a mere $40 considered by financial editors worthy of special mention?

Because the transaction was news. And it was news because it was the first acquisition of securities listed on the New York Stock Exchange under a new idea—a new concept which has been described as the "most significant" in personal financial planning in decades.

The idea is the Monthly Investment Plan, developed by the member firms of the New York Stock Exchange and inaugurated on January 25, 1954.

Why "most significant"?

Shortly after the Plan began, Harold L. Bache, senior partner of Bache & Co., referring to the "growing family of small investors," expressed the conviction that only through creation of a large group of investors who will provide private venture capital will the nation be able to maintain and increase the level of business activity and thereby insure uninterrupted employment and a prosperous economy.

"I am optimistic, even enthusiastic," said Mr. Bache, "about the prospects for a large increase in the number of small investors. In this connection, only recently and after many

Mr. and Mrs. Norman Hoffman buy 1.1794 shares of Anaconda to inaugurate the Monthly Investment Plan on January 25, 1954—cost: $37.74. Their purchase gave them part-ownership of this famed open-pit copper mine, the Berkeley, in Butte, Montana.

months of painstaking planning, the Monthly Investment Plan for purchase of securities went into effect. This Plan may well be a great forward step in initiating the new investor into the nation's economy as well as providing a stabilizing factor in the securities markets. This is the age of the 'little financier'."

Why is the Plan considered one of the most forward-looking developments ever originated in the securities business? For the reason that the Plan introduces to the American public a method of buying stocks which conforms with recognized buying habits of the public at large—a method which requires only small monthly or quarterly payments.

The Plan, it may be stated here, does not only have its roots in a desire to expand the business of the Stock Exchange and its member firms—although that purpose certainly is praiseworthy and in the American tradition. It goes much deeper than that. It is rooted in the conviction that public ownership of the nation's plants and industrial machinery—that is, widespread ownership of the securities of the nation's corporations—is "an idea with the power to combat and kill the virus of Communism, the power to keep our country strong and free, the power to give our people an unending supply of the good things of life and the leisure to enjoy them."

How the Plan works

Widespread ownership of securities perforce means ownership by persons of average means —and the Plan is designed for them.

Under the Plan one may invest any amount from $40 to $1,000 monthly or quarterly in any of the approximately 1,200 stocks listed on the New York Stock Exchange. (The broker is glad to assist the investor in the selection of sound securities, and does this without charge.)

For example: let us assume the investor elects to invest $50 monthly. The initial $50 will purchase 2.6206 shares of an $18 stock or 0.2621 shares of a $180 stock, and also pay the broker's commission. If the price of the stock is higher at the time of the next monthly investment of $50, the second payment will buy a smaller amount of shares and, conversely, if the stock is lower in price the second payment will buy a larger number of shares. This is dollar cost averaging. The money is invested immediately in the selected stock, regardless of the price of the stock, whether it sells for $180 a share or $18 a share.

The shares so acquired are owned outright by the investor. He can take possession of the shares at any time. He can sell them at any time—in whole or part. There is no borrowing involved—it is pay-as-you-go. Hence, the Plan is not an installment purchase; it is non-contractual—the investor can stop at any time.

ADOLPH WOOLNER graduated from Yale in 1930 and entered the Harvard Graduate School of Business Administration. He became a partner of Bache & Co. in 1945 and is now a senior partner. Mr. Woolner was instrumental in the formation of the Monthly Investment Plan.

He can invest by mail. His dividends will be mailed to him or automatically reinvested, as he directs. His stocks will be voted at annual or special meetings of stockholders in strict accordance with his written instructions.

How is the Plan doing?

At the end of 1959, after some five and a half years of operation of the Plan, approximately 196,000 individual plans had been started. Almost 3,500,000 shares have been purchased using this investment technique for a total of over $135,000,000 invested. During 1959, a banner year, new plans came in at the rate of about 200 per day—more were started (36,758) in the first nine months than were started in any previous twelve-month period.

Of the accounts now in operation, about half have been terminated, some because the investor reaches a goal he has set in one stock and then often starts a new Plan. 88% call for the dividends to be reinvested automatically, thus adding on to the holding of the investor. Another interesting aspect of the present day MIP investor is the size of payment. A recent check of these showed the average payment received is $85.00—considerably greater than the $40 minimum.

MIP dramatizes stock ownership

MIP has dramatized common stocks and stimulated their sales. In addition to MIP investors, thousands of individuals who responded to MIP publicity and advertising have opened regular accounts or bought mutual funds.

Experience to date indicates that the Monthly Investment Plan is helping to change the public attitude toward stocks—who can buy them and how to buy them. It is also making the public aware of the fact that our member firms are glad to do business with both large and small investors—that people everywhere have the opportunity to own their share of American business.

The type of stocks popular with MIP investors indicates that quality is a prime consideration*—an interesting point in the light of the fact that the Stock Exchange has emphasized MIP not as "a get-rich-quick scheme," but a "new way to accumulate income-producing capital." Another development in MIP has been the adaptation of the Plan to make it possible for individuals in a number of companies listed on the Exchange to make their MIP payments automatically through employee payroll deductions.

*As of June 26, 1959, the latest official compilation available lists such public favorites and blue chips as: General Motors Corp., General Electric Co., Dow Chemical Co., Standard Oil Co. (N.J.), Tri-Continental Corp. and Sperry Rand Corp.

On the basis of results during the first growth years, the Plan, in my opinion, is helping toward attainment of the principal objective of combating Communism through a broadening of public ownership of corporate securities. A recent Stock Exchange report estimated that "90% of MIP members are new investors."

Here then, it may be assumed, are people who in the future will have a much closer personal contact with American corporate management than they have had heretofore. That contact is certain to arouse a keener awareness and appreciation of what American free enterprise is and does for all of us. The contact—through attendance of stockholders at annual meetings, personal conversation or correspondence with corporation officials, receipt of dividend checks, reading of annual reports—can hardly fail to inspire an interest in economic affairs, which in turn should stir up an active, militant participation in all efforts to preserve and strengthen the American capitalistic system.

A good start, then, it is agreed by many, has been made. But much remains to be done, for the surface of the field has scarcely been scratched. According to recent studies, 12,940,-000—only 11.5%, or about 1 out of 8 of the adult population—held publicly owned stocks. On the other hand, it is estimated that 124,000,000 individuals own life insurance; 50% of the 56.8 million spending family units have savings accounts; 20% of the spending units own "E" bonds and there were 19,000,000 beneficiaries of pensions or annuities. These figures speak for themselves—and they add up to the fact that the undeveloped market for MIP plans is practically unlimited.

PHOTO CREDITS

Aerojet-General Corporation 12, 16, 20 Aluminum Company of America 30, 82, 83 American Can Company/Fairchild Aerial Surveys 147 American Cyanamid Company 73 American-Saint Gobain Corporation 97 The American Stock Exchange/Tommy Weber 48, 49, 67, 71, 73, 107, 159, 167 American Telephone and Telegraph Company 36 The Anaconda Company 147, 190 Bache & Co./Paul Blacker Studio 190 Fabian Bachrach 29, 124, 130, 154, 184 Bethlehem Steel Company 87 Blackstone Studios 76, 122, 141, 180 Brown Brothers 47, 48, 49, 55, 57, 63, 135, 154, 157 Burns and Roe, Inc 107 Buschke-Selick Studio 157 Careers Incorporated/Maynard Frank Wolfe 175 Chase, Ltd 62 Chase Manhattan Bank 25, 35, 50, 58, 85, 99, 159 Cities Service Company 30, 111, 125 Coca-Cola Company 20 New York Commodity Exchange, Inc 25, 179 Conference of Eastern Railroad Presidents 13, 110, 146, 147 Connecticut General Life Insurance Company/John Haley 145 Conway Studios 56 Jerry Cooke 173 Cotton Exchange 133, 178 Culver Service 48, 76, 86 87, 116 Delta Airlines 73 Doremus & Company 154 Dun & Bradstreet 133 The Dreyfus Fund, Inc 143 Eastman Kodak Company 4-5 Ebasco/Washington Water Power Company 107 Engels Studio 89 Fairchild Aerial Surveys 137 Austin Field 72 Ford Motor Company 12, 51, 70 Ewing Galloway 16 Maurey Garber 188 General Electric Company 12, 80, 109, 120, 156, 189 Gresser & Dunlop 172 Ideal Cement Company 107, 133 Illinois Tollway 107, 129 Inland Steel Company 13, 111 International Business Machines Corporation 174, 175 International Finance Corporation 29, 33 International Telephone and Telegraph Corporation/Handy-Boesser 107 Kidder, Peabody & Co 13, 159 Carl M Loeb, Rhoades & Co./Blecker-Amster 119 Los Angeles Chamber of Commerce 12, 31, 88, 135 Manufacturers Trust Company 157 Maier Studio 94 Merrill Lynch, Pierce, Fenner & Smith, Inc./Dick Hanley 45, 69, 70, 159, 163, 168, 170, 172, 173, 174, 175, 176, 179, 184, 186, 187, 188 Museum of the City of New York 15, 42, 48, 80 The National Archives 18, 45, 46, 58 National Biscuit Company 13, 133 New Jersey Turnpike Authority 87, 107 The New York Historical Society, New York City 44, 45, 46, 47, 54 New York State Thruway Authority 75 New York Stock Exchange 13, 35, 37, 38, 40, 41, 45, 46, 47, 71, 159, 160, 161, 163, 164 The New York Times 184 New York University/William Simmons 193 Pepsi Cola Company 20, 131 Prudential Insurance Co of America 156 Pan American World Airways 20, 31, 73 The Port of New York Authority 12, 35, 88, 90-91, 111, 126, 133 Radio Corporation of America 35, 110, 117, 147 Joan Raeburn 115 Raytheon Company 123 Reynolds & Co 170, 175 Santa Fe Railway Careers Incorporated 73 Bill Schrapp 37 Securities and Exchange Commission 66 Smithsonian Institution Museum of Natural History 12 Spanish National Tourist Department 64 Squibb & Sons/Careers Incorporated 73 Standard Oil Co (N J) 30, 59, 73, 74, 80, 91, 98, 107, 146, 177, 181 Stanford University 26 Time Incorporated 43 United States Air Force 17, 116 United States Department of Agriculture (Office of Information) 12-13, 20 United States Department of the Treasury 46 U S Rubber Company 12, 13, 30, 39, 73, 75, 110, 111, 133, 171 Dan Weiner courtesy of Fortune Magazine 104, 105 Western Union Telegraph Company 172 West Virginia Pulp and Paper Company 35 Wide World (from The New York Times) 60 Yale University News Bureau 156

Text of the address by the President, delivered at the Economic Mobilization Conference conducted by the American Management Association, at the Hotel Astor, New York City, Tuesday, May 20, 1958, at 9:30 P.M. EDT.

Cover: Eastman Kodak Company

BIBLIOGRAPHY

The following list of references is designed as a guide for students and others to further reading in the areas covered by the several sections of Wall Street/20th Century. The references are divided on the basis of the six sections of the book and are intended to include at least one reference for each specific article.

The reference list was prepared by Dr. Julian G. Buckley, Associate Professor of Finance, New York University. Dr. Buckley, a 1928 graduate of Harvard University, is familiar with Wall Street and its operations, having worked as senior analyst for Delafield & Delafield, as portfolio manager for the Fiduciary Trust Company of New York, and as a special assistant at the Federal Reserve Bank of New York. For several years, he has been associated with the Graduate School of Business Administration of New York University.

PART I—ECONOMICS AND FINANCE

Brooks, J., *Seven Fat Years: Chronicles of Wall Street.* New York: Harper and Bros., 1958.

Clews, H., *Fifty Years in Wall Street.* New York: Irving Publishing Co., 1908.

Committee For Economic Development (Research and Policy Committee), *Economic Development Abroad and the Role of American Foreign Investments.* February 1956.

Daniel, J., *Private Investment.* New York: McGraw-Hill Book Co., Inc., 1958.

Duesenberry, J. S., *Business Cycles and Economic Growth.* New York: McGraw-Hill Book Co., Inc., 1958.

Grayson, T. J., *Leaders and Periods of American Finance.* New York: John Wiley & Sons, Inc., 1932.

Mayer, M., *Wall Street Men and Money.* New York: Harper and Bros., 1955.

Noyes, A. D., *Forty Years of American Finance, 1865-1907.* New York: G. P. Putnam's Sons, 1909.

Randall, C. B., *Foreign Economic Policy for the United States.* Chicago: University of Chicago Press, 1954.

Schumpeter, J. A., *Capitalism, Socialism and Democracy.* Third Edition. New York: Harper and Bros., 1950.

Studenski, P., and Kroose, H. E., *Financial History of the United States.* New York: McGraw-Hill Book Co., Inc., 1952.

Wright, C. W., *Economic History of the United States.* Second Edition. New York: McGraw-Hill Book Co., Inc., 1949.

Wright, David McCord., *Capitalism.* New York: McGraw-Hill Book Co., Inc., 1951.

PART II—WALL STREET

Bogen, J. I., ed. *Financial Handbook.* New York: The Ronald Press Co., 1957.

Dice, C. A., and Eiteman, W. J., *The Stock Market.* New York: McGraw-Hill Book Co., Inc., 1952.

The George Washington University Law School. *Securities and Exchange Commission Silver Anniversary Commemorative Symposium.* Volume 28. Number 1. October 1959.

Hayek, F. A., ed. *Capitalism and the Historians.* Chicago: University of Chicago Press, 1954.

Leffler, G. L., *The Stock Market.* Second Edition. New York: The Ronald Press Co., 1957.

Mises, Ludwig von., *Human Action.* New Haven: Yale University Press, 1949.

Robinson, L. R., Adams, J. F., and Dillin, H. L., *An Introduction to Modern Economics.* New York: The Dryden Press, 1952.

Securities and Exchange Commission: *Annual Reports.*

PART III—INVESTMENT BANKING

Badger, R. E., and Guthmann, H. G., Fourth Edition. *Investment Principles and Practices.* New York: Prentice-Hall, Inc., 1951.

Childs, C. F., *Concerning U. S. Government Securities.* Chicago: C. F. Childs and Co., Privately Printed, 1947.

Curvin, W. S., *Manual on Municipal Bonds.* New York: Smith Barney and Co., Privately Printed, 1956.

Dewing, A. S., *Financial Policy of Corporations.* Fifth Edition. Two Volumes. New York: The Ronald Press Co., 1953.

Foster, M. B., Rodgers, R., Bogen, J. I., and Nadler, M., *Money and Banking.* Fourth Edition. New York: Prentice-Hall, Inc., 1956.

Guthmann, H. G., and Dougall, H. E., *Corporate Financial Policy.* Third Edition. New York: Prentice-Hall, Inc., 1955.

Investment Bankers Association, *Fundamentals of Investment Banking.* New York: Prentice-Hall, Inc., 1949.

Medina, Harold R., C. J. *Corrected Opinion February 4, 1954 on United States of America v. Henry S. Morgan, et al.* United States District Court (New York, Southern District).

Pizer, L. M., *U. S. Government Bond Market Analysis.* New York: Transcripts of Lectures Given at New York Institute of Finance, (1955).

PART IV—ANALYSIS AND EVALUATION OF SECURITIES

Chatters, C. H., and Hillhouse, A. M., *Local Government Debt Administration.* New York: Prentice-Hall, Inc., 1939.

Edwards, R. D., and Magee, J., *Technical Analysis of Stock Trends.* Springfield, Mass.: Stock Trend Service, Inc., 1958.

Fisher, P. A., *Common Stocks and Uncommon Profits.* New York: Harper and Bros., 1958.

Graham, B., *The Intelligent Investor.* New York: Harper and Bros., 1959.

Graham, B., and Dodd, D. L., *Security Analysis.* Third Edition. New York: McGraw-Hill Book Co., Inc., 1951.

Hillhouse, A. M., *Municipal Bonds, A Century of Experience.* New York: Prentice-Hall, Inc., 1936.

Knappen, L. S., *Revenue Bonds and the Investor.* New York: Prentice-Hall, Inc., 1939.

Loeb, G. M., *Battle for Investment Survival.* New York: Simon and Schuster, Inc., 1957.

Plum, L. V., ed. *Investing in American Industries.* New York: Harper and Bros., 1960.

Wheelan, A. H., *Study Helps in Point and Figure Technique.* New York: Morgan Rogers and Roberts, Inc., Privately Printed, 1954.

PART V—THE MONEY MANAGERS

Bullock, H., *The Story of Investment Companies.* Calvin Bullock, Privately Printed, 1959.

Cam, G. A., *Survey of the Literature on Investment Companies 1864-1957.* New York Public Library, 1958.

Johnson, A. W., *Intermediate Accounting.* New York: Rinehart and Co., Inc., 1958.

Kurnow, E., Glasser, G. J., and Ottman, F. R., *Statistics for Business Decisions.* Homewood, Illinois: Richard D. Irwin, Inc., 1959.

Lennon, T. F., *Factors in Investment Management.* Article. Commercial and Financial Chronicle, September 21, 1950.

Nadler, M., Heller, S., and Shipman, S. S., *The Money Market and Its Institutions.* New York: The Ronald Press Co., 1955.

Samuelson, P. A., *Economics.* Fourth Edition. New York: McGraw-Hill Book Co., Inc., 1958.

BIBLIOGRAPHY—*continued*

Wiesenberger, A., *Investment Companies. 1959.* (Annual Editions) Arthur Wiesenberger and Co.

PART VI—HOW THE MARKET PLACE WORKS

Commodities. Bache and Company, Privately Printed, 1958.

$40 and I'm An Owner of Common Stocks. New York Stock Exchange, 1959. (Pamphlet)

Friend, I., *The Over the Counter Securities Market.* New York: McGraw-Hill Book Co., Inc., 1958.

Gold, G., *Modern Commodity Futures Trading.* New York: Commodity Research Bureau, Incorporated, 1959.

Hardy, C. O., *Odd Lot Trading on the New York Stock Exchange.* Washington, D. C.: Brookings Institute, 1939.

Lea, V. L., *The Commodity Futures Markets.* Boston: Paine, Webber, Jackson and Curtis, Privately Printed, 1954.

Lohman, P. H., and Ricciardi, F. M., *Wall Street Explains Its Operations.* New York Institute of Finance, 1951.

Now About the Specialist. New York Stock Exchange, 1958. (Pamphlet)

Odd Lots. Carlisle and Jacquelin, Privately Printed, 1959.

The Story of MIP, The Monthly Investment Plan. New York Stock Exchange, 1959. (Pamphlet)

Understanding the New York Stock Exchange. New York Stock Exchange, 1958. (Pamphlet)

ACKNOWLEDGING...

In sincerest appreciation, the debt owed to Mrs. Robert C. Finnie for her invaluable editorial assistance in collection of photographs for this volume; to Mr. Frank C. Kline, and the staff of Careers Incorporated, for their cooperation and patience during the production of this book; to Miss Neil Collins of the New York Stock Exchange and Mr. Tom Sherman of "We the People" for particular help with pictorial problems; to the following for assistance too valuable and varied to be recounted: Miss Margaret Pallesen, Mrs. Patricia Shebell, and Miss Geraldine Micallef, all of Kidder, Peabody & Co.; Mr. Richard Paynter of Doremus & Company; and Mrs. Edna Costonguay of Blair & Co. Incorporated.

The Staff

PRINTER'S NOTE

This volume was set in Linotype Century and Spartan type-faces, with the headings cast in Ludlow Tempo bold capitals and Bodoni light italics. The book was composed, printed, and bound by the Majestic Press, Inc., Philadelphia. The cased edition was bound by the National Publishing Co., Philadelphia. Body design, typography, and binding design by WILLIAM H. OTTLEY.

LITHO IN U S A.
MAJESTIC PRESS
PHILA., PA.

MARYGROVE COLLEGE LIBRARY
Wall Street, 20th century.
332.4 Y1
3 1927 00101220 9
332.4
Y1
Yale Daily News
Wall Street 20th century
332.4
Y1

MARYGROVE
LIBRARY
DETROIT, MI

CPSIA information can be obtained
at www.ICGtesting.com
Printed in the USA
BVHW051244130223
658403BV00003B/273

9 781013 797675